# THE HISTORICAL AND PHILOSOPHICAL CONTEXT OF RATIONAL PSYCHOTHERAPY

# THE HISTORICAL AND PHILOSOPHICAL CONTEXT OF RATIONAL PSYCHOTHERAPY
## The Legacy of Epictetus

*Arthur Still and Windy Dryden*

**KARNAC**

First published in 2012 by
Karnac Books Ltd
118 Finchley Road
London NW3 5HT

British Library Cataloguing in Publication Data

A C.I.P. for this book is available from the British Library

ISBN-13: 978-1-78049-023-6

Typeset by V Publishing Solutions Pvt Ltd., Chennai, India

Printed in Great Britain

www.karnacbooks.com

# CONTENTS

# ACKNOWLEDGEMENTS

We would like to thank those people—colleagues, clients, and others—with whom we have discussed the ideas presented in this book. We would also like to thank:

Sage Publications for permission to use and modify the material of the following articles, which appear as Chapters Three and Six, respectively:

Still, A. W. & Dryden, W. (1998). The intellectual origins of Rational Psychotherapy. *History of the Human Sciences*, 11: 63–86.

Dryden, W. & Still, A. W. (1999). When did a psychologist last discuss "chagrin"? America's continuing moral project. *History of the Human Sciences*, 12: 93–110.

Springer for permission to use and modify the material of the following articles, which appear as Chapters One, Two, Four, Eight and Nine, respectively:

Still, A. W. & Dryden, W. (1999). The place of rationality in Stoicism and REBT. *Journal of Rational-Emotive & Cognitive-Behavior Therapy*, 17: 143–164.

Still, A. W. & Dryden, W. (2003) Ellis and Epictetus: dialogue vs. method in psychotherapy. *Journal of Rational-Emotive & Cognitive-Behavior Therapy*, 21: 37–55.

Dryden, W. & Still, A. W. (1998). REBT and rationality: philosophical approaches. *Journal of Rational-Emotive & Cognitive-Behavior Therapy*, 16: 77–99.

Still, A. W. (2001). Marginalisation is not unbearable. Is it even undesirable? *Journal of Rational-Emotive & Cognitive-Behavior Therapy*, 19: 55–66.

Dryden, W. & Still, A. W. (2006). Historical aspects of mindfulness and self-acceptance in psychotherapy. *Journal of Rational-Emotive & Cognitive-Behavior Therapy*, 24(1): 3–28.

Wiley for permission to use and modify the material of the following articles, which appear as Chapters Five and Seven, respectively:

Dryden, W. & Still, A. W. (2007). Rationality and the shoulds. *Journal for the Theory of Social Behaviour*, 37: 1–23.

Still, A. W. & Dryden, W. (2004). The social psychology of "pseudo-science": A brief history. *Journal of the Theory of Social Behaviour*, 34: 265–290.

# ABOUT THE AUTHORS

**Arthur Still** taught psychology at the University of Durham until 1988. He then trained as a counsellor and psychotherapist and currently works in private practice in Edinburgh and the Scottish Borders. He was co-founder and editor of the journal *History of the Human Sciences.*

**Windy Dryden** was the first Professor of Counselling in Britain, and is now a Professor of Psychotherapeutic Studies at Goldsmiths College, University of London, where he runs the MSc course in Rational-Emotive and Cognitive Behaviour Therapy. He has authored or edited 195 books, and edited twenty book series. He was the founding editor of the British Journal of Cognitive Psychotherapy in 1982 and is now editor of the Journal of Rational-Emotive and Cognitive-Behavior Therapy.

# INTRODUCTION

This book is about Albert Ellis (1913–2007) and Epictetus (*c.* 55–*c.* 135 CE) and the relationship that exists between them across nineteen centuries. It is also, more generally, about the relationship between the Stoicism represented by Epictetus and the cognitive approach to psychotherapy represented by Ellis. Ellis and Epictetus are thus a synechdoche for a much broader relationship between ancient and modern thought and practice. We focus on the intellectual context, rather than the battles Ellis fought to establish himself, and the social and economic changes that made that possible, although these cannot be kept entirely separate.

Our interest is not mainly in the apparent similarity between Stoicism and modern cognitive therapy, which has often been pointed out, and is explored at length in Robertson (2010). Instead, the focus will be on the historical relationship between them. Why is there a similarity, and what are the differences? To borrow a contrast from evolutionary theory, we are interested in homologies rather than analogies. The eye of an octopus is remarkably similar to the mammalian eye, so it is analogous. However, they are not historically connected, so not homologous. On the other hand, it is hard to find much analogy between the ossicles of the mammalian middle ear, and the articular and quadrate jawbones of reptiles, but it turns out that they are homologous—the jawbones evolved into the ossicles. Analogy and homology are different kinds of argument. Homology is always in principle exact, true or false, although the evidence may be inherently vague and uncertain. Analogy is more subjective—one person may find similarities where another finds differences—and it can be impossible historically or scientifically to decide between them. However, it often provides *prima facie* evidence for homology.

## Life of Albert Ellis

Ellis was born in Pittsburgh, Pennysylvania in 1913, but his family moved to the Bronx in New York when he was four. In his own account, Albert describes a thoroughly dysfunctional Jewish family, with a bipolar mother and a mostly absent father. He was often seriously ill, yet had the responsibility for looking after his two younger siblings. At the time of the Depression, he was forced to work to support both himself and his family, but managed to acquire a BA in business studies from what is now City University of New York in 1934. His upbringing, it seems, far from crushing him or leaving him an emotional wreck, became the making of him as a therapist. It is as though he learned early on to step back from the potentially lethal attachments of his childhood, and to find his own solutions to the emotional problems confronting him. The most famous illustration of this came in his late teens when, to overcome his shyness with women, he made himself talk to 100 women in a month. He failed to date any of them, but overcame his fear of rejection. This is one of the key origin myths of Rational Emotive Behavior Therapy (REBT), and expresses an insight that stretches well beyond the range of psychotherapy, in its shift from the Great American Dream of self-esteem and happiness through positive thinking and material success, to a different kind of happiness: self-acceptance even in the face of failure. More traditional was the cure of his own phobia about public speaking by *in vivo* desensitisation, by forcing himself to speak, a technique he learned from reading J. B. Watson; in this case he succeeded and self-acceptance was not tested.

He read widely during the 1930s, especially in philosophy, by which he meant not the modern academic practice dominated by logical positivism at the time, but the Ancients who approached philosophy as a way of life (Hadot, 1995). He read the later Stoics, Epictetus, Seneca, and Marcus Aurelius, who were readily available in cheap translations. He also read and wrote on Marxism, studied Buddhism, and became a sex therapist. For several years he was an intellectual entrepeneur— and not a very successful one. He wrote prolifically—twenty full length manuscripts, including novels, plays, a question and answer version of *Das Kapital*, *The Case for Sexual Promiscuity*, and *A History of the Dark Ages: The Twentieth Century*. However, he had nothing published and "got a variety of small and unimportant jobs to keep from starving to death".[1]

In 1941, he enrolled as a graduate student in Columbia's psychology department, and a year later transferred to Teachers College, where he gained his MA and PhD. His doctoral thesis was on personality questionnaires, after his initial proposal for research on the love emotions of college women had been turned down. During the 1940s, Ellis was employed by the State of New Jersey as a clinical psychologist and taught at New York University and Rutgers. He also worked as a psychotherapist, dealing especially with sex and relationship problems. He began to publish on this, first in academic journals, and later in a series of popular books (*The Folklore of Sex* (1951); *The American Sexual Tragedy* (1954); and *Sex without Guilt* (1958) in the 1950s—with at least four more appearing during the 1960s). He published his research on personality tests in *Psychological Bulletin*, in a style familiar to readers of his later work. In particular, the use of a rhetorical device, the long, numbered list of arguments, appears there and throughout Ellis's work. It was not generally used by Ellis to drive relentlessly to a conclusion, but dialectically, to qualify any claims to absolute truth in himself or others.[2] This was an important survey of personality tests at the time, and could have launched his career as an academic psychologist.

However, in 1947 he began a training analysis with Richard Hulbeck at the Horney Institute. This was apparently not a success. A successful analysis probably requires the right kind of childhood, where a sense of reality becomes tortuously entangled with the vicissitudes of emotional attachment, and this is what Albert had managed to avoid. But he started practising as an analyst and wrote papers on how psychoanalysis might be made scientific, as well as his books on sex therapy. By 1953, he was disillusioned with psychoanalysis, and began to try other methods, calling himself a rational psychotherapist instead of a psychoanalyst. The range of methods he had to select from was listed in great detail by Ellis (1955a, 1955b). In these two extensive reviews of the psychotherapy literature the dialectical style is again striking. Contradictory dogmatic statements are deliberately juxtaposed, with supporting references for each, but little comment and no attempt to reconcile them. Whatever the intention, the impact of this style creates an ironic undermining of the dogmatic claims of all current schools of psychotherapy. Each claim is neutralised by, and neutralises, its opposite. Thus, Ellis maps out and defuses a rhetorical minefield that he proceeded to stride boldly across. It is probably significant, therefore, that Rational Psychotherapy does not figure in these two literature reviews, although he had started to use it in 1954 (Ellis, 1962, p. 14).

Articles on Rational Psychotherapy appeared in 1957 and 1958, and soon he had published two of his major books, *A Guide to Rational Living* (1961) and *Reason and Emotion in Psychotherapy* (1962). Since then Rational Psychotherapy (later Rational Emotive Therapy (RET) and now Rational Emotive Behavior Therapy (REBT)) has been one of the most widely used psychotherapies in North America. The Institute for Rational Living in New York was founded in 1959, and this, rather than a university (McMahon, 1996), remained his base throughout his career. Before then Ellis published in several academic psychology journals, but later his audience changed. Beside his many books and popular articles, he wrote for specialist non-academic psychotherapy journals, including the Institute's house journal *Rational Living*, and the *Journal of Rational-Emotive and Cognitive-Behavioral Therapy*. These later writings were often in a challenging and combative style,[3] and he has excited much hostile criticism from within clinical psychology and psychotherapy. But clinical psychology honoured him, and his autobiographical chapter is the first in the first book of the new series, *History of Clinical Psychology in Autobiography*. Academic psychology largely ignored him, and he did not write a chapter for the series *History of Psychology in Autobiography*, nor did he accumulate the impressive list of honorary doctorates typical of writers in that series.

A few years after Ellis had started to practise Rational Psychotherapy, Aaron Beck launched Cognitive Psychotherapy. As Cognitive Behaviour Therapy (CBT), this has become the best-known cognitive therapy, perhaps because it has relied more on academic affiliations, and benefited from the opportunity this brings for research, mainly outcome studies. The advantages and disadvantages of this are discussed in Chapter Nine. Although both therapies make use in practice of Ellis's ABC schema (see p. 47), there is an important theoretical difference between

REBT and CBT. Ⓐ is the activating event, Ⓑ is the belief, which leads to Ⓒ the consequence. For example, a student is excessively, unhealthily anxious about an exam. The A is the exam and the thought of it and of failure; B is that it would be absolutely awful to fail; the C is anxiety. The defining philosophy of REBT lies in the irrational B, which always contains a demand about the self, the other, or the world. Such demands can colour a person's whole life, and a recognition of this can lead to what Ellis called a "philosophical change", a release from the shackles of the shoulds in general. This has a moral flavour absent in the more pragmatic CBT (Chapter Nine).

## Life of Epictetus

Epictetus (ca 55–135 CE) also had a long and eventful life, but virtually nothing is known for sure about the details. He started life as a Greek slave of a Roman master, and there is a well-known story that Epictetus's master broke his legs in a fit or rage. As a result he remained crippled and in pain throughout his life. For a Stoic such a bodily state was categorised as an "indifferent"; there was nothing to be done so Epictetus accepted it, and was able to live happily in spite of the pain. This is a characteristic use of Stoic reason, bringing about harmony between the person and the world. This differs from Platonic reason, which is directed more towards other-worldly realities than practical care of the self. After being freed from slavery, and learning Stoic philosophy from Musonius Rufus, Epictetus became a teacher in Rome. Around 93 CE he had to leave Rome following the banishment of all philosophers by the emperor Domitian. He set up a school in Nicopolis in Greece, where his most famous pupil Arrian recorded his teachings in the *Discourses* in the form of dialogues between him and his pupils. Epictetus is said to have written a lot, but the writings that have come down to us are these dialogues, a collection of his sayings, the *Enchiridion* (or *Handbook*), and a brief collection of *Fragments*. The "legacy of Epictetus" refers to the impact of these writings, rather than to Epictetus the man. It is possible, for instance, that Arrian constructed the dialogues as a vehicle for his own philosophy, rather as Plato used the dialogues of Socrates.

The analogy between Epictetus and Ellis is fairly clear. It starts with the dictum from Epictetus that "Men are disturbed not by things, but by the views which they take of things' (Epictetus, 1955, p. 19)", which is cited by both Ellis and Beck as their starting point. It is the B in the ABC model that causes emotional disturbance, so the cure for disturbance, in both Epitetus and Ellis, is to change the beliefs. Assumed in this is that people can change their beliefs, and therefore are responsible for their emotional disturbances.

Can this analogy be explained by homology? Quoting Epictetus is hardly sufficient. The quote was well known before Ellis and Beck, and the view it expresses is familiar in Western philosophy and does not originate with Epictetus. We need evidence that Ellis actually read Epictetus and other Stoic writers, and that this had an impact on his thought and practice. This is considered in Chapters One and Two. To complicate matters there are less obvious cultural influences: the culmination of a long history of writing about rationality and the role of shoulds and oughts in moral discourse. These are considered in Chapters Four, Five and Six. Behind the argument in those chapters is that, although Ellis's views emerged out of this cultural background, and not just from his reading of the Stoics, the background itself was conditioned by Stoic thinking, which entails a more complex, less direct homology than that provided by his reading of Epictetus. This implicit line of influence is not considered in detail in the following chapters, but it is an important framework for the book, and we outline it here.

## The Christian Stoics

The cultural background we have in mind is the Christian background that dominated human life in the West until science began to replace it as a source of wisdom around the end of the sixteenth century. After the conversion of the emperor Constantine in 312 CE, and the reforms of Augustine (354–430 CE), the Church instituted an intellectual dictatorship that regarded the pre-Christian philosophies of the Pagans with great suspicion. Through the offices of the Roman Empire, it was able to police the thinking and reading of its devotees on a scale that had never been possible before. Aristotle and Plato were allowable guides in worldly matters, but not in theology. The Stoic theory of human nature, as inseparable from the universe as a whole, and with the capacity to live in harmony with the world by the exercise of reason alone, was anathema. But before this clampdown the Stoic impact was extensive, as the early Christian writers turned to the Stoics in their struggle to discover practical ways of controlling thoughts and feelings. Even Paul seems to have been affected. When he spoke to the Athenians he spoke of a god in whom "we live, and move, and have our being" (Acts 17.28), which accords with Stoic philosophy, not with the Christian God who is like a person, a loving and all-powerful father who won't allow us to die provided we are good!

And what is it to be good? Here the Stoics helped provide the framework, with a cognitive theory rather than a *diktat* like the Ten Commandments. One basis of the Stoic theory was the separation of physiological reactions to events from the thinking about them. Seneca referred to these as "first movements", which just happen, and for which we cannot be responsible. Writing 200 years after Seneca, the Christian Origen (*c.* 185–254 CE) followed him in referring to first movements, but these were not so clearly distinct from thoughts.[4] Whether they are connected immediately with thoughts or not, the key lies in the nature of the thoughts that follow. An initial annoyance at the behaviour of a colleague may develop into nothing more and pass, but if we think about it in a certain way it will develop into lasting anger. The same applies to other first movements, and the classification of the triggers of these movements by later Stoic Christians became the basis of the seven deadly sins. These do not appear in the bible, and the first to give a list (of eight rather than seven) was probably Evagrius (*c.* 345–399 CE) who was followed by John Cassian (*c.* 360–435 CE). Both seemed to have used them as a way of categorising different sequences of thoughts in terms of their undesirable consequences, analogous to the list of unhealthy emotions (anxiety, depression, jealousy, etc.) in REBT. They were about spiritual change and development, rather than about avoiding hell as they later became, along with associated absolute "musts".

Cassian introduced monasticism to the Western Church after an investigation of the desert hermits of the Eastern Church, and of the psychological problems they faced in their spiritual exercises. For instance, he wrote on the anger that can arise when the peace of mind achieved in the desert is shattered by living with other monks, and the irritations this involves (Folsom, 1984). He recognised that through our thought processes we are responsible for our anger and other passions, as the Stoics argued, and used Evagrius' list as a way of categorising the thoughts that can take us over in this way. Both he and Epictetus used the moneychanger, carefully evaluating the coinage as a metaphor for the vigilance required over such thoughts.[5]

The start of the fourth century was evidently a lively and progressive time for the cognitive investigations by these Christian Stoics, and the most famous of them was the British monk Pelagius (c. 354–430 CE). He spelt out even more clearly the belief that people can choose to live a good life without divine assistance. God's grace is unnecessary, since He has already given human beings the gift of this capacity of reason and choice (Wiley, 2002). This doctrine was attacked vigorously and successfully by Saint Augustine, and was declared heretical. The official dogma became that human reason is insufficient to overcome the taint of original sin, and that God's grace is necessary to live a good Christian life. So further investigation along the lines of Cassian and Pelagius was suppressed, but, by this time, the Stoic stress on cognitive awareness and control had infiltrated Christian morality. The thinkers behind it were not honoured: Pelagius' memorial is the heresy to which he gave his name; Cassian was a dismissed as a semi-Pelagian (not a full one, since he acknowledged that God could be of some help); and Origen was neither canonised nor considered one of the Church fathers. The seven deadly sins became one of the chief instruments of coercion through the "shoulds" and the "musts" of Christian morality.

## Stoicism after the Renaissance

During the Renaissance, when the Greek and Roman texts became widely available, Stoicism was revived (de Montaigne, 1991; Jones, 2006). It formed the basis of many of the theories of sociality and natural law that became prominent in the eighteenth century (Haakonssen, 1996). In ethics, it was not linked with the Christian Stoicism discussed above, although this aspect of the familiar Christian framework undoubtedly made the new Stoic ideas more readily acceptable. In the United States, Stoicism helped the development of an individualism breaking away from control by the Church and rejecting the doctrine of original sin. A return to Pelagianism perhaps, although nobody claimed that for themselves, and even today it remains a dismissive insult. It is present in Benjamin Franklin's (1706–1790) explicit search for moral perfection, through practical reason rather than prayer, and by following the example of the Roman Stoic, Cato. The Stoicism became more explicit in Ralph Waldo Emerson (1803–1882), as in his declaration that:

A man contains all that is needful to his government within himself. He is made a law unto himself. All real good or evil that can befall him must be from himself.

(cited in Richardson, 1995, p. 152)

This was fertile ground for the American self-help tradition,[6] including the Englishman James Allen's *As a Man Thinketh*,[7] and the works of Dale Carnegie and Norman Vincent Peale in the twentieth century. Carnegie's *How to Stop Worrying and Start Living* (1948) was published in the States in 1944; Peale's *The Power of Positive Thinking* (1996) was first published in 1952. Allen and Peale were ardent Christians (semi-Pelagian one might say), Carnegie less so, and one of his well-known catchphrases—"Our life is what our thoughts make it"—was taken from the Stoic Marcus Aurelius. This quote is referred to by the title of Chapter Eleven of Carnegie (1948): "Eight words that can transform your life". The role of thoughts in making us what we are was thus widely familiar, and what Ellis added to this was the specific Stoic view that we are responsible for our emotions. He also made it clear in many places that the kind of therapeutic thinking he had in mind was nothing like the positive thinking of Peale, a Right Wing bigot whose virulent anti-Catholic attacks on Kennedy led to Adlai Stevenson's famous remark. "I find the Apostle Paul appealing and the Apostle Peale appalling" (QuotesL.com, n.d.).

## Ellis and his contemporaries

At this point, the homology metaphor begins to falter. In biology, a homology is historical fact, take it or leave it. But in intellectual history, even if we accept a homology between Stoicism and REBT, it might turn out to be trivial compared to other influences. To evaluate this, the direct or indirect influence of Stoicism must be weighed against non-Stoic influences, including Ellis's reading of contemporary writers during his formative years, and the effects of his education and training. These are considered in Chapter Three. But this source of influence was not complete at the time Ellis launched Rational Psychotherapy in the late 1950s. Much happened between then and the far more elaborate REBT when he died in 2007. He and other REBT practitioners had participated in, drawn from, or opposed several contemporary movements in psychology, psychotherapy, and the philosophy of science. During this time, REBT had reacted against much of what was on offer, but assimilated some of it, and occasionally accommodated to it.[8]

Although Ellis broke with psychoanalysis in 1953, in some ways the break was not as important as the apparent reaction to the so-called Humanist tradition represented by Carl Rogers. Ellis remained scornfully critical of psychoanalysis but his practice was influenced by it. Already in the States, the neo-Freudians were focusing on the ego's attempts to adjust to the environment, rather than on the detailed analysis of the unconscious processes that undermine this. Karen Horney (1991, p. 64), the founder of the Horney Institute where Ellis was analysed, had written of the "tyranny of the should" in 1950 (discussed further in Chapters Three and Five). She described how the neurotic is trapped behind demands masquerading as moral principles, and it was not a big step for Ellis to focus treatment on changing these demands, rather than on the unconscious structures behind them. He did not deny the truth of psychoanalysis, with its focus on intricate past detail, but for the purposes of treatment he lumped[9] together all the diverse developmental routes into a single terminus, the irrational demands on self, others, and the world. But his attitude to psychological dysfunction remained similar to Freud's. When Ellis announced that we are all fucked up human beings and therapy can help us to recognise this and attain self-acceptance, there is an echo of Freud's tough-minded pessimism about therapy. In addition, like Freud and like the Stoics, Ellis believed that we can use reason to overcome our emotional difficulties, by becoming aware of and eradicating the irrationalities in our thinking.

Rogers, by contrast, had a more optimistic view of human nature (but not of the power of human reason). Echoing a Christian ideal (e.g., Yeoman, 1991), there is an inner self or spirit that is held prisoner by the critical demands of socialisation. Roger's Person Centred Counselling provides a social setting in which the criticism is lifted, and the self can begin to recognise itself and articulate its genuine feelings and needs, leading to self-actualisation. Reason takes a back seat, and the core conditions of unconditional positive regard, empathy, and congruence are sufficient for therapeutic change to take place. Rogers too was influenced by the psychoanalytic thinking developing in the States, especially Otto Rank (De Carvalho, 1991), and perhaps he too should be considered a lumper, making the relationship of the transference the crucial part of psychoanalysis to be isolated and reconstructed as a new method of counselling or psychotherapy.

Rogers was acclaimed as one of the prophets of Humanistic Psychology, a movement prominent during the 1960s and 1970s. It was presented as a third way between psychoanalysis and mainstream Experimental and Biological Psychology, and was linked with phenomenology as well as Carl Rogers. It was also vaguely linked with an attitude of tender-mindedness, favouring optimistic spiritual values and radical but peaceful political change, and cultivating empathy. Ellis, by contrast, was seen as tough-minded and confrontational, a contrast exemplified by the widely shown Gloria video, in which a single client, Gloria, was recorded with a succession of three therapists, Rogers, Ellis, and the founder of Gestalt Therapy, Fritz Perls. Ellis did not come off well, and there was little of the quick rapport that he could achieve in other recordings, especially those of his Friday night workshops, in which Ellis would spend a few minutes discussing a problem with a volunteer from the audience. The Gloria video has been widely shown during introductory courses on psychotherapy. As Ellis recognised, this did not help his reputation with those who favoured a humanistic approach. However, as he also recognised, the contrast was misleading, and he went on to describe REBT as humanistic (Ellis, 1974). Unlike sympathy, empathy, which is insight into the viewpoint of the client, is neither tough nor tender minded. So if twentieth-century humanism is based on empathy that is because, like its predecessor during the Renaissance, it advocated seeing things from the point of view of the individual human being, rather than that of powerful institutions, whether those of Christianity, psychoanalysis, or Laboratory Psychology.

This argument between humanist and non-humanistic is important for this book but is not explicitly spelt out. Instead there are two chapters on issues arising from the tension, pseudoscience (Chapter Seven) and the fashionable interest in mindfulness (Chapter Eight), starting with Kabat-Zinn (1990) during the 1980s. Ellis has rightly claimed that his humanistic notion of self-acceptance captures the therapeutic essence of mindfulness, but he was not alone in this. It was explicit in Gestalt Psychology (Perls et al., 1972; first published in 1951), Person Centred Therapy (PCT), and indeed in all the therapies that claimed to be humanistic. Both Ellis and Perls seem to have been influenced by Buddhist practice, and their notion of self-acceptance (Beisser, 1972) is close to Kabat-Zinn's stress on being non-judgemental. But the term "mindfulness" was studiously avoided in psychotherapeutic circles because of its familiar connection with a religion, Buddhism, until Kabat-Zinn drew upon the emotional capital already invested in the word, while insisting that it can be abstracted from its context without loss.

The interest in pseudoscience arose from the "demarcation" problem in the philosophy of science and from the tradition of exposing cranks using scientific rhetoric in order to convince the gullible. The tradition goes back to nineteenth-century investigative journalism, but became a more academic study with the work of Martin Gardner, starting in 1952. Psychoanalysis was always a strong candidate for the label, and Ellis himself, when still a psychoanalyst, wrote papers on how it could be made more scientific. He certainly used scientific rhetoric in writing about REBT, but also recognised how far it fell short in this respect. Wessler (1992, 1996), an apostate from Ellis's REBT, criticised REBT as being pseudoscientific. This is briefly analysed in Chapter Two, and a detailed account of what "pseudoscience" amounts to in late twentieth-century thought is given in Chapter Seven. This is not in order to define Ellis as scientific or pseudo-scientific, but rather to convey some of the general cultural tensions that Ellis had to contend with. More specific tensions are discussed in Chapter Nine, in which we describe how REBT preserved its original philosophical core while trying to hold its own in the marketplace against Beck's CBT, whose looser theoretical structure enables it better to adapt to the changing demands of "evidence-based practice".

## Historiography

One of the difficulties with this kind of history of ideas and practices is that we assume that the original (or translated) words of the Stoics mean the same as their modern equivalents. Does the Stoic "Reason", for instance, mean the same as the modern word used by Albert Ellis, and what is implicit in the "Rational" of REBT? In general, there are two ways around this. The first is to assume that there is a common human reality, independent of culture, and that language reflects the changing ways of describing this reality. This assumes a real human invariant, reason, although words used to describe it change. History then traces these changes. This is a traditional method for the history of science in the English-speaking world, but there are many problems with it, stemming from the view that language affects experience, which is an essential assumption of REBT itself. The follower of Stoic philosophy aspired to Sagehood, and *ataraxy* or peace of mind, whereas the typical modern client for psychotherapy desires to get rid of his or her depression or anxiety in order live a more fulfilling life. How much can we assume that the words used to aid these different processes and goals share common meanings unaffected by context?

The second way is to accept that our language and concepts affect how we experience the world, and write a history of concepts themselves, with no assumption of any common experience of reality. This way prospered in France during the twentieth century, following the work of Gaston Bachelard and Georges Canguilhem (Nicolson, 1991; Tiles, 1984). Later Michel Foucault applied it to the social sciences, and shook the complacency of the English-speaking historians of these disciplines when translations of his work began to appear. The first to appear was *Madness and Civilization* in 1965. Instead of assuming a fixed category, madness, referring to a definable human condition, and then writing about increasingly scientific ways of describing it, Foucault instead examined the concept itself, and its changing relationship to rationality and irrationality, and the emerging Western civilisation founded upon the Enlightenment belief in the powers of reason. The concept of madness, the way it is used, and the practices it supports, is part of a discourse that reflects the interests of a culture invested in this belief. It is not an isolated referent, but is part of a discursive formation that determines the thinking and practices of its users. The meaning of the word is not given by a reality to which it corresponds, but to its place in the discursive formation. Similarly, the meaning of practices, such as those linked with the relationship between client and therapist, have their meaning within a modern discursive formation. Therefore we cannot take a word or practice out of one discursive formation (e.g., that of Stoic philosophers) and assume it means the same as the supposedly equivalent word or practice in another discursive formation. Such ideas were not novel to English readers. They are similar to Wittgenstein's (1953, p. 5) "language games", and are present in Quine's (1953) work on translation and in Kuhn's (1962) notion of incommensurability. However, compared with those writers, Foucault was energetically political and showed the radical implications of such thinking, not only in psychiatry, but for all those human sciences where we are tempted to assume that human nature is a bundle of unchanging essences, rather than a social construction.

The notion of discursive formation has been prominent in the work of Kurt Danziger, one of the leading historians of psychology of the last fifty years. He writes of "networks of categories", where to understand a word it is necessary to understand the linguistic and cultural network of which it is a part. He has explained this as follows:

> [S]ingle terms are always embedded in a network of semantic relationships from which they derive their meaning and significance. In such a network, changes in the meaning of one term are not independent of changes in the meaning of others, and the significance of each term depends on the position it occupies in a larger whole that is best thought of as a *discursive formation*. By this I mean a language that constitutes an integrated world of meanings in which each term articulates with other terms so as to form a coherent framework for representing a kind of knowledge that is regarded as true and a kind of practice regarded as legitimate.
>
> (Danziger, 1997, p. 13; emphasis in original)

Such networks or discursive formations[10] change as a whole, a change in a part necessitating an adjustment in other parts, rather like an evolving biological species. Recently he has applied this to a history of memory, where he examines the context and use of the *memoria* of the Ancients, making clear that it has been a serious mistake in histories of psychology to assume that it means the same as our modern "memory" (Danziger, 2008, *passim*).

The general proscription from this work on discursive formations is "don't judge one discursive formation by the standards and meanings of another". It can certainly be illuminating to compare and contrast analogous concepts from different discursive formations, but misleading to use one as a yardstick to evaluate the other. This applies to the writing of history but also to different discursive formations that exist side by side, within the same culture. In Chapter Four, we use the concept of "discursive formation" in this way for a detailed analysis of rationality. We argue there, against writers who have criticised Ellis for his use of rationality in a therapeutic context, that they are confusing concepts of rationality from different discursive formations. Following the Stoics we may stress the importance of reason for the conduct of everyday life, but it is often dysfunctional (in fact, irrational) to apply the demanding canons of scientific rationality to the conduct of intimate relationships. Stoic (and REBT) and modern scientific rationality come from different discursive formations.

These views seem especially appropriate as a guide to comparing the work of our two main discursive formations, those of Epictetus and Albert Ellis. They are different in many respects, but both stress the conceptual interconnectedness that is central to the concept of discursive formation. This is compatible with what has come to be known as "constructivism" in psychology and psychotherapy (Mahoney, 2004, *passim*), which assumes that cultures and individuals within cultures construct their own way of perceiving the world through language and concepts. Ellis (1994) considered himself a constructivist, and throughout his career (as discussed in Chapter Three) he stressed the interdependence of his concepts, and the effect of language on our view of the world is an essential tenet of REBT. Likewise the concepts of Hellenistic and Roman Stoicism were self-consciously interconnected, even across disciplines, so that, for instance, changes in logic would be reflected by a change in the whole system, and hence in the ethics. As Diogenes Laertius puts it, in his first century BC summary of Stoic doctrine: "No part of philosophy is separate from another part; they all combine as a mixture" (Long, 1974, p. 118).

One of the dangers of getting carried away by useful terms like "discursive formation" and "constructivism" is of ignoring their own history as part of the old dualist debate between idealism and realism. Users of these terms easily find themselves unwittingly taking on a crude anti-realist stance,[11] and to avoid this we adopt a mutualist position (Still & Good, 1992, 1998) which situates the origin of the real in neither the mind nor the outer world, but in the dynamic relationships between them. One problem in doing this is we cannot draw on modern psychology, with its roots sunk deep in a dualist tradition, to theorise changes within discursive formations. So in Chapter Five, in which we look at the history of the relationship between rationality and deontological words like "should" and "ought", we develop an *ad hoc* psychology suited to mutualism, by putting together Giddens' (1976, p. 121) concept of "duality of structures" with Bakhtin's (1981, p. 424) distinction between "authoritative discourse" (AD) and "internally persuasive discourse" (IPD).

## Notes

1. This quote and information on Ellis' early life and career comes from Ellis (1991).
2. "Either/or, rather than this-and-that, seems to be the only realistic description of necessary conditions for basic personality change that can be made at the present time" (Ellis, 1962, p. 119). This characteristic conclusion belies his unusually confident style, both in speech and writing. However, throughout his career he has been consistent both in his confidence, and in his careful qualifications.
3. "Psychoanalytic horseshit" became his standard dismissal of psychoanalysis, familiar to many from his taped recordings of public lectures. Like a comedian's catchphrase, it was guaranteed to raise a laugh, and it contrasts sharply with the respectful tone with which he wrote about psychoanalysis even after he had begun Rational Psychotherapy. He readily acknowledged a debt in his more considered writings.
4. Sorabji (2000, p. 346). We draw freely from Sorabji's excellent account of the Stoic influence on early Christians.
5. Martin et al. (1988, esp. pp. 16–49). In Epictetus, according to Foucault, you apply evaluative rules to the thought itself, but Cassian goes beneath the surface, examining the root of the thought, to see whether its apparent innocence masks evil origins, analogous perhaps to Beck's idea of core beliefs, and the downward arrow technique in REBT.
6. The British self-help tradition of Samuel Smiles was different, and seems to have owed little to Stoicism, focusing more on education and practical improvement in the tradition of utilitarianism, and perhaps William Cobbett (1823).
7. Allen was English and seems to have been more influenced by Tolstoy and Buddhism than Emerson and Stoicism. However, his huge and continuing popularity in the States rather than Britain suggests a ready receptivity there that makes him part of the tradition we have in mind. The following quote from one of the many websites on Allen illustrates this: "James Allen's philosophy became possible when liberal Protestantism discarded the stern dogma that man is sinful by nature. It substituted for that dogma an optimistic belief in man's innate goodness and divine rationality" (Self-improvement-ebooks.com, n.d.).
8. "Accommodation" and "assimilation" is a pair of terms from biology, much used by Piaget (1971) in his theory of child development. An organism may assimilate material from its environment (e.g., food) without actually changing, or it may accommodate by changing itself to meet new conditions, as a child does during intellectual development.

9. The use of this word "lumped" points to another metaphor from the history of biology, the distinction in classification between "lumpers" and "splitters". Lumpers prefer a few broad categories, ignoring small differences, whereas splitters insist on the importance of these differences by creating distinct categories (Endersby, 2009; Mayr, 1982). We return to this distinction in Chapter Three, where it is used to distinguish between different views on appropriate units of analysis in psychology.

10. Although "network of categories" is more elegant and self-explanatory, we prefer to use "discursive formation". "Network of categories" implies verbal categories only, whereas "discursive formation" refers in addition to various non-verbal practices.

11. Or being perceived as doing this. Like many wars, the anger generated in science wars described in Chapters Three and Eight were a product of this kind of perception.

# CHAPTER ONE

# The place of rationality in Stoicism and REBT

## An outline of Stoicism

A discursive formation as defined in the introduction may be examined in two ways: by analysing the contemporary usages and interrelations of its concepts and practices; or by studying its evolution. Here we adopt the latter approach by comparing REBT with a discursive formation from Hellenistic and later Stoic philosophy. Using the distinction from evolutionary biology made in the Introduction, we will be asking whether the two discursive formations are truly homologous, rather than just analogous.

In his writings, Albert Ellis often referred to his early interest in philosophy, and to his reading of Stoic writers.

> I inducted this principle of the ABCs of emotional disturbance from working with hundreds of clients from 1943 to 1955. But I also took it over from many philosophers I studied from 1929 (when I was 16) onwards ... Clearest of all amongst the ancients were the Greek and Roman Stoics, especially Zeno of Citium

(the founder of the school), Chrysippus, Panaetius of Rhodes (who introduced Stoicism into Rome), Cicero, Seneca, Epictetus, and Marcus Aurelius.

(Ellis, 1994, p. 64)

The Stoics were one amongst many Hellenistic schools (including the Cynics, Epicureans, and Pyrrhonian Sceptics) whose philosophy centred on practical recipes for happiness[1] and for dealing with emotional disorders, during a period when the more theoretically oriented Peripatetics (followers of Aristotle) were in decline. Zeno of Citium was the founder, who around 300 BC started to teach while walking in the Painted Colonnade (Stoa) at Athens. Chrysippus ("the most important of all the Stoics" (Long & Sedley, 1987, p. 3)) was the leader of the school during the second half of the third century BC and developed a systematic philosophy in his many books, none of which survived the decline of Stoicism after 200 AD. Like Zeno, his works exist only in fragments, and through the accounts of other writers.

The authority of Zeno and Chrysippus was usually accepted by the later Stoics, but there were significant changes. The philosophy became more exclusively practical, and politically conservative. The ethical philosophy of the Hellenistic founders was practical, but also directed towards an ideal, that of the Sage whose actions are entirely in harmony with nature. They accepted that there have been no ideal Sages in reality, except perhaps Socrates, and Panaetius and Posidonius developed a more down to earth aspect of Stoicism during the second century BC, designed for those with no aspirations to Sagehood.

Politically, Zeno and Chrysippus were critical of hierarchy, notably the institution of slavery, which had been supported as part of a harmonious society by Plato and Aristotle (Erskine, 1990). Corresponding to this, we shall see below that they did not follow Plato in his hierarchical, dualistic psychology, which hinged on his use of an ordered society and its distinct classes as a metaphor for mind. Reason and emotion, for instance, correspond to the ruling and military castes. This Platonic view and this metaphor, with appropriate changes of detail, have been one of the dominant models of the mind in Western thought for over 2,000 years.

The later Stoicism was not just more practical than the earlier, it also accorded better with the hierarchical nature of Roman imperialist society. Its theory of mind, too, differed, following Plato's tripartite division of the soul rather than Chrysippus (Long, 1974, p. 115), although they were distinctly Stoic in their practical arguments and recommendations for cultivating virtue and happiness. These views, realistic and conservative in their acceptance of the political status quo, were generally followed by the later Latin Stoic writers, especially Seneca[2] and Marcus Aurelius; and by Cicero, who was not himself a Stoic, but who wrote extensively and sympathetically on Stoicism, and is of great value as a source for earlier writers.

Epictetus' saying that "[m]en are disturbed not by things, but by the views which they take of things" (Epictetus, 1948, p. 19) is sometimes cited as a hallmark of REBT, and even given to clients during the early sessions, as a succinct way of capturing this starting point. Through the exercise of reason, we can change "the views we take of things" and in this chapter we will examine the discursive formation constructed around this programme, and reflected in Stoic writings. We do not argue that Ellis's discursive formation is the same as that of the Stoics, but that it is similar in structure and historically related—so there are homologies, not just analogies.[3]

## The prevalence of Stoicism

In intellectual history, the proclivities of the audience are as relevant as those of the writer in determining the success of a text or movement. It is therefore important to recognise that Ellis was not digging up forgotten masterpieces read by none but a few scholars for nearly 2,000 years. For hundreds of years the best known Stoic masterpieces have been a huge popular success, and influenced many of the movements of thought that are taken to define Western culture. As we saw in the introduction, Stoic ethics and psychology were thoroughly assimilated by Christianity during its formative years. The Stoic emphasis on acting in harmony with nature and emotional constraint had lasting appeal, and could be readily abstracted from the pagan basis of Stoic philosophy. With the revival of Greek and Latin humanism from the twelfth century onwards, Stoic ethics was again studied directly and reabsorbed into Christian thinking. The texts that had survived, notably those of Cicero, Seneca, Epictetus, and Marcus Aurelius became prominent during the Renaissance. Later these works were translated into English and other European languages, and "were read and reread by those who had time to read in the sixteenth, seventeenth and eighteenth centuries" (Long, 1974, p. 107). Writers like Petrarch in the fourteenth century, Montaigne in the sixteenth, Shaftesbury, Bishop Butler, Hume, and Kant in the eighteenth, who built up their moral stance in debate with, rather than simply as followers of, Stoicism, were widely read by every hero of cultural change from Shakespeare and Thomas More to the great American moralists, Benjamin Franklin and Ralph Waldo Emerson.[4] Partly through these, and building on the earlier influx described in the introduction, Stoic ethics became assimilated into British and American culture, where it fused with the eighteenth- and nineteenth- century utilitarianism of England and Scotland.

The Stoics have continued to be read in modern editions right up to the present and "Stoicism" has entered European languages as a widely recognised ethical position. When we speak of someone being "philosophical" in the face of misfortune, it is the Latin Stoic moral philosophers who are implicitly being referred to, not the modern professors of philosophy. The Middle English "reasonable", of thinking things through, and avoiding extreme emotions, has a clear Stoic resonance. It reflects that sense of "rational" which means acting thoughtfully and with commonsense, rather than according to some logical ideal. Stoic thinking has been assimilated into our language, and it is no accident that Rudyard Kipling's (1977, pp. 257–258) "If", a stirring exhortation to Stoic virtues as seen by a late Victorian Englishman, was recently voted Britain's most popular poem. When Ellis drew on Stoicism as he began to write about Rational Psychotherapy during the 1950s, he was not preaching to the unconverted—the Stoicism contained in popular morality ensured a ready audience for what he had to say. The hostility he experienced was fired by intellectual investments in opposed conceptions of therapy, especially Person Centred Therapy, and of the relation between thought and emotion, not puzzlement at the unfamiliar (Still & Dryden, 1998).

## Emotions and responsibility

A central feature of Stoic ethics is that we are responsible not just for our actions, but also for our emotions. The psychological theory behind the ethics was worked out in considerable detail by the earlier Stoics. In the version of the theory outlined later by Seneca, there is a "first movement" akin to a physiological response like a startle or salivation, followed by a judgement of assent, which makes the whole process similar to the modern "emotion". This is demonstrated in different ways, but a common move is to show that undesirable emotion is not caused by its supposed source since we are unmoved by worse events in a different context:

> [W]hy do you shudder at the shouting of a slave, at the rattling of bronze, or the banging of a door? Although you are so sensitive, you have to listen to thunder ... These same eyes ... that cannot tolerate marble unless it is mottled and polished with recent rubbing, that cannot tolerate a table unless it is marked by many a vein, that at home would see under foot only pavements more costly than gold—these eyes when outside will behold, all unmoved, rough and muddy paths and dirty people ... and tenement walls crumbled and cracked and out of line. Why is it, then, that we are not offended on the street, yet are annoyed at home, except that in the one case we are in an unruffled and tolerant state of mind, and in the other are peevish and fault-finding?
>
> All our senses ought to be trained to endurance. They are naturally long-suffering, if only the mind desists from weakening them.
>
> (Seneca, 1928, p. 339)

Such inconsistencies demonstrate that we are responsible for our undesirable emotions. One of Seneca's recommendations was to summon the mind to give an account of itself at the end of every day: "Anger will cease and become more controllable if it finds that it must appear before a judge every day" (Seneca, 1928, p. 340). The details of Stoic remedies may differ from those offered by Ellis, but both give a special place to responsibility and to the rationality that makes responsibility possible—to disciplined observation and reflection on the workings of the mind, in the hope and expectation of leading a happier and more satisfactory life. This is achieved through the control of the emotions, by witholding assent to the first movements. However, this is not usually control through the forcible suppression of unruliness, but by exercising reason and altering the source of emotional unruliness in the environment or in the mind.

## Reason and emotion in Plato

This view that we are responsible for our emotions, and can therefore use reason therapeutically, contrasts with a widely accepted view amongst some modern psychotherapists that reason and intellect are part of the problem, certainly not the solution. Implicit in such a view is that emotion and reason are separate, so that emotions can be triggered and can run their course in psychological isolation. A possible source of such faculty psychology, familiar to the early Stoics, was Plato. In *The Republic* he described the mind as containing three distinct parts. He (or his mouthpiece Socrates) distinguished reason, desire, and emotion. Reason and desire are distinct, claimed Socrates, because they are sometimes in opposition. He began by distinguishing in this way between thirst as a desire which unequivocally pulls the person towards drinking, and a prohibition "derived from reasoning", which forbids drinking. Socrates concluded:

> Then we may fairly assume that they are two, and that they differ from one another; the one with which a man reasons, we may call the rational principle of the soul, the other, with which he loves and hungers and thirsts … may be termed the irrational or appetitive.
>
> (Plato, 1970, p. 213)

His example to illustrate the separation of desire and emotion[5] (passion or spirit) is more complicated, but of great interest.

> Leontius … observed some dead bodies lying on the ground at the place of execution. He felt a desire to see them,[6] and also a dread and abhorrence of them; for a time he struggled and covered his eyes, but at length the desire got the better of him; and forcing them open, he ran up to the dead bodies, saying, Look, ye wretches [i.e., his eyes], take your fill of the fair sight … The moral is that anger at time goes to war with desire, as though they were two distinct things.
>
> (Plato, 1970, p. 215)

Thus, both reason and emotion differ from desire, but is emotion a kind of reason? No, since:

> We may observe even in young children that they are full of spirit [or passion] almost as soon as they are born, whereas some of them never seem to attain to the use of reason, and most of them late enough.
>
> (Plato, 1970, p. 215)

Reason and emotion are distinct because emotion occurs in animals and children but not reason. Thus, for Plato, at the start of a great tradition of thinking about the mind, reason, emotion, and desire are distinct faculties, and rationality is contrasted with, and may be opposed to, emotion and desire. They may affect one another, but each is independently acted upon by the environment or bodily changes, rather than being part of a single system.

## Right and wrong reason in Chrysippus

For Chrysippus, the most influential of the Hellenistic Stoics, the relationship between reason, emotion, and desire was very different. They are not distinct faculties and cannot be opposed to one another since they are intrinsically related as part of a system.

The tight organisation of the discursive formation is brought out in a fragment preserved in a text by Galen. It is cited in Inwood (1985), whose gloss emphasises the semantic interconnections:

> This explanation [by Chrysippus] makes it plain that "irrational", "unnatural", "disobedient to reason", and "excessive" (which are all specifications of the kind of impulse which constitutes a "passion") must be elucidated in terms of one another. It also makes it clear that Chrysippus dealt with the doctrine of the passions in the broad context of the proper goal of man's life and the place of a rational animal in a rational universe.
>
> (Inwood, 1985, p. 155)

The passage from Chrysippus is as follows:

> We must first keep in mind that the rational animal is by nature such as to follow reason and to act according to reason as a guide. Nevertheless, he often moves[7] towards some things and away from some things in another way, disobediently to reason, when he is pushed too far [or to excess]. Both definitions, [sc. the one mentioning] the unnatural movement which arises irrationally in this way and [the one mentioning] the excessiveness in the impulses, are in terms of this movement. For this irrationality must be taken to be obedient to reason and turning its back on reason.

> And it is in terms of this motion that we also say in ordinary usage that some people are "pushed" and "moved irrationally without reason and judgement".

> (cited in Inwood, 1985, pp. 155–156)

A problem of interpretation in this passage, a problem which Chrysippus himself is struggling with, lies in two senses of "reason" or "rational". In Stoic human psychology, "impulses" (towards or away from some object) are never in conflict with reason, since they are themselves always the product of reason. The presence of reason is what differentiates the adult human from a child or an animal, and is the Stoic interpretation of Aristotle's definition of human beings as a rational animal. Like non-human animals, children are governed by pre-rational impulses. Impulses are directed desires—not just hunger, for instance, but hunger directed towards a plate of food. They are a product of a sense impression (triggering a "first movement") and "assent", and the process of assent includes what we call appetite and emotion. When a sense impression (food and salivation) is assented to, it becomes an impulse (eat).

In adults, the process of assent is a product of reason. As Chrysippus put it: "Reason supervenes as the craftsman of impulse" (Long & Sedley, 1987, p. 346; cited in Long, 1974, p. 173). It supervenes as part of a developing system, a possibility overlooked by Plato in his argument for the separation of reason and emotion. In Cicero's account of Stoicism, there are five stages in this process of development. Initially there is a mere turning towards what accords with nature. Second, this becomes consolidated (a sub-stage of Seneca's first movement). Third, it is consciously chosen—reason is now involved, but choice entails the possibility of choosing wrongly. Fourth, the choice becomes a habit. Finally, for the sage, it is "unwavering and in harmony with nature" (Cicero, 1991, p. 37). At the third stage there may be an "excess" (controlled by "passion"), when the impulse is disobedient to reason. For the Stoics, "passion" corresponds not to emotion in general, but seems similar to the "inappropriate" or "unhelpful" emotions of REBT, and the judgements that go with these (Dryden, 1990, p. 7). "Passions are 'false judgements' which have as their predicate very good and very bad … Fear is 'judgement of an impending evil which seems to be intolerable'" (Long, 1974, p. 176). So we get the paradox of an irrationality which is "obedient to reason and turning its back on reason" (Inwood, 1985, p. 156).

There seems agreement amongst interpreters of Chrysippus that the paradox is resolved by a distinction between right and wrong reason (Inwood, 1985, p. 156), and a wavering between the two (rather than a direct clash) on the part of all adult humans except the sage. This difference between right and wrong reason may be illustrated with an example that could come from REBT.

> At one moment (someone) may assent to the true Stoic proposition that pain is not a bad thing; but if this judgement is insecurely based it will not be strong enough to reject a contrary judgement, that pain is something very bad, which comes to mind and is accompanied by a bodily reaction as the dentist starts drilling his tooth.
>
> (Long, 1974, p. 177)

Thus whereas for Plato, and most psychology since Plato, the conflict is between reason (going to the dentist serves my long-term goal to be healthy) and emotion (fear), in Chrysippus the conflict is between two impulses, each a system of (we would say) reason, emotion, and sense impression. On the one hand, asssent to "it's worthwhile going in spite of the pain" plus unpleasant anticipation on hearing the drill; on the other, assent to "I can't stand it" plus panic and terror. Although different in detail, this example has the same structure as the play of rationality in REBT; making appropriate substitutions to the quotation from Long we get:

> At one moment (someone) may assent to the true REBT proposition that pain (A) is unpleasant but not awful and absolutely unbearable; but if this belief (rB) is insecurely based it will not be strong enough to reject a contrary belief (iB), that pain is absolutely unbearable, which comes to mind and is accompanied by a bodily reaction (C) as the dentist starts drilling his tooth.

Thus, just as in REBT an emotional or behavioural consequence is always (or nearly always) a product of belief (B), which may be rational or irrational, so in classical Stoicism choice is always controlled by reason, which may be right or wrong reason. When conflict occurs, it is not between reason and emotion, as in Plato, but between right and wrong reason, and the corresponding impulses, which contain within them what we call desire or appetite and emotion.

### Classical Stoicism and the conflict between impulses

Given these theoretical differences between the Platonic view and the classical Stoic theory of mind, represented by Chrysippus, how do they differ in practice? Chrysippus agreed with Plato's developmental point that reason does not occur in animals or children, but did not see this as an argument for treating the mind as consisting of distinct parts. Instead, as we have seen, the struggle is not between reason and desires, but a problem of ensuring that impulses are moulded in accordance with right reason. His interpretation of the story of Leontius would be that the struggle is not between desire, passion, and reason, but a wavering between different impulses, as assent is given to one and then the other. Reason is always involved when assent is given, although it may be right or wrong.

Suppose, having read the evidence connecting smoking with illness, someone decides to give up; but when she meets friends she accepts the offered cigarettes. Plato would see this as a conflict between reason and desire, with passion coming into play in the guilt at having given in again. But for Chrysippus, if there is a struggle, it is between two impulses, one moulded by right reason ("I get a lot of pleasure from smoking and it will be painful to give it up, but the health risks far outweigh these short-term gains"), and the other by wrong reason ("Just one won't do any harm, and I really need one just now to steady my nerves"). A third impulse may come into play after failing to resist temptation ("I've given in again, what a worm I am"); this is homologous to the self-talk by Leontius as he berates his eyes, as though it is the claims of their appetite he has succumbed to: "Look, ye wretches, take your fill of the fair sight."

In a detailed discussion of Chrysippus' theory, Nussbaum (1994) takes bereavement as an example to illustrate how it works, and concludes as follows.

> On the parts-of-the-soul view, conflict is viewed as a struggle between two forces, different in character and simultaneously active within the soul. Reason leads this way, desire pushes that

way … [If the grieving person is striving to be a good Stoic] the parts view will say that her irrational element is doing the grieving, while the rational part is thinking philosophical thoughts and endeavouring to restrain her from grief … Chrysippus would urge us, instead, to regard the conflict as an oscillation of the whole soul between recognition and denial … "not the conflict and civil war of two parts, but the turning of a single reason in two different directions, which escapes our notice on account of the sharpness and swiftness of the change". At one moment, [the mourner] assents (her whole being assents) to the idea that an irreplaceable wonderful person has departed from her life. At another moment, she distances herself from that knowledge, saying, "No, you will find someone else."

(Nussbaum, 1994, pp. 384–385)

## Stoicism and REBT—homologies, analogies, and differences

How alike is this Stoic discursive formation to that of REBT? We have already noted significant parallels, and in both rationality is a crucial ingredient in living happily through the cultivation of healthy or appropriate emotions. This general similarity is potentially homologous rather than analogous since Ellis drew some of his account of the control of emotions by reason directly from Stoic writings, and from the Stoicism present in popular morality.

More specifically, Ellis appears to share with Chrysippus the view that conflict is between right and wrong reason (or rational and irrational beliefs) rather than between reason and emotion. Chrysippus developed this into a distinct psychological theory of impulses and conflict between impulses, whereas in practice Ellis seems less consistent than the early Stoics in maintaining that reason and emotion are essentially linked and not separate faculties. In this section, we focus on some surface differences between Stoicism and REBT in order to tease out the striking homologies still present in the midst of divergence.

### Interdependence of reason and emotion

According to REBT, we disturb ourselves with irrational beliefs in the form of demands, which are themselves illogical and unrealistic.

We have seen that this is homologous to the Stoic "wrong reasons", which are linked with "passions" and "excess", and hence irrational. In Stoicism, an impulse consists of sense impression and assent, and assent involves reason (right or wrong) so cognition is an integral part of an impulse. The impulse is a system involving sense impression, reason, and emotion, so that for the Stoics, unlike Plato, thinking and emotion are essentially (not just causally) interdependent. Ellis too has always stressed the interdependence of thinking and emotions (in both Ellis, 1962, and in Ellis, 1994), but in practice this is easily lost in the implicit independence of A, B, and C in the ABC model (see p. 47). As a guide for practical intervention it has proved convenient to identify A, B, and C as though they were distinct.

However, in the 1962 edition of *Reason and Emotion in Psychotherapy,* Ellis explored a conceptual inseparability of reason and emotion, when he distinguished between "strong" and "weak" cognitions and later equated this with Abelson's computer simulation of "hot" and "cool" cognitions. In the 1994 edition, he writes:

> Adapting and adding to Abelson, I now talk about three kinds of cognitions to my clients and in my lectures and workshops on REBT: (1) "Cool" or descriptive cognitions—e.g., "This is a table" or "This is the round table." (2) "Warm" or evaluative cognitions— e.g., "I like this table" or "I dislike this table." (3) "Hot" or strongly evaluative cognitions—e.g., "I like this table very much and must use it!" or "I hate this table and must destroy it!"
>
> (Ellis, 1994, p. 60)

This sounds as if the cognitions contain the emotion, as in Chrysippus, but Ellis (1994, pp. 60–61) goes on to write that the cognitions "almost always accompany" or "tend to go with" the emotions, which suggests that there are exceptions, and the relationship is contingent. Ellis has developed this pervasive use of qualifiers ("almost", "always", etc.) in order to avoid any sign of dogmatism or absolutist thinking. But strict avoidance of unqualified assertion can itself become absolutist, and if Chrysippus (as we interpret him) is right it is correct and not absolutist to say that a hot cognition like "I hate this table and must destroy it" is always accompanied by (or better "is part of") a certain kind of emotion. What this amounts to is that hot emotion is one of the necessary signs of a hot cognition—the heat is not just in the words, and "I hate this table and must destroy it" said coolly and without corresponding emotion is, by the definition we are attributing to Chryssipus, not a hot cognition. Conversely, "I dislike this table", spat out with angry venom, already contains the emotion and is a hot cognition.

This is an extremely important point theoretically, since it marks the difference between a systemic account of the relationship between cognitions and emotions, and the faculty account which we have ascribed to Plato, and which has dominated psychological thought in the West. Ellis's affiliation remains ambivalent. In theory, he gave a systemic account, but in practice in the ABC model, it looks more like a faculty account.

## Sexual asceticism and permissiveness

In both editions of *Reason and Emotion in Psychotherapy* Ellis lists the Stoic thinkers to whom he is indebted, but in the second he adds a caveat.

> Watch it, however! Although I largely adapted REBT's ABC theory of emotional disturbance from Epictetus and other Stoics and although I made Epictetus one of the patron saints of cognitive behavior therapy ... I am hardly a Stoic. I favor, in addition to Epictetus, Epicurus, who emphasized pleasure as the main good and the end of morality, but who, as Webster's Biographical Dictionary states, held "that the genuine life of pleasure must be a life of prudence, honor, and justice."
>
> (Ellis, 1994, p. 65)

This seems to be what Ellis favours as "long-term hedonism", although in both editions he ascribes this to Stoicism, referring to one of his main tenets as "[t]he Stoic principle of long-range rather than short-range hedonism" (1962, p. 363). He agrees with the Stoics on high frustration tolerance, but "many of their writings on sex, love, and marriage show that they are too ascetic for my taste" (Ellis, 1994, p. 65).

There are misunderstandings here, perhaps based on the texts available to the youthful Albert Ellis, but also because of contrasting contexts. According to Diogenes Laertius' exposition of Stoic ethics, "some existing things are good, others are bad, and others are neither of these" (Long & Sedley, 1987, p. 354). Health, beauty, wealth, etc., are usually preferred but not in themselves good, since they can be used well or badly. They, like pleasure and pain, are indifferent to the virtuous life, which, according to both Stoics and Epicureans, is a life of prudence, honour, and justice. The difference between them is that for the Epicureans the ultimate good is pleasure, whereas for the Stoics it is virtue itself, which is living in accordance with nature; in the case of human beings this is to live rationally (according to right reason). Generally, the rational person will prefer pleasure to pain, and since virtue accords with rationality, it may be part of a virtuous life to choose pleasure, including sexual pleasure. However, pleasure itself is morally neutral. A person suffering chronic pain or unable to enjoy sexual pleasure, is in no way morally inferior because of it; nor is such a person morally superior, although he or she may be in a better position to lead a virtuous (and therefore happy) life, since he or she is less likely to be ensnared by passion.

Given this, there was a variety of views about sexual asceticism amongst the Stoics. Their views evolved partly from the Cynics, who shared the Stoic belief that to live in accord with (human) nature is to live rationally (Long, 1974, p. 110). The Cynics were famous for sexual permissiveness. There is a well-known story that the founder of the school in the fourth century BC, Diogenes of Sinope, used to masturbate openly as soon as he felt the urge, sometimes in crowded streets. Crates was noted for having sexual intercourse in public with Hipparchia (one of his followers), as well as for an early shame attacking exercise described by one of the great writers on Stoicism in the early modern era.

> In the midst of a discussion, and in the presence of his followers, Metrocles let off a fart. To hide his embarrassment he stayed at home until, eventually, Crates came to pay him a visit; to his consolations and arguments Crates added the example of his own licence: he began a farting match with him, thereby removing his scruples and, into the bargain, converting him to the freer stoic school from the more socially oriented Peripatetics whom he had formerly followed.
>
> (de Montaigne, 1987, p. 165)

Crates was one of the teachers of the founder of Stoicism, Zeno of Citium, who continued the radical tradition by proposing to dispense with marriage and sexual taboos. As Erskine (1990) explains, these "impose unnecessary restrictions on the behaviour of the wise man or woman, who should be perfectly capable of freely making his or her decision on the matter" (p. 25). The resulting promiscuity would have the advantage that since fathers would not know who their children were, they would be encouraged to take an interest in all of them. Unlike many other philosophers, then and since, the Stoics did not believe that women differed from men in their potential for virtue, and did not support different sexual moralities for men and women (Nussbaum, 1994, Chapter Nine). This was true throughout classical Stoicism, and the asceticism to which Ellis objects, which has come to seem characteristic of Stoicism, does not seem to have been marked until the patrician Roman Stoics of the first century AD. Their austere version of Stoic ethics, which is the one we are most familiar with, fitted their role as politically active members of an imperial ruling class. Marcus Aurelius was emperor, and Seneca held high office within the empire. It is partly from these Stoics that the founding fathers of Christianity, such as Clement and Augustine, took their strict sexual morality and their disapproval of contraception and masturbation, both practices which make the goal of sex pleasure rather than propagation, and which are therefore seen as contrary to nature (Brown, 1989, p. 21). But, by this time, "nature" had become linked to the will of God, an interpretation far removed from the "nature" followed by Diogenes the Cynic when he masturbated in the public highway.

However, this strict code is not essential to Stoic ethics, and is not always how Stoicism has been viewed. Montaigne, writing in the sixteenth century, actually uses the laxity of early Stoics in his arguments for moral relativism; they behaved in ways that would be regarded as unbecoming in a grave philosopher of the sixteenth century. He writes: "Chrysippus said that, for a dozen olives, a philosopher will turn a dozen somersaults in public, even with his breeches off" (de Montaigne, 1987, p. 165). More immediately to the point, he cited Seneca's criticism of the sexual looseness of other Stoics (de Montaigne, 1987, p. 164). Seneca was reacting against the liberal attitudes of earlier Stoics, whereas Ellis is moving in the opposite direction, against the American puritanism whose remote ancestor was the ascetism he criticises in the Stoics he otherwise admires. But, for the Stoics and for Ellis, the moral target was not sex as such, but the irrational passion associated with sexual love. In this respect, there may be homology, but it exists against backgrounds of very different cultural attitudes towards sex and asceticism.

### Hedonism, self-preservation, and oikeosis

Like most classical philosophers, Stoics and Epicureans were Eudaimonist—they believed that happiness is an ultimate goal. However, the Epicureans believed that this is achieved through the cultivation of pleasure, and the Stoics believe that it is achieved through the exercise of virtue. In Stoicism, virtue is "in accordance with nature" and in practice this includes self-preservation. According to Diogenes Laertius, writing on Stoicism and drawing from Chrysippus, "pleasure ... is a by-product which arises only when nature all by itself has searched out and adopted the proper requirements for a creature's constitution, just as animals [then] frolic and plants bloom" (Long & Sedley, 1987, p. 346). For the Stoics, "pleasure" was limited to the satisfaction of the appetites and a pleasure principle only comes into play, if at all, when the animal is at home with itself in its proper environment. Until then its activities are directed towards this rather than pleasure, and the psychological component of this prior principle is *oikeiosis*. This has proved hard to translate but has connotations of concern, of being at home with, or being well disposed towards (Pembroke, 1971). Seneca gave as examples a baby trying to stand and a tortoise on its back, which "feels no pain, but desire for its natural state makes it restless, and it does not stop struggling and shaking itself until it stands on its feet" (Long & Sedley, 1987, p. 347).

Some twentieth-century psychologists, following Freud and utilitarian theories of action, would see no distinction between the pain/pleasure principle and *oikeiosis*. In Hull's (1943) influential learning theory of the 1930s and 1940s, for instance, both would be included under drive and drive reduction. And for Ellis too, when he writes:

> Just about all existing schools of psychotherapy are, at bottom, hedonistic, in that they hold that pleasure and freedom from pain are good and preferably should be the aims of thought and action. This is probably inevitable, because people who do not believe in a hedonistic view would continue to suffer intense anxiety and

discomfort and would not come for therapy. And therapists who did not try in some manner to alleviate the discomfort of those who did come for help would hardly remain in business for very long.

(Ellis, 1994, p. 292)

Here Ellis implies that comfort/discomfort, pain/pleasure, and anxiety/freedom from anxiety are variations along a single hedonistic dimension. This is the dimension he links with Epicurus' hedonism, and the quote from *Webster's Dictionary* given above suggests he sees it as of the long-range variety (Ellis, 1994, p. 65). He appears to assume that relieving discomfort is a hedonistic activity, but the Stoics too tried to alleviate the discomfort of those who came for help, without being hedonists; and the fact that later in *Reason and Emotion in Psychotherapy* Ellis refers favorably to the "Stoic principle of long-range rather than short-range hedonism" (p. 292) suggests that the distinction between pleasure and happiness is unimportant for Ellis.

However, for the Stoic discursive formation the distinction between pleasure and happiness is crucial. Their ethical system hinges upon it. The tortoise struggling to right itself acts in accordance with nature and for self-preservation, according to the principle of *oikeiosis* rather than the pleasure/pain principle. In adult humans the use of right reason accords with human nature, and the virtuous person will follow *oikeiosis* in seeking to act rationally. For them, "pleasure" is the satisfaction of appetite, not *oikeiosis*. Satisfaction of appetites, like health and wealth, will play an important part in the life of a virtuous person, but they are not essential to a virtuous life. Ellis's utilitarian hedonism is a product of modernity, but not obviously an advance over the theory of *oikeiosis*. Ethologists have exposed flaws in Hull's theory of drive reduction (Hinde, 1970), and few theorists of motivation nowadays would rely on a single dimension, whether it is pleasure or drive reduction.

## Acceptance and fatalism

In both editions of *Reason and Emotion in Psychotherapy* Ellis rejected the common criticism of the Stoics that they are too fatalistic. It is true he criticised Marcus Aurelius for being "irrationally over-fatalistic", but

> Epictetus ... did not say or imply that one should calmly accept all worldly evils and should stoically adjust oneself to them. His view

was that that people should first try to change the evils of the world; but when they cannot successfully change them, then they should uncomplainingly accept them.

(Ellis, 1994, pp. 290–291)

However, for Ellis, it is not always expected that you actually cultivate an active wish (rather than passive acceptance) for the conditions you have failed to change, but this seems fundamental to the sagehood aimed for by Stoicism. "Demand not that events should happen as you wish; but wish them to happen as they do happen, and you will go on well" (Epictetus, 1955, p. 20). The first part of this recommendation is close to REBT. The second half suggests a difference between Stoicism and REBT. In Stoicism, to wish events to happen as they do happen (if they cannot be changed) is to be in harmony with nature, and follows from the cultivation of realistic desires, and acceptance of yourself and of the vicissitudes of the world. To wish otherwise is to assent to an impulse through wrong reason or irrationality. However, in REBT there is a tendency to accept the client's likes and dislikes as a given, and to confine "irrationality" to the corresponding demand. Thus "I like cigarettes" is not irrational in the same way as "I must have cigarettes", since the latter is not logical (it does not follow from "I like cigarettes"), nor empirically valid (there is no law that I must have what I want), nor helpful. Similarly, in REBT, "I want to be perfect in everything" or "I dislike this chronic pain" is rational, but "I must be perfect" or "I can't stand this chronic pain" is irrational.

Two arguments suggest that Ellis's views are nevertheless close to the Stoics in this area. The first is that there are some cases where likes and dislikes (or at least acting on them) are irrational. The second is that the Stoic wish that things happen as they do happen is not the same as cultivating a liking for the events.

i. The range of thoughts and actions regarded as irrational varies in Ellis's writings. There are, so to speak, different discursive subformations, the therapeutic and the guide for rational living. For Ellis the therapist "I like cigarettes" is (we are assuming) just a true factual statement, hence not irrational, even as a statement of intent. However, for Ellis in his more general role as guide to rational living it is irrational. Thus his comprehensive list of irrationalities includes poor health education; drug advertising;

drug promotion; neglect of medical research; leading a carousing, playboy or playgirl type of life at the expense of other more solid enjoyments; ignoring the dangers inherent in going for immediate pleasures; and refusing to work against a harmful addiction because of the immediate discomfort of giving it up (Ellis, 1976). These are the kind of antecedent conditions that lead to the true assertion "I like cigarettes", and the rational course would be to try to undo the effect of these conditions, and (in Stoic terms) to cultivate the wish to do without them. In this sense, "I like cigarettes" is irrational, and, in this instance, which involves the cultivation of good health, Ellis's view accords with the Stoics.

ii. Seneca recommended cheerfully eating whatever food you are given, rather than refusing it or wishing for something else. "It is necessary that one grow accustomed to slender fare … To have whatsoever he wishes is in no man's power; it is in his power not to wish for what he has not, but cheerfully to employ what comes to him. A great step towards independence is a good-humoured stomach, one that is willing to endure rough treatment" (Seneca, 1962, p. 425). Seneca here seems to be echoing Epictetus' recommendation to "wish events to happen as they do happen", without going so far as to recommend liking the food (although that may follow, like learning to enjoy taking coffee without sugar). Similarly, Seneca advocated putting up with pain for the sake of long-term goals, without actually recommending that we like or enjoy it (Seneca, 1962, p. 437). Again we can practise accepting the pain, rather than getting drawn emotionally into the wish that it were otherwise, and this acceptance, perhaps, is what Epictetus meant by wishing events to happen as they do happen. If so then to "wish events to happen as they do happen" amounts to the same as the REBT recommendation that we accept inevitable pain, where to accept the pain is not to like it but to avoid any demand that it be otherwise.

## Conclusion

We have seen that there may be important homologies between Stoic recipes for virtuous living and REBT, but these can be hard to evaluate against the different historical contexts. For the Stoics the use of reason was natural to human beings, so to follow their recipes for the conduct of life was to live in accordance with human nature. Two thousand years later, the use of reason is sometimes opposed to "being natural", and Ellis's acclaim for rationality was set against an opposition that gave it a very different force and meaning from that of the Stoics. Likewise, Ellis's hedonism slots into a historical background of utilitarianism and materialism that has no exact parallel in antiquity, and which offers no equivalent to the Stoic *oikeiosis*.

The psychology of the early Stoics, notably Chrysippus, made emotion and reason essentially interdependent, in opposition to the faculty psychology that eventually dominated Western psychology. Ellis's psychology also stresses the essential interdependence of emotion, but there is no evidence that he derived this from his reading of the Stoics, and hence that it is homologous with the Stoic theory. More likely, he was following an approach popular when he began to write on REBT, and opposed to the dominant stimulus response theories of the time. Similarly, Ellis's sexual ethics is part of the liberal reaction to constraints on sexual expression which is peculiar to the present time, and hard to compare with any of the varying views of Ancient Stoicism.

These differences in historical context certainly make a difference to the respective discursive formations, but, to some extent, they can be understood historically and allowed for. This would not render the discursive formations equivalent, even in part. It would probably be impossible nowadays to adopt the Stoic attitude to sex, or hedonism, since to adopt such an attitude in a modern context would mean something different from what it did over 2,000 years ago. But given these historical differences we might claim that, apart from the importance of *oikeiosis* to the Stoics, the discursive formations of REBT and Stoicism are as close as it is possible to get, and that they are sometimes homologous rather than merely analogous, partly because of the pervasive influence of Stoicism on modern thought, and partly because of Ellis's own close study of Stoicism. Above all, the two discursive formations share a confidence in the application of reason for removing psychological barriers to happiness.

Earlier in this chapter we expressed the hope that the parallels we find will throw mutual light on REBT and on the conceptual apparatus that guided Stoic thinkers in their search for happiness. The perspective of Stoic philosophy helped us to focus on the ambivalence in Ellis's views on the interdependence of reason and emotion, and on the possible limitations in his hedonistic philosophy, as well as helping us bring out that neither this hedonism nor Ellis's modern sexual liberalism are essential to REBT. At the same time, REBT gave us a model of Stoicism in practice against which to articulate the practical philosophy of Chrysippus and his Roman successors. Historians of philosophy are already accustomed to taking a more general psychotherapy as their model in this way (Long, 1974; Nussbaum, 1994; Pannizza, 1991), and the use of REBT would add precision to these attempts to clarify Stoic practices to a modern audience. In the next chapter we look at another aspect of the Epictetan legacy, the emphasis on dialogue and practice rather than absolute philosophical truth, which leads to a reflection on the differences between REBT and Beck's CBT.

## Notes

1. We don't have to go far before the problem of finding a modern equivalent to classical words arises. The general goal for the Hellenistic philosophers was *ataraxia,* usually translated as peace of mind. A Stoic goal on the way to this was freedom from passions, which were homologous to, but not the same as, our modern "emotions" (Dixon, 2006, p. 3 *et passim*). For Aristotle, happiness was *eudaimonia,* which was equivalent to *eu zên* or living well (Kraut, 2010).

2. Although Inwood (1993) has argued that Seneca does not follow Plato in his tripartite division of the soul.

3. Panizza (1991) writes on Petrarch's Stoicism as psychotherapy, and the link between Stoicism and psychotherapy has been pointed out by several classical scholars (Long, 1974: Nussbaum, 1994; Sorabji, 2000). The connection with REBT and CBT has been explored in our earlier papers (Still & Dryden, 1999, 2003—this chapter and Chapter Three are revised versions of these) and in Robertson (2010).

4. See, for example, Eliot (1951); Emerson (1977); and Richardson (1995, pp. 152–153).

5. There are complications in translation from the Greek that we ignore for the purposes of our argument. We treat both "passion" and "spirit" in Jowett's translation of Plato as equivalent to "emotion". The modern word "emotion" may belong to a different discursive formation, but the tripartite model we are discussing appears to be homologous to the separation of emotion and appetite that has formed the framework of modern psychology.

6. Why a desire? A possible explanation is that Leontius was attracted to deathly pale youths, and this was well-known to Socrates' audience (Price, 1994, pp. 52–53).

7. This is not the "first movement" but the impulse that follows assent.

# CHAPTER TWO

# Ellis and Epictetus: dialogue *vs.* method in psychotherapy

*Introduction*

Having made the case for homologies between Stoicism and Ellis's REBT, in this chapter we use a more detailed historical analysis in order to tease out other aspects of the legacy, as well as some of the differences between REBT and the more popular CBT founded by Aaron Beck. Some recent commentators have found problems in the scientific status of REBT, which seem not to be present in Beck's CBT. We argue that this may be partly because they drew differently from the traditions of thought available to them, which appears most clearly in their first published papers. Beck's were more in the modern medical tradition, whose history forms part of the search for method leading to abstract knowledge and control that has been so powerful a feature of Western culture. Ellis was more discursive in style and drew on the dialogic tradition, in which obstacles to self-awareness and freedom are removed by enlisting the power of reason through question and answer. Socrates and Epictetus are the classical representatives of this tradition, and Ellis's first paper shows clear signs of being modelled on Epictetus. Later, however, although continuing in this tradition in his personal style and popular self-help books, Ellis also developed abstract models and methods that belong to the medical tradition. His dual allegiance, his attempt to balance distinct discursive formations or language games, has made him vulnerable to criticism from both sides.

The similarities between Aaron Beck's CBT and Albert Ellis's REBT are very clear. Both were trained as psychoanalysts, and both attempted to short-circuit the process of analysis by going straight to the thoughts themselves and trying to change them directly. Both therapies are a mixture of cognitive and behaviour therapy, both use an ABC model, and both explicitly take as their starting point the famous maxim of Epictetus that "[m]en are disturbed not by things, but by the views which they take of them". But recently, there has been debate about differences, and a 2001 special issue of the *Journal of Rational-Emotive and Cognitive-Behavior Therapy* took as its starting point the marginalisation of REBT compared with CBT (discussed further in Chapter Nine). Even after forty years, the theories of CBT and of REBT are still not seen by some writers as fully converged, although in daily practice the modern followers of the two schools may sometimes be hard to distinguish. Our purpose in this chapter is not to give a detailed account of apparent differences, but to focus on Ellis and those aspects of his theory and practice that have militated against full assimilation into a common, scientific framework of cognitive and behavioural therapy.

One writer who has addressed this is Wessler, as part of a critique of REBT. He became disenchanted after years as a prominent practitioner of REBT, and attempted to explain this in a series of papers (Wessler, 1992, 1996). He found Ellis's use of "rational" ill-defined and inconsistent, and charted the perceived shortcomings of REBT through a pair of dichotomies, rationalism *vs.* constructivism, and science *vs.* pseudo-science. For Wessler "rationalism" does not have the traditional philosophical meaning, but the one popularised by Mahoney.

> Like Zen Buddhism, the constructivistic position maintains that humans construct a private reality and that objective reality is unknowable if it exists at all. The rationalistic position holds that humans are more or less accurate perceivers of an objective reality.
>
> (Wessler, 1992, p. 620)

Mahoney had implied that the theories of both Beck and Ellis are rationalistic (Mahoney & Gabriel, 1987), but Wessler argued the opposite, that both are in theory constructivist, citing their common appeal to the above quote from Epictetus, "who might be called the patron philosopher of constructivists" (Wessler, 1992, p. 622). However, he found that in practice Ellis (unlike Beck) is rationalistic, since he insists that his version of one aspect of reality is correct; this is the musturbation axiom, "that absolute musts have a pivotal role in any form of psychological disturbance" (Wessler, 1992, p. 624). In a later paper, Wessler detected a second dogma unsupported by evidence, the parallel process model of emotions.

> Unique to RET [as it was when Wessler wrote] is the untested and unsupported hypothesis that there are qualitative differences between certain similar emotions, and that each is mediated by a different type of belief. For example, sadness is appropriate and depression is inappropriate, and each is mediated by a distinctly different type of belief.
>
> (Wessler, 1996, p. 48)

Thus, following bereavement, it is rational to recognise how much the person meant to you and the pain of the loss, so that you may feel extremely sad for a time. It is irrational to believe that the loss is absolutely awful and unbearable; such beliefs, if unchecked, are likely to lead to depression. Dogmas like the parallel process model of emotion, as well as Ellis's unwarranted assumption that human goals are universal, led Wessler to describe RET as a pseudoscience; it is in Wessler's words "a set of non-empirical assertions masquerading as a scientific psychotherapy" (Wessler, 1996, p. 52).

But even if justified, this exposure of Ellis's assumptions hardly disqualifies REBT from scientific status, certainly not to a constructivist. Nowadays even realists (or what Wessler refers to as rationalists) can agree with Lakatos that every science has a hard core of assumptions which are treated as unquestionable, and which are protected from scrutiny by the language and practices of what he called the "protective belt" (Lakatos, 1970, p. 131). Furthermore, an untested and unsupported hypothesis at the heart of REBT is not necessarily a "non-empirical assertion". A non-empirical assertion usually means one that *cannot* be tested empirically, and although more sympathetic to REBT than Wessler, Bond and Dryden (1996) made this more serious objection. They argued that the PM (the "primacy of the musts") hypothesis is untestable, and went further by deducing this difficulty from a more general problem with the core hypothesis of REBT, which is that "beliefs are at the core of psychological disturbance and health" (Bond & Dryden, 1996 p. 30). It is a problem because of the interdependence principle, that is, "that cognition, emotion, and behaviour cannot be regarded as separate psychological processes" (Bond & Dryden, 1996 p. 30).

> If cognition (which includes irrational beliefs), emotion, and behaviour form an interdependent system that determines psychological function, then how can elements of that system (i.e., cognition, emotion, and behaviour) be isolated and their separate effects on psychological function be measured?

> (Bond & Dryden, 1996, pp. 30–31)

However, even if the PM hypothesis may not be testable through experimental analysis in the laboratory, it is not unsupported, since the use of the therapy by Ellis and others has proved successful for a large number of clients; it has effectiveness, if not proved efficacy (Seligman, 1995). Like Maxwell's field theory of gases and Darwin's theory of natural selection, it works, even if it is not possible to break it down into elements that can be separately manipulated for a traditional psychological experiment.

Summarising these points, it would appear that Ellis has been understood by some writers as making important assumptions that are not made, or certainly not stressed, by Beck. Cognition, emotion, and behaviour are parts of an interdependent system, and there are two kinds of emotion, which might correspond to two distinct states of the system. In the rest of this chapter, we argue that these perceived differences are related to a split which goes deeper than issues of science *vs.* pseudoscience, or rationality *vs.* constructivism. It is deeper in the sense that it stretches back in time long before such distinctions, if they existed, had anything like their modern meanings. Beck and Ellis, for all their similarities, drew differently from the traditions of thought confronting them, and these differences have continued to colour their written and spoken presentations, and those of their followers.

## Two philosophical traditions

"Philosophers are not very philosophical." This joke, common amongst philosophy students, may well be old. It depends upon an ambiguity in the word "philosophy", which derives from two distinct traditions of thought, both originating in the Socrates of Plato's *Dialogues*. Until the sixteenth century, Plato, and his pupil Aristotle, were read and drawn upon, or taken as a starting point, by Christian philosophers. Theirs was an intellectual search for knowledge and the foundations of knowledge, and later academic philosophy has never quite succeeded in breaking away from this, hence Whitehead's famous remark that "[t]he safest characterization of the European philosophical tradition is that it consists of a series of footnotes to Plato" (Whitehead, 1978, p. 39). As "Natural Philosophy", however, one part of this search for knowledge became science, which has been no footnote but the main text of the last 400 years.

This is the major tradition. The second, minor and marginalised, is of a practical, personal philosophy, concerned with how to live rather than with knowledge. It also originated in Socrates, but it is more from the way Socrates lived and expressed his thinking through dialogue, described by Xenophon as well as Plato, than through the products of his thought. By encouraging reason and self-scrutiny in dialogue, Socrates believed that a person can be enabled to live well. Thus, someone can be a great philosopher in the first sense, but not in the second, by living badly and far from the Socratic ideal.

The course of the second tradition has been very different from the first. Instead of the emergence of new forms of knowledge, held together through historical continuity, it has depended upon the availability and return to certain key texts, used as a guide to living. Socrates has remained a moral ideal in this tradition, but the Hellenistic schools have provided some of the best-known sources (Long, 1986). These include the works of Epicurus and his follower Lucretius; Sextus Empiricus' account of Pyrrhonic scepticism; and the later Stoics, especially the Greek Epictetus, and the Romans Seneca and Marcus Aurelius. As we have seen, Epictetus is the writer cited by both Ellis and Beck, and his work has been frequently compared with modern psychotherapy by authors who make no mention of cognitive therapy (Long, 2002; Sorabji, 2000; Xenakis, 1969). We take Epictetus as representative of this tradition, especially his *Discourses*, which consist partly of dialogues on the Socratic model.

## Method and the decay of dialogue

Modern academic philosophy is but a small part of the legacy of ancient philosophy, like the surviving streets of an ancient city now dwarfed by the vast buildings of more recent times. The great constructions of science grew out of philosophy, but up to the seventeenth century they were still part of the same attempt to order the world. In 1637, Descartes' *Discourse on the Method* was published. This was his reply to the anti-rational scepticism of the late sixteenth century in France, especially in the writings of Montaigne, who had drawn on the recently published Latin translations of Sextus Empiricus (Curley, 1978).

Descartes described at length his own moral preparation for the task, which draws closely and accurately on his reading of Epictetus (Jones, 2006; Long, 2002, pp. 264–266), although the method itself, as we shall see, undermined the dialogic teaching favoured by Epictetus and Socrates. The full title of Descartes' ambitious book was *Discourse on the Method of Rightly Conducting one's Reason and Seeking the Truth in the Sciences, and in Addition the Optics, the Meteorology and the Geometry, which are Essays in this Method* (Cottingham, Stoothoff & Murdoch, 1985, p. 109). The method was spelt out in more detail in *Rules for the Direction of the Mind* (Cottingham, Stoothoff & Murdoch, 1985, pp. 7–78), and Descartes was so confident in it and himself that he believed he would eventually "explain all the phenomena of nature, i.e., all of physics" (Cottingham, Stoothoff & Murdoch, 1985, p. 109). This confidence in method did not arise in a vacuum. By Descartes' time, it was a fashionable topic that had developed out of the push by Petrus Ramus and others in the sixteenth century towards formalising the processes of logic into spatial arrangements that foreshadow modern flowcharts (Lenoir, 1979). It was not that method was a new discovery, but that making it explicit had been given a massive boost through the invention of printing, and the wide dissemination of knowledge that this made possible. The drive was not primarily towards science, which did not exist then as a concept, but towards an emphasis on didactic ways of teaching, rather than the full range of dialogue used, as we shall see, by Epictetus. In this way understanding became much more thoroughly a matter of learning rules or methods, and also facts, from textbooks, and less likely to be acquired directly out of dialogue. Method was here to stay, although Descartes' faith in his own version was over-optimistic, since he failed to recognise that the acquisition of knowledge would require a lot of steady empirical grind rather than a few flashes of theoretical insight. The teaching and practice of medicine and the expansion of science into specialist disciplines were the main beneficiaries of this slow revolution, whose distant legacies include manualisation and evidence-based practice in psychotherapy.

One result of these changes, as indicated in the title of Ong's *Ramus, Method and the Decay of Dialogue*, was the decline of dialogue as a pedagogic ideal (Ong, 1983). Obviously, teachers continued to speak to pupils to impart knowledge, but there was less faith in Socratic question and answer directed to self-observation and designed to awaken reason and intellectual insight. Yet such dialogue was kept alive in the minor, marginalised tradition of philosophy, by the readers of the Socratic dialogues and Epictetus concerned with how to live rather than with philosophical knowledge. Epictetus had belonged very firmly to this dialogic tradition.

These two traditions of method and of dialogue cut across the more familiar philosophical distinctions such as empiricism and rationalism, and epistemology and ontology. Both traditions can be empirical: dialogue because it appeals to self-observation and experience, including trial and error; method because it has created science out of experience, and science includes specialised systems of observation and classification, as well as experimental method.

## Epictetus and Socratic dialogue

Epictetus used Socrates to illustrate his maxim that "[m]en are disturbed not by things, but by the views which they take of them".

> Thus death is nothing terrible, else it would have appeared so to Socrates. But the terror consists in our notion of death, that it is terrible.
>
> (Epictetus, 1955, p. 19)

However, Socrates was not just a source of edifying examples to illustrate this central dictum of Epictetus' philosophy. He was also the source of Epictetus' dialogic style, which is so distinctive that we will refer to it as "Epictetan dialogue".

The work of Epictetus has come down to us only through the accounts given by his pupil, the historian Arrian. The longest and most detailed account is in the *Discourses*. This is less well known than the *Handbook*, which is a collection of maxims extracted from the *Discourses*.

In addition, there is a brief collection of *Fragments*. In all three books, the writings are concerned with how to live; not just the nature of the good life, but how in practice to achieve it. But the *Discourses* has something else, a pedagogic style based on Socrates. In several places Epictetus spells out his version of the Socratic method, which includes *protreptic*: exhortation, through monologue or questions and answer, "designed to make people rethink their ethical beliefs and convert to a fundamental change of outlook and behaviour" (Long, 2002, p. 54); and *elenctic*: refutation, "showing people the inconsistencies or conflicts they are caught up in, and showing that they do not know what they thought they knew" (Long, 2002, p. 55). Both are distinct from the didactic or doctrinal style, which is imparting information or principles rather than appealing to the listener's own powers of reason. Therefore, in Epictetus' *Discourses*, as recorded by Arrian, there is not just a set of principles that urge us to take responsibility for our emotions as well as action, and thereby to live well, but also instruction in disseminating these principles, both by example and through explicit discussion. Can principles and dissemination be separated? Epictetus was of his time, and for him they were not separable, since to behave virtuously it is not enough to know what is good or true and what is bad or false; it is necessary also to understand the means of distinguishing them.

[Question]:  [M]ere speech is not enough, but it is necessary that we should become able to test and distinguish between the true and the false and the doubtful?
[Answer]:  It is necessary.

(Epictetus in Gill, 1995, p. 19)

And this was achieved by Epictetus through dialogue, as even in this example, which is part of a chain of questions and answers.

If, as social constructionists believe, the social world is constructed through discourse (Potter & Wetherell, 1987), this traditional reliance on dialogue lends credence to Wessler's belief that Epictetus could be the patron philosopher of constructivists. However, Epictetus was not a private world constructivist as defined by Wessler. He was impatient of scepticism and questions of whether external reality is knowable.

I never, when I want to take a loaf, take a broom; but go directly to the loaf, as though to a target. And do yourselves, who deny all evidence of the senses, act in any other way? Who of you when he intended to go to a bath, ever went to a mill?

(Epictetus in Gill, 1995, p. 60)

He was not saying such that philosophical argument can be simply ignored.

> If the sophisms of Pyrrho and the Academy [i.e., scepticism] are what afflict us, let us bring forth what can aid us against them ... But it must be done by one who has the ability, who has the leisure; but he who is fearful and perturbed, and whose heart broken within him, must employ his time on something else.

(Epictetus in Gill, 1995, pp. 60–61)

Epictetus used his commonsense realism as an appeal to obstinate opponents, who hesitate when asked whether imprisonment and death are evils, and whether "ignoble and faithless speech, the betraying of a friend, or the flattering of a tyrant" (Gill, 1995, p. 240) are indifferents. For Epictetus the former are out of our control and therefore indifferents (to be treated as such) while the latter are in our control and therefore evils. However, this is too stark for his audience, and Epictetus gave them a diatribe (the Greek word translated as "Discourses" is *diatribai*) in the *protreptic* style.

> For do you ever stop to consider whether black is white, or light heavy? Do you not follow the plain evidence of your senses? Why, then, do you say that you are now considering whether things indifferent are to be avoided rather than evils?

(Epictetus in Gill, 1995, p. 241)

The point is that impressions are not the same as judgements, and only judgements are always in our control.

> The way things look to the mind (what philosophers call "impressions") have an immediate psychological impact and are not subject to one's wishes, but force human beings to recognise them by a certain inherent power. But the acts of approval (what philosophers call "assents") are voluntary and involve

human judgement. So, when some terrifying sound comes from the sky or from a falling building, or when sudden news comes of some danger, or something of this sort happens, even the wise person's mind is necessarily affected, shrinks back, and grows pale for a moment, not because he forms a judgement that something bad is about to happen, but because of certain rapid and unconsidered movements which prevent the mind and reason from functioning.

(Epictetus in Gill, 1995, pp. 309–310)

Elsewhere he said, directing his listener to the self-observation that is so characteristic of Socrates:

Observe yourself carefully, and see how you take the news, not, I say, that your child is dead (for how could you endure it?) but that your oil is spilled, your wine drunk up. You react in such a way that somebody standing by, as you fall into a passion, might say this: "Philosopher, you talk otherwise in the lecture-hall. Why are you deceiving us?"

(Epictetus in Gill, 1995, p. 241)

This is Stoicism with a human face, acknowledging the emotional force of a severe loss where correct judgement may take time to have an impact, but constrasting it with a trivial loss where being upset is the result of false judgement. Notice also the self-observation, which was characteristic of Epictetus (following Socrates), and the potential for a parallel process theory of emotion and reason, as discussed in Chapter One. On the one hand, there is the natural reaction tempered eventually by correct judgement; on the other, there is the same reaction but amplified by incorrect judgement.

## *Dialogue* vs. *method: the persisting influence of Epictetus*

As we saw in the Introduction, Stoicism had a deep though often unacknowledged influence on early Christian thinkers, especially in ethical matters, so it is not surprising that there are parallels in modern ethical thought in the West, conditioned as it is by Christianity. However, there is a more direct influence, through the continued reading of a few classic texts in translation, especially Epictetus. This modern tradition began at the same time as the decay of dialogue in the mainstream tradition, with the widespread translation of Greek texts into Latin at the beginning of the sixteenth century, and later into the vernacular.

Epictetus was translated into Latin in 1497, and into modern European languages throughout the sixteenth century. Montaigne (1533–1592) was an early reader of the new Latin translations, and his essays (de Montaigne, 1991) in turn have been widely read since that time. He headed one of his essays with the quote from Epictetus favoured by Ellis and Beck. The essay is "That the taste of good things and evil things depends in large part on the opinion we have of them". He took the quote as a hypothesis, and demonstrated that death and pain are not intrinsically evil by giving examples, mainly from classical literature and his own observations, of suicides and self-inflicted pain. The logic is similar to that in REBT, although the examples are more robust than even Ellis would allow himself to use. By the time Shakespeare wrote at the end of the sixteenth century it is clear that knowledge of Stoic philosophy was widespread, both as a source of wisdom (Hamlet's "There is nothing either good or bad, but thinking makes it so") and as a source of conduct (Brutus in *Julius Caesar*, who displays his Stoicism by his fortitude in war and his composure on hearing of his wife's death). The powerful undercurrent of Stoic influence, especially Epictetus, surfaces in a diverse collection of writers who have explicitly acknowledged his influence; these include Chapman, Pascal, Shaftesbury, John Dryden, Thomas Jefferson, Adam Smith, Henry James, Walt Whitman, and Matthew Arnold (Gill, 1995; Long, 2002).

However, not only writers and philosophers read Epictetus. Frederick the Great carried a copy of the *Handbook* throughout his campaigns, and in this way, as a private guide to living in difficult circumstances, it has been published repeatedly, as a volume small enough to be fitted into the side pocket of a rucksack. In spirit, this is still dialogic. The book is not read in order to gain knowledge abstracted from everyday living, but to help readers recruit their own powers of reason in dealing with the situation being faced. A striking modern example of this is Jim Stockdale, who has written of how he discovered Epictetus, and came to use his writings in order to survive years of imprisonment and torture in North Vietnam. A basic principle was taken from the start of the *Handbook*—"There are things which are within our power, and there are things which are beyond our power" (Epictetus, 1955, p. 17)—and he very soon discovered the limitations of our power. It was not in anyone's power to withstand the subtle torture practised by the interrogators, and he was thereby confronted with the reality of another maxim from Epictetus: "Look not for any greater harm than this: destroying the trustworthy, self-respecting well-behaved man within you" (Stockdale, 1995, p. 8). Faced with this and his responsibility as senior officer in the prison, he worked out a plan of resistance that would enable himself and his fellow prisoners to retain self-respect even after being subdued by torture. First consolidating themselves as a group by communicating in every way possible, and then, as one of the other prisoners put it:

> [W]e deserve to retain our self-respect, to have the feeling we are fighting back. We can't refuse to do every degrading thing they demand of us, but it's up to you, boss, to pick out things we must all refuse to do unless and until they put us through the ropes again.
>
> (Stockdale, 1995, p. 9)

This was within their power:

> Epictetus said, "The judge will do some things to you which are thought to be terrifying; but how can he *stop you* from taking the punishment *he threatened*?" That's *my* kind of Stoicism. You have a right to make them hurt you; and they don't like to do that.
>
> (Stockdale, 1995, p. 9; emphasis in original)

The choice was to submit and despair or submit and use reason to work out a plan of continued resistance; Stockdale did the latter through a kind of dialogue with Epictetus. When he described his experiences to the British Institute of Classical Studies "many of the scholars present felt they had gained a better understanding of Stoicism from discussions with him" (Stockdale, 1995, p. 1). For Stockdale it was "a laboratory of human behavior. I chose to test [Epictetus'] postulates against the demanding real life challenges of my laboratory. And as you can tell, I think he passed with flying colours" (Stockdale, 1995, p. 11).

## Beck and Ellis: the early papers

Beck's first two papers on thinking and depression were published in 1963 and 1964, respectively. His medical stance is apparent in the first paragraph of the second article, in his use of the concept of "thought disorder".

> (In a previous article) [i]t was suggested on the basis of clinical observation that many of the phenomena in depression may be characterized in terms of a thought disorder. This conclusion was drawn from the consistent finding of systematic errors, such as arbitrary inferences, selective abstraction, and overgeneralization in the idiosyncratic conceptualizations of the depressed patients.
>
> (Beck, 1964, p. 561)

In psychiatry, it was assumed before Beck that while schizophrenia is characterised by thought disorder, in depression thought is intact, and the disorder is primarily affective. This had been confirmed by psychological tests of thinking disorder, and although disturbances in thought and behaviour may occur, they were seen as a result of the disturbance in mood. Beck's originality lies not just in his "clinical finding of a thinking disorder at all levels of depression" but in reversing the direction of the presumed causal connection, so that "the way an individual structures an experience determines his affective response to it" (Beck, 1963, p. 44) rather than the other way around. This structuring or organisation of experience through thinking derives from

> The activation and dominance of certain idiosyncratic cognitive patterns (schemas), which have a content corresponding to the typical depressive themes in the verbal material.
>
> (Beck, 1963, p. 332)

Beck studied a control group of non-depressed patients in therapy, and these showed similar logical idiosyncrasies, although they differed from the depressed patients in the theme of their thinking. In his conclusion, he foreshadowed a programme of research that continues to expand.

> The thesis was advanced that the various nosological groups could be classified on the basis of the degree of cognitive distortion and the characteristic content of their verbalized thought.
>
> (Beck, 1963, p. 333)

In the second of the pair of papers, Beck elaborated on the notion of schema, and the therapeutic implications of a causal link from thinking to affect. He considered the spiralling effect if there is a two-way connection, so that affect influences thinking as well as vice-versa, but his focus was on ways of changing the thinking by identifying and challenging the automatic thoughts. The patients' thinking is usually based on faulty generalisations or theories about themselves in the form of schemas. The initial task therefore is to make thinking more inductive, "to form ... judgements more in terms of objective evidence and less on the basis of biased assumptions and misconceptions" (Beck, 1964, p. 571), and eventually to correct "the underlying misconceptions and biased assumptions" (Beck, 1964, p. 571).

Ellis was trained as a scientific psychologist, but the tone in his paper introducing "Rational Psychotherapy" was different from Beck's more medical stance. He began with a humanist declaration that may owe something to Rogers as well as his own reading in existentialism and phenomenology.

> The central theme of this paper is that psychotherapists can help their clients to live the most self-fulfilling, creative, and emotionally satisfying lives by teaching these clients to organize and discipline their thinking.
>
> (Ellis, 1958, p. 35)

No hint here of a thought "disorder", and later Ellis made clear that irrational thinking is not an illness, but the norm.

> [H]uman beings are the kind of animals who, when raised in any society similar to our own, tend to fall victim to several major fallacious ideas; to keep reindoctrinating themselves over and over again with these ideas in an unthinking, autosuggestive manner; and consequently to keep actualizing them in overt behavior ... the ideas were ingrained, or imprinted, or conditioned, before later and more rational modes of thinking were given a chance to gain a foothold.
>
> (Ellis, 1958, p. 40)

If this is mental illness it belongs to the culture, although in his later writing he argued that the tendency towards irrational thinking is biological, so part of the human condition. Fortunately, as Socrates and Epictetus realised, human beings also have the capacity for reason and self-scrutiny, so that through dialogue they can come to see the irrationalities and change them.

> The concept of neurosis only becomes meaningful ... when we assume that the disturbed individual is *not* deficient or impaired but that he is theoretically capable of behaving in a more mature, more controlled, more flexible manner than he actually behaves.

> (Ellis, 1958, p. 38; emphasis in original)

This implies that adults do not need to be taught to reason from scratch, so that dialogue rather than didactic instruction is the appropriate means (although Ellis is not consistent in this respect, and at other points he wrote as if rationality has to be taught). As Socrates and Epictetus believed, and tried on numerous occasions to demonstrate, the power of reason is present in everyone. However, being overshadowed by "the habit you have acquired from the beginning" (Epictetus in Gill, 1995, p. 241), it needs to be cajoled or gently shaped into use. If for Ellis in 1958 therapy was medical, it was mainly in the same metaphorical sense that it was for Epictetus, who frequently compared himself to a physician. Just as the physician removes the cause of illness, so Epictetus and Ellis try to enable people through dialogue to remove obstacles to living well, but without assuming any kind of medical model.

The psychological part of Ellis's argument was theoretical, demonstrating that, amongst other ways of calming oneself, it is possible to "reason oneself into a state of calmness" (Ellis, 1958, p. 35) since reason and emotion are closely linked.

> Rational psychotherapy is based on the assumption that thought and emotion are not two entirely different processes, but that they significantly overlap in many respects and that therefore disordered emotions can often (though not always) be ameliorated by changing one's thinking.

> (Ellis, 1958, p. 36)

This is a clear argument for the systemic process that Bond and Dryden (1996) pointed out. The "therefore" indicates that disordered emotions can be ameliorated not because there is a causal link between two independent processes, thought and emotion, but because they are part of the same process. Reason, and therefore beliefs based on reason, gains a foothold through dialogue. The typical client enters therapy with a repertoire of irrational thinking, and Ellis listed this in familiar detail. The irrationality is shown in talk of "dire necessity", in "shoulds" and "musts", and in what later became known as "musturbation" and low frustration tolerance, and in taking no responsibilty for emotions. Epictetan dialogue opens the way to self-scrutiny, to recognition of the effects of irrational thinking, and the realisation that such thinking can be changed.

## Conclusion

What Ellis described in his 1958 case study is akin to Epictetan dialogue. The aim is to demonstrate to the client the consequences of his or her irrational thinking and to open the way to living well, through dialogue in which the client is persuaded to engage in self-scrutiny. This can be done in many ways, and Ellis describes equivalents to the *protreptic* and *elenctic* styles. The former corresponds to what is usually nowadays referred to as "didactic", the latter to the modern "Socratic". Epictetus' didactic or doctrinal style is similar to modern pronouncements within a medical framework. Thus, Epictetus made a distinction that seems to have been lost today: between a didactic assertion which is open to challenge, as in dialogue, and one which is based on authoritative knowledge possessed by the speaker but not the listener. Modern examples of this are the medical knowledge possessed by a physician. The evolution of specialised method has made this form of it possible, but it is by no means a modern phenomenon. In earlier times, the authority was likely to come from the Church.

The structure is Epictetan, but the doctrines are different. The principles that Ellis derives from his rational philosophy are not universal, as Wessler recognised. They are those of modern liberal individualism, although there are clear affinities with the Stoics due to the pervasive influence of their thought on Western culture, as well as to his own reading of Epictetus and others. What he largely avoided in his early work is any dogmatic appeal to method—methods of enquiry and discovery to which he but not the client has access—which would undermine the Epictetan dialogue that depends on activating the client's own powers of reason, which in turn draws on everyday talk about psychological processes. An extreme case of such "non-dialogue" is therapeutic talk shaped entirely by evidence-based practice or medical prescription. What would be lost in this extreme case is the idea of tapping into the power of human reason, as in Socrates and Epictetus, and in Ellis of this early paper. There would be no room for Epictetan dialogue. Reason has been handed to the care of the therapist or physician, and the patient's role is compliance. Relinquishing reason in this way is usually rational in the case of a broken leg, but more questionable in psychotherapy. Stockdale is unlikely to have benefited much from an adviser trained to rely solely on evidence-based methods.

However, it is now 400 years since method replaced dialogue as the most prolific and approved vehicle for human reason, and if Ellis had been totally committed to Epictetan dialogue he would have had a struggle to survive. Even in 1958 he was ambivalent about the need to teach reason (as opposed to allowing it to emerge), and it is inevitable that he and others should be drawn towards a more medical approach, like that favoured by Beck. In 1962, Ellis made use of the ABC model, which hovers uneasily between being a useful didactic and dialogic metaphor, and a psychological or medical model that appears on the surface flatly to contradict the interdependence principle. If B and C are conceptually interdependent the link between them can be investigated through dialogue, and there will necessarily be two kinds of C to correspond to the two kinds of B, irrational and rational. But articulating them as A, B, and C invites the reader or listener to treat them as independent processes, whose causal connection is a matter of *a priori* postulation (which Wessler found objectionable), or empirical investigation (which Bond and Dryden found problematic). The ABC model may have pointed the way to formal research of the kind favoured in medicine and experimental psychology, but REBT's success in this respect has been less than that of CBT (see Chapter Nine).

Ellis kept his link with Epictetan dialogue in his self-help books, and the more obviously dialogic workshops. He was notably charismatic, and his relish in encounters with clients and colleagues is well known through his public "performances" and his recordings. There he remained a modern Epictetus of the following portrait.

> In his methods of teaching Epictetus is at his most effective as a shock psychologist. His *Discourses* abound in acute analysis of mental states and problems. Suppose a man wants to change his mode

of life but fears that old drinking companions will think badly of him for avoiding their company. Well, says Epictetus, he must make a choice. He can't have it both ways. "If you don't drink with those you used to drink with you can't be liked by them as much as before; so choose whether you want to be a boozer and likeable to them or sober and not likeable." In presenting the demands of the moral life he uses metaphors and examples that may alternate between hyperbole and bathos but rarely fail to seize attention and banish complacency.

(Long, cited in Gill, 1995, p. 339)

But difficulties arise in trying to ride two traditions at the same time, in retaining some allegiance to the spirit of Epictetan dialogue, as well as to the demands of modern science. Ellis has become vulnerable to attack from two sides: on the one hand, from those who believe that the purpose of psychotherapy is to help release the client from domination by reason; on the other, from those who evaluate Ellis from a medical point of view, and fail to recognise that Epictetan dialogue belongs to a different discursive formation or language game. Thus "getting a client to contract to eat a tablespoon of feces if he failed to do what he agreed to do" is certainly "bizarre and dangerous" (Wessler, 1996, p. 53) if taken as a prescription from within medical discourse, where compliance is nowadays expected in return for a guarantee of evidence-based practice. However, the same talk in the Epictetan dialogic tradition has a very different purpose and meaning. It is understood by both therapist and client as "shock psychology". This aspect of REBT suggests a homology that goes beyond philosophical analogues, but neither these nor the dialogic tradition can be attributed solely to Ellis's reading of Epictetus and other Stoics. In the next chapter we put the Stoic legacy into perspective, by considering homologies with twentieth-century movements drawn upon by Ellis that have little obvious connection with Stoicism.

# CHAPTER THREE

# The intellectual origins of Rational Psychotherapy: twentieth-century writers

*Introduction*

In the previous two chapters we attempted to establish a homology between Epictetus and Albert Ellis. However, there were important influences on Ellis from other twentieth-century writers, and these need to be considered in order to put the Stoic influence in perspective. They belong to the discursive formations of the time, rooted in the post-Enlightenment urge to put the world to rights and restore the American Dream through individual or political transformation. Ellis drew on a number of popular intellectual movements: operationalism, General Semantics, the holistic theory of emotion, cognitive psychology, psychoanalysis, and the self-help tradition. The pervasive influence of Stoicism cannot be excluded, especially from the self-help writers. Thus, Dale Carnegie, the best selling author, whose *How to Stop Worrying and Start Living* was published in 1948, took one of his catchphrases ("Our life is what our thoughts make it") from the Stoic Marcus Aurelius.

Our model of "influence" is of an active seeker of resources, rather than the passive imbiber assumed in some histories of psychology, which treat the passing down of knowledge as like the inheritance of biological characteristics.[1] Innovation is a mutual process, since success depends not just on the writer's rhetorical skills, but also on the audience's receptivity to what is on offer. Both writer and audience are potentially exposed to the same cultural resources, and the innovator's skills include an ability to take advantage of the receptivity. A complete account would include investigations of the reception Ellis's work received, the way this effected his development, the setting up of his own institution, and so on. In this chapter, we do not explore this unfolding over time, but the intellectual resources and his use of them that enabled him to make the transition from psychoanalysis to Rational Psychotherapy during the 1950s.

## Lumpers and splitters

An important contrast in style of argument, especially important to an understanding of Ellis's intellectual development during the 1950s, is between lumpers and splitters, suggested in the Introduction (p. xxvii) as a way of describing his shift in the focus of change in psychoanalysis. Instead of focusing on the lengthy uncovering and reworking of the individual's personal history, he lumped these together into their result, the demands in self-talk by which the client is currently disturbed. In psychology the atomism of associationism and the holism of Gestalt theory are the best-known instances of splitter and lumper arguments respectively, but the arguments range more widely than this. In the history of biological taxonomy

> Some authors consider even relatively minor differences as justifying the recognition of new genera, families and higher taxa. They are referred to as "splitters" in the taxonomic jargon. The majority of taxonomists prefer rather large, comprehensive taxa, as being better able to express relationship and reducing the burden on the memory. They are referred to as "lumpers".

> (Mayr, 1982, p. 240)[2]

In psychology, there are arguments about classification and measurement directly analogous to those in biological taxonomy. Psychiatric classification hinges on the lumper argument that different cases show common features that justify lumping them together. A recent diagnostic manual (American Psychiatric Association, 1994) traces its history from a simple dichotomy in the 1840 United States census (presence or absence of "idiocy/insanity"), through the split into seven categories of the 1880 census, to the 400 or more categories and sub-categories of modern diagnostic systems.

However, splitting and lumping also occur in discourse regarded as theoretical rather than classificational. Splitters follow language in treating the objects of thought as distinct. In psychology, thought and emotion, mind and body, conscious and unconscious, sensation and perception, have all been treated as separate following the application of splitters. Because the labelling function of language itself seems to endorse the splitter, and the isolation of topics in the laboratory is a cornerstone of experimental psychology, it has often been taken for granted until challenged by a lumper. In his chapter on the reflex arc of 1896, John Dewey provided such a challenge. He used a lumper to demonstrate that stimulus and response can only be regarded as distinct when defined as such by the physical setup of the laboratory; in reality, they are inseparable since the response alters the stimulus that alters the response, etc., in a continuous flow. But Dewey did not succeed in establishing a unit of analysis[3] to rival those of associationism or Pavlovian conditioning as the basis of an empirical research programme, and in the stimulus–response learning theories of the 1920s and 1930s splitter arguments predominated. This trend has continued in the theories of modern cognitive science. These are usually based on splitters, since they separate the inputs from the cognitive processing that follows, although in the period under discussion in this chapter there was much lumping as well as splitting within cognitive psychology (Murray, 1995; Neisser, 1967).

But even during the heyday of stimulus–response theory, there were research programmes based on units of analysis derived from lumpers. The best known was the perceptual Gestalt of Gestalt Psychology, which focused attention on structural properties rather than analysis into elements. Pursuing lumper arguments against stimulus–response theories, Tolman distinguished between molar and molecular behaviour during the 1920s. At the molecular level, psychologists studied muscle twitches, glandular secretions, or bodily movement; at the molar level they studied goal-directed action. In moving from molecular to molar, the theorist lumps together instances at one level in a single category at another level. Tolman (1932) lumped together different movements of an animal as instances of or as part of a single goal-directed action, and his focus was on this molar level. Skinner's definition of the operant was similar in structure. In the case of the operant, "raising the head to a specified height" is defined as "a set of acts defined by the property of the height to which the head is raised" (Skinner, 1953, p. 65). The details ("topographies") of the acts that fit this description are ignored, being lumped together as a single operant. From this, Skinner developed a language that proved effective in the control and prediction of behaviour, but later splitter arguments exposed shortcomings. Research on "constraints on learning" showed that confining description to the operant can mask important differences between species in what can be learned and how it is learned (Hinde & Stevenson-Hinde, 1973).

## The origins of Rational Psychotherapy

During the early part of his intellectual career Ellis read widely, attended lectures, joined in discussions, was formally tutored, listened to tapes, was psychoanalysed, and so on. In this way, a variety of discursive practices became available to him. Such availability is not just based on a set of rules for generating responses, but involves the sensitivity to potential audiences which gives knowledge of how and when to apply the practices. They include arguments (e.g., lumpers and splitters), appeals to authority, ways of talking, rhetorical devices, etc. These are the raw material from which Rational Psychotherapy derived.

Most psychologists are trained in a set of arguments and appeals to authority, and stay with these, and subsequent variations on them, throughout their careers. They may be said to "become" cognitive psychologists or behaviourists, and it is often a simple matter to trace "influences".[4] Ellis's career cannot be understood in this way, partly because his early training was not of this kind. We are not so much interested in tracing influences as in identifying the arguments that Ellis used, how he selected from the pool of widely familiar arguments and beliefs, and how his selection was shaped to launch Rational Psychotherapy—shaped not just by Ellis in an ivory tower, but through interaction with its actual and potential recipients of his talk and writing. However, our present concern is with the early stages, when the interactions were with clients and sometimes colleagues, rather than the wider debates that came later—it is in the arguments and the appeals to authority that made possible and eventually acceptable his turn from psychoanalysis to the beginnings of Rational Psychotherapy in 1954.

## The turn to Rational Psychotherapy: a case presentation

Our starting point in this chapter is Ellis's account of a moment of therapeutic insight with a client he had been giving psychoanalytic psychotherapy to for two years. The date is around 1954, and the case was presented as a turning point. It was based on verbatim transcripts, but was abridged and edited, allowing for a more rhetorically polished presentation than would be provided by the transcripts themselves.

The client was a thirty-seven year-old woman who believed the world was against her, having been taught by her parents to "be suspicious of others and to demand a good living from the world" (Ellis, 1962, p. 23). She was hostile towards her husband and felt worthless and inadequate. After understanding the origins of her problems, she was given homework assignments to try to see her husband's point of view and to do better in the office. This seemed to work up to a point, but she still felt as worthless as ever.

> "I still feel basically the same way that there's something really rotten about me, something I can't do anything about, and that the others are able to see."

> (Ellis, 1962, p. 24)

At this stage, over a year into therapy, there was a breakthrough. But first Ellis had his own moment of insight.

> "Yes, come to think of it—" and, suddenly, I did come to think of it myself, as I was talking with this patient. "—all human disturbances seem to be of the same definitional nature. We assume it is horrible ... if ... we are imperfect or someone else is not acting in the angelic way we think he should act. Then, after making this assumption, we literally look for the 'facts' to prove our premise. And invariably, of course, we find these 'facts'".

It was the patient who then drove the insight home with a question.

> "Would you say, then ... that my disturbance stems directly from these, my own sentences?"
>
> "Yes," I replied with sudden enthusiasm. "You give me an idea ... every human being who gets disturbed really is telling

himself a chain of false sentenses [*sic*] … And it is these sentences which really are, which constitute his neurosis."

"Can you be more precise? What are my own exact sentences, for instance?"

The dialogue continued until the client summed up her agreement thus:

"So when my parents tell me I'm no good, by word or by gesture, I quickly say to myself: 'They're right. If I don't love them dearly and don't sacrifice myself to them, I'm no good, and everyone will see I'm no good, and nobody will accept me, and that will be awful!'"

"Right. And it is these phrases or sentences of yours that create your feeling of awfulness—create your guilt and your neurosis."

"But how? What exactly is there about my own sentences that creates my awful feeling? What is the false part of these sentences?"

"The last part, usually. For the first part, very often, may be true. The first part, remember, is something along the lines of : 'If I don't completely love my parents and sacrifice myself for them, many people, including my parents, will probably think that I'm a bad daughter—that I'm no good.' And this part of your sentences may very well be true."

"Many people, including my parents, may really think that I'm no good for acting in this way—is that what you mean?"

"Yes."

(Ellis, 1962, pp. 27–28)

So it is the last part that is false, and causing the client's problems. People may think she should be a perfect daughter, and no good if she isn't, but it doesn't follow that she is no good. At Ellis's suggestion, she changed her sentences.

Maybe they are right about their thinking I am worthless if I am not a much more self-sacrificing daughter, but what has that really got to do with my estimation of myself? Would it really be terrible if they continue to think this way about me? Do I need their approval that much? Should I have to keep hating myself if I am not more self-sacrificing?

(Ellis, 1962, p. 31)

The client tried this out, and "within several weeks … improved far more significantly than she had done in the previous two years" (Ellis, 1962, p. 31). Two or three years later Ellis could confidently refer to the activities of "the Rational Psychotherapist" whose "main task is to make patients aware—or conscious of their inner verbalizations" (Ellis, 1957a, p. 39).[5]

This case presentation proved a rhetorical *tour de force*, in which a lumper argument, merging the painstaking details of an analysis into a single "should", led to a practical solution of the client's problems. However, its power did not reside simply in the argument itself, or the manner of its appearance in print, eight years later. Ellis was a trained psychoanalyst, carrying on an analysis weighed down by the momentum of his own massive investment in training, as well as two years' worth of time and money on the part of the client. He was part of a well-paid profession with a rapidly increasing clientele, an important new industry whose theories had already become part of intellectual and popular culture. All of this depended on the validity of the tortuous proceedings of analysis, and the splitter assumption that the minutiae are essential. It was no small matter therefore to take seriously the assertion of his client that her "disturbance stems directly from these, my own sentences," rather than from the memories painfully and painstakingly uncovered during the analysis. It would have been easy to treat this as naive with a grain of truth—superficially the sentences, yes, but more deeply what they express, their underlying meaning, so it could only almost seem as if the sentences are the neurosis. Nothing remarkable, or original about "almost seeming as if", but for Ellis there was no qualification, the sentences really are the neurosis. There had been other apostates from psychoanalysis, such as Fritz Perls and Eric Berne, who went on to make a name for themselves with their own brand of psychotherapy, but none had portrayed the initial step with the rhetorical flair displayed by Ellis.

## Further aspects of the original theory; the ABC model

In his 1958 manifesto, Ellis laid down the principles of Rational Psychotherapy. He recommended that therapists teach their clients to "discipline their thinking" (Ellis, 1958, p. 35).

> The effective therapist should continually keep unmasking his client's past and, especially, his present illogical thinking or

self-defeating verbalizations by (a) bringing them to his attention or consciousness; (b) showing the client how they are causing and maintaining his disturbance and unhappiness; (c) demonstrating exactly what the illogical links in his internalized sentences are; and (d) teaching him how to rethink and re-verbalize these (and other similar) sentences in a more logical, self-helping way.

(Ellis, 1958, p. 39)

This remains a clear and accurate nutshell statement of the practice of Rational Psychotherapy, although much of the most familiar terminology is absent. There is no ABC model there, and it is thoughts in general rather than beliefs that are irrational and changed in therapy. Currently, the ABC model is used in therapy to communicate the structure of the therapy to the client and to students (Introduction; Dryden, 1990). A of ABC stands for Activating event, B for Belief, and C for Consequence. If A is "Exam tomorrow" and C is intense anxiety, the client may think that A causes C. The therapist endeavours to convince the client that this is not so, but that C results from an irrational B, such as, "I absolutely must do well in the exam." B is said to be irrational because it is untrue,[6] does not help the client to achieve his or her goals, and gives rise to an unhealthy emotion. The client is taught to substitute a rational B, such as, "I would like to do well, but I don't have to." This gives rise to "healthy" concern rather than anxiety.

The ABC model did appear briefly in Ellis (1962) in order to explain to a client why he is impotent.

"[V]irtually all emotional disturbance is as simple as A-B-C—if you clearly see the A-B-C of what is occurring to you. At point A something happens—the girl you are with, for example, makes a comment about the small size of your sex organs or indicates that she is difficult to satisfy sexually and that perhaps you're not going to make the grade. At point C, you become impotent. Erroneously, then, you believe that A causes C—that her remarks cause you to fail sexually."

"What does cause C, or my impotence, then?" my patient asked.

"B does," I replied. "And B is what you tell yourself—and in this case the utter nonsense you tell yourself—about A."

(Ellis, 1962, p. 176)

Thus in this stage of the history of the ABC model, the letters were used to mark events in time, rather than standing for distinct processes. Only later did B come to stand for "beliefs"—the theoretical concepts were chosen to fit an abbreviation, rather than the other way round.

## Perpetuation of irrational thinking

To distinguish the goals and methods of Rational Pyschotherapy from those of psychoanalysis, Ellis pointed out that the latter looks for origins—"How do [clients] originally get to be illogical?"—whereas Rational Psychotherapy asks, "How do they keep perpetuating their irrational thinking?" and "How can they be helped to be less illogical, less neurotic?" (Ellis, 1958, p. 38). The theories may therefore be compatible, but questions about origins take a long time to answer, and often the answer has no effect; whereas the other two questions (whose answers are "by repeating the same old irrational sentences to themselves" and "by changing the sentences to rational ones") lead to more rapid and effective therapy.

If "[t]he therapist's main task is to make patients aware—or conscious of their inner verbalizations" (Ellis, 1957a, p. 39), then these verbalisations are presumably unconscious when having their upsetting effects. Ellis agreed, but they are not in the deep unconscious of psychoanalysis and "can, in almost all instances, be quickly brought to consciousness" (Ellis, 1962, p. 174). There was no "Unconscious" in Rational Psychotherapy, but sometimes desires are repressed because they conflict with other values.

> [B]eing ashamed [clients] sometimes do repress or actively look away from (in Harry Stack Sullivan's words "selectively inattend") their "shameful" urges.
>
> (Ellis, 1962, p. 354)

In such processes, thought and emotion are hard to distinguish, and in both the 1958 article and the book, Ellis was at pains to stress their inseparability.

> A large part of what we call emotion, in other words, is nothing more or less than a certain kind—a biased, prejudiced, or strongly evaluative kind—of thinking.
>
> (Ellis, 1958, p. 36)

This lumper view was quite widely held at the time, and after a brief review of the current literature on the topic in his 1962 book, he concluded:

> Emotion, then, does not exist in its own right, as a special and almost mystical sort of entity; it is, rather, an essential part of an entire sensing-moving-thinking-emoting complex. What we usually label as thinking is a relatively calm and dispassionate appraisal (or organised perception) of a given situation, an objective comparison of many of the elements in this situation, and a coming to some conclusion as a result of this comparing or discriminating process. And what we usually label as emoting, as I pointed out in my earlier article ... is a relatively uncalm, passionate, and strong evaluating of some person or object.
>
> (Ellis, 1962, p. 47)

This theory of emotions was held by Ellis before the move to Rational Psychotherapy, and he continued to insist on it in 1994. In Ellis (1994) he repeats his discussion of emotion from the 1962 edition, and adds the same quotation from Ellis (1956) to show that his view predates Rational Psychotherapy. The 1956 paper was written in 1954, "just before I originated REBT" (Ellis, 1994, p. 57), or "just as I was becoming a rational-emotive psychotherapist" (Ellis, 1962, p. 44).

Thus, in its original form, Rational Psychotherapy supposed that "sentences" give rise to emotional upsets, which can be changed by changing the "sentences" or thoughts of the client. Emotions are not isolated processes in the organism, but an essential part of an entire sensing-moving-thinking-emoting complex. At the heart of the theory therefore are two lumpers, denying the relevance of analysis. However, in the development of the therapy a splitter (the ABC model) qualifies this by offering a new mode of analysis.

### The pool of arguments

The persuasive force of Ellis's therapy depended in part upon the popularity and prestige of the arguments that went into its presentation— arguments about operationalism, psychoanalysis, general semantics, emotion, and cognition. These arguments were the resources drawn upon from Ellis's intellectual environment. Following Skinner (1945) and Stevens (1935, 1939) operationalism was still important during the 1950s as a philosophical base for experimental psychology (Garner, Hake & Eriksen, 1956). Psychoanalysis was extremely familiar in the States; it had had a powerful impact on academic psychology, in development, personality, and learning theory (Dollard and Miller, 1950; Mowrer, 1950); it was still dominant in psychotherapy, and new therapies tended to situate themselves by reference to it (Berne, 1961; Perls, Hefferline & Goodman, 1951). The interest in language was increasing in academic psychology, and General Semantics had a wide, non-academic audience. The holistic theory of emotion was linked to the lumper arguments of John Dewey, which were enjoying a minor vogue at the time (e.g., Dewey and Bentley, 1949), although soon to be forgotten as advances in technology increasingly underwrote the splitters of the "cognitive revolution".

## Operationalism

At the beginning of the 1950s, Ellis was practicing psychoanalysis, but was often fiercely critical rather than a loyal devotee. In 1950, he published an article for a psychological audience advocating a more scientific approach to psychoanalysis (Ellis, 1950). At that time operationalism in psychology promised a way of doing justice to mental concepts without sacrificing the parsimony of behaviourism. Bridgman, whose *The Logic of Modern Physics* of 1927 is often referred to as the starting point, had based the philosophy on Einstein's famous and successful exposure of the contradictions implicit in the classical notions of space and time. These contradictions turned out to be contained in the processes of measurement, the very operations upon which experimental physics is based. Clearly, it seemed, much conceptual progress was possible through an examination of those practical aspects of a science that were usually taken for granted.

Bridgman was at Harvard and the philosophy was applied to psychology by two research students there in the early 1930s, Skinner and Stevens. Skinner appealed to operationalism applied to the concept of the reflex to justify his theory from its inception (Skinner, 1931). He used history in order to try to show that the essence of the reflex is not some underlying process, the reflex arc, but the observed regularity that had been isolated and studied as reflexology. His eponymous box and his radical criticism of liberal shibboleths in *Beyond Freedom and*

*Dignity* made him famous or notorious beyond psychology, and both evolved from a consistent application of his own version of operationalism. He contributed to a well-publicised symposium on the subject in 1945, organised by Boring (Skinner, 1945), and by 1950 the arguments of operationalism had considerable prestige.

Ellis's paper on the operationalisation of psychoanalytic terms was published alongside a paper by Skinner in the book of a symposium held in 1954 (Feigl & Scriven, 1956). Another contributor was Paul Meehl, famous as the author of a paper with Kenneth MacCorquodale on the distinction between hypothetical constructs and intervening variables; later Meehl encouraged Ellis in his work on Rational Psychotherapy, and used it in his own practice (Ellis, 1991). Ellis attempted "to reformulate the main tenets of psychoanalysis in operational language" (Ellis 1956, p. 131), and discussed whether to treat the psychoanalytic concepts as intervening variables or as hypothetical constructs. He was not yet ready for the radical revision contained in the lumper argument favoured by Skinner, in which the minutiae of mental or stimulus–response processes are classified together as operants, defined as effects upon the environment. Ellis's paper was written just as he was becoming a rational-emotive psychotherapist (Ellis, 1991, p. 14). Within a short time, he was to reject psychoanalysis, and to follow Skinner in seeing the concepts of psychoanalysis as inconvenient fictions, masking the significant locus of psychological change. Just as Skinner's "operant" lumped together the different topographies that had the same effect on the environment, so for Ellis the sentence incorporating the irrational belief lumped together the many possible life histories that could eventuate in the same causally operative "sentence". He marked this new insight with a well-proven rhetorical device—the published demonstration of superior efficacy, reported in standard scientific form with statistical tests (Ellis, 1957b).[7]

## The appeal to language and "General Semantics"

In the twentieth century, the appeal to language has proved a powerful argument. Some years ago, Rorty (1967) gave the title *The Linguistic Turn* to a collection of readings. This was in philosophy and the authors included in that edited volume were selected from the limited population of Anglo-American and Scandinavian philosophers. What is apparent forty-five years on is that the linguistic turn was a much more universal affair, and embraced most of the social sciences throughout the century, in continental Europe as well as America and Britain. Linguistics itself had come to seem increasingly important, even by the 1920s, and its influence has been popular as well as academic, especially in North America in the work of Benjamin Lee Whorf and in General Semantics. At an even more popular level, the vogue for Couéism and auto-suggestion involved the self-therapeutic use of language. Ellis was well aware of these, but distanced Rational Psychotherapy from their "positive thinking", and it is the arguments used by General Semantics in particular that were drawn upon by him—something that is especially obvious in the dawning recognition of the importance of "sentences" in the case history cited above.

General Semantics was about applying, in principle at least, the manipulation of language to psychological well-being. Such titles as *People in Quandaries: The Semantics of Personal Adjustment*, *General Semantics and Psychotherapy*, *General Semantics and Group Therapy*, and *General Semantics and the Control of Affective Processes in Education* (all advertised in the third edition of Korzybski, 1948), convey the intended practical appeal of this movement. Ellis has acknowledged his debt and refers frequently to its founder Korzybski's *Science and Sanity* (1948).

Korzybski's was a speculative theory about the evolution of the mind and scientific progress, marked by a calm sense of certainty and a readiness to translate the most general propositions about humanity into mathematics. Mental evolution was explained as a movement in thought from Aristotelian identification to non-Aristotelian non-identification. In its simplest terms, Pavlov's dogs identify bell and food, while more developed thought recognises the difference, and such primitive, affective identification is always mistaken. In Korzybski's abstract terms, Aristotelian logic was two-valued while his own non-Aristotelian logic was infinite-valued. As Ellis put it in 1962:

> [A]s Korzybski … and many of his followers have shown, Aristotelean logic has its own distinct limitations and does not fully cover the laws of thinking. The world does not just consist of A and not-A, but often consists of A1, A2, A3, etc.
>
> (Ellis, 1962, p. 156)

Neuroses and insanity are the result of regression to primitive identification, so that "[a]ll psychotherapy, with its manifold theories, each contributing its share, is a semantic attempt to influence 'feeling' by 'thinking'" (Korzybski, 1948, p. 298). What changes because of therapy is what Korzybski calls "the s.r", the semantic responses—or adustments—to the world based on perceived meanings or evaluations. He proposed an experiment to verify his prediction that more spontaneous recoveries will occur in psychiatric patients given retraining in s.r.

> A physician who himself has undergone a [non-Aristotelian] training should attempt to re-train the s.r of one group. The other group should not be retrained, but treated in the average passive and standard way,- [sic] it would be the control group. One physician should be in charge of both wards and keep a detailed record of the cases and treatment. It is to be expected that at the end of the year, in the ward trained in the [non-Aristotelian] standards of evaluation, a larger number of unexpected and spontaneous recoveries would happen than in the untrained ward.

> (Korzybski, 1948, pp. 532–533)

If the methods of Rational Psychotherapy can be taken as retraining in s.r., Ellis (1957b) carried out the proposed study. Ellis's own use of "evaluation" (Ellis 1956, pp. 138–139, 1962, p. 44), and of identification through association (Ellis 1962, pp. 56–57; Ellis's argument was the same as Korzybski's though he doesn't use the term "identification") suggest that the methods are indeed close to retraining in s.r. Ellis seemed to accept this: "Rational-emotive psychotherapy ... parallels much of the thinking of the General Semanticists." But he added: "[I]t also provides a detailed technique of psychotherapy which is so far absent among the followers of Korzybski" (Ellis, 1962, p. 328).

While it is true that detailed techniques were absent, the possibilities for therapy were recognised. Of all the books published by General Semanticists, Hayakawa's *Language in Action* of 1941, which was thoroughly revised and expanded ten years later as *Language in Thought and Action* was the most popular. It is a self-help guide to applying the principles of General Semantics. Hayakawa cited the sad story of a man who died of wounds received when his car would not start and he angrily punched his fist through its rear window. This was not a simple response but "his reacting to his own abstraction ('that mean old car') rather than to the actualities of the car itself" (Hayakawa, 1952, p. 187).

He spelt out the way what we say to ourselves determines whether we get upset, or put ourselves down.

> [N]otice the difference between "I am a filling-station attendant" (which is a report) and "I am only a filling-station attendant" (which involves a judgement, implying that I ought to be something different and that it is disgraceful that I am what I am).
>
> (Hayakawa, 1952, p. 301)

Self-help consists of learning to recognise the way we upset ourselves with words, and changing this, but Hayakawa did not envisage this as a conventional therapeutic procedure. The therapist can help, but only by passing no judgement.

> [H]e helps us change the judgement, "I am only a filling-station attendant and therefore I am not much good," back into the report, "I am a filling-station attendant." … As a result of the psychiatrist's or counsellor's acceptance of us, we are better able to accept ourselves.
>
> (Hayakawa, 1952, p. 301)

Writing around 1950 Hayakawa's model counsellor was Carl Rogers (whose *Counseling and Psychotherapy* was published in 1942). He cited Rogers' theory of self-concepts that may be "realistic" or "unrealistic". If we act on unrealistic self-concepts, we cannot fulfil our full potential, so the client's task is to build more realistic self-concepts. As Hayakawa saw it, the Rogerian therapist did not actively facilitate the change, but tried to provide the secure emotional environment in which the client can safely explore and change his or her self-concepts.

The work of another General Semanticist and psychologist, Wendell Johnson (1939, 1946), came even closer to practical therapy, and was cited by both Korzybski and Ellis. Johnson explored the way that stuttering can be brought on in a child by the anxieties of adult listeners, and their evaluative definitions of speech hesitations as stuttering and as therefore undesirable. The child comes to internalise these definitions and to view him or herself as a stutterer. Struggling against this, the innocuous speech hesitations become more marked, and end up as stuttering. By redefining the speech hesitations as just that, and getting the child to relax the struggle against them, Johnson hoped to check the escalation into a stutter. Likewise, in adults Johnson identified the "taboo against stuttering" as the source of the perceived problem. Speech therapists of his time reinforced this taboo by teaching various tricks to avoid stuttering, and

> [t]he resulting speech, while usually free from "stuttering", is frequently more or less grotesque … What the so-called speech correctionist says, in effect, is this: "Don't stutter. Whatever you do, don't stutter. You can even talk in this strange manner that I am suggesting, but don't stutter."
>
> (Johnson, 1946, p. 459)

Ellis's solution would be to train the stutterer to drop the demand that "I must not stutter". Johnson did not focus so directly on this demand, but more generally on changing the "semantic environment". The stutterer becomes "a person who stutters" and "the fearful effort, exaggerate hesitancy, etc., which we call well-developed stuttering" (Johnson, 1946, p. 459) is interpreted as the result of attempting to avoid "repetitious speech". His therapy technique was a version of what has come to be known as "paradoxical intent". In paradoxical intent, the client tries to carry out the behaviour that he or she is trying to avoid. The stutterer is encouraged to "deliberately imitate his own stuttering" and to develop "a forthright, unhurried, deliberate performance of what would otherwise be done under protest and with tension" (Johnson, 1946, pp. 462–463). Paradoxical intent is used within modern forms of Rational Psychotherapy, since it entails giving up the demand "I must not stutter"—typically the client is encouraged to stutter while disputing the demand. This explicit focus on demands is not present in Johnson's work.

However, even if Wendell Johnson's procedure had been the same as Ellis's, it by no means follows that they were doing the same thing. An individual thinker immersed in institutional structures is constrained to follow certain practices. Failure to follow the constraints is a potential threat to the unity of the institution that may trigger self-preservative action. The individual may be censured, and excluded from participation. He or she can then attempt to reshape the deviancy in order to fit institutional requirements, or try to revolutionise the institution.

In the latter case a schism may result, as with Lacan and the French psychoanalytic association (Turkle, 1979), or a new therapy, as with Fritz Perls and Gestalt Therapy (Perls, Hefferline & Goodman, 1972), Eric Berne and transactional analysis (Berne, 1961), and Albert Ellis and Rational Psychotherapy. Thus for Ellis the psychoanalyst to step back in the middle of an analysis and launch into Rational Psychotherapy, by dramatically discovering (according to his own account) that it is sentences that cause neurosis, is different from tentative probings by Johnson, based on a detailed hypothetical aetiology of a specific problem. Whatever credit Johnson deserves for the details of his therapeutic work, it would add little to our understanding of Ellis's step from psychoanalysis to Rational Psychotherapy, over and above the close intellectual links we have already found in General Semantics. It is the latter, and its popular reception, that provides the pool from which Ellis fished his rhetorically effective account of the effect of "sentences".

## Psychoanalysis

Soon after Ellis had turned to Rational Psychotherapy in 1954, he wrote a paper listing similarities to Adler's individual psychology (Ellis, 1957a). Detractors of Adler present him as at best a rebel against psychoanalysis, but as Ellenberger (1970) has convincingly documented, he had already developed his own therapeutic practice when he met Freud. Unlike Freud, the specialist in neurological diseases, Adler had been a General Practitioner in Vienna, well aware of the social and practical difficulties faced by his relatively poor clients. He was prepared to try out quick solutions, based on change in conscious cognitive processes, and was less dedicated than Freud to the ideal of scientific achievement for its own sake. This general approach, rather than details of Adler's theories, was available as an important precedent for Ellis and his successful exploitation of the potential market for brief therapy. But more relevant for our detailed purposes is the work of Karen Horney, and not just because Ellis's analyst had been trained at the Karen Horney Institute.

In *The Neurotic Personality of Our Time*, Horney (1937, pp. 107ff.) had identified what she called "the neurotic need for affection". In an important departure from Freud, she used this concept to displace the Oedipus complex as a primary explanatory principle, and as a universal stage of development. Instead of explaining the neurotic personality in terms of an unresolved Oedipus complex, she explained the Oedipus complex as one amongst many possible examples of the neurotic need for affection: "The Oedipus complex in these cases is not then the origin of the neurosis, but is itself a neurotic foundation" (Horney, 1937, p. 161). Thus, in general the therapeutic focus became directed on the current need itself, rather than on an inevitable origin in the Oedipus complex.

If we think of classical psychoanalysis as laboriously disentangling the knots of an unresolved Oedipus complex, rational pychotherapy might be thought of as a way of bypassing that completely, of cutting off the entangled parts, and joining the remaining ends. Horney's theory in 1937 was a step in that direction by making the therapeutic goal the relaxing of the neurotic need, rather than an inevitable unravelling of the Oedipal tangle. The move is one away from the associationist, splitter view of ideas as distinct entities or atoms, which can lurk in the unconscious as pathogens set up by early pathogenic experiences. Instead, there is a constantly reactivated need that is taken for granted and outside the patient's awareness.

In *Our Inner Conflicts* of 1945, Horney had moved even further away from classical psychoanalysis, and the therapeutic task was more clearly focused on the present "predominant attitude" (Horney, 1945, p. 220). What she called the "neurotic character structure" is a "protective edifice built around the basic conflict" (Horney, 1945, p. 220). She explicitly separates work on the character structure from work on the conflicts themselves. For the latter:

> We would have to show him how he shuttles between extremes; how, for instance, he alternates between being overstrict with himself and overlenient; or how his externalized demands upon himself, reinforced perhaps by sadistic drives, clash with his need to be omniscient and all-forgiving, and how in consequence he wavers between condemning and condoning everything the other fellow does; or how he veers between arrogating all rights to himself and feeling he has no rights at all.

> (Horney, 1945, p. 221)

For Horney the conflict between wishes was primary, and not a possible outcome of a clash between underlying instinctive forces. The therapeutic task therefore is to uncover the conflicting wishes and to seek ways of resolving them. Therefore, the basic neurotic conflict "is possible of resolution ... provided the sufferer is willing to undergo the considerable effort and hardship involved" (Horney, 1945, p. 38).

Such conflicting wishes are likely to be wrapped up in moral values, which "were to Freud illicit intruders in the realm of science. In line with his convictions, he strove to develop a psychology devoid of moral values" (Horney, 1945, p. 39). Later still this focus on moral (or pseudo-moral) demands and self-abasement became even more direct in what she called "the tyranny of the should"[8] (now established in the literature of Rational Emotive Behavior Therapy as "the tyranny of the shoulds"). Here the pathogen was expressed in the form of conflicting propositions.

> Thus any request plunged him into an inner conflict: he should accede to it and be very generous and also he should not allow anybody to coerce him. The irritability was an expression of feeling caught in a dilemma which at that time was insoluble.
>
> (Horney, 1991, p. 81)

But even then Horney did not see the "should" as a direct target for change. Instead she was more interested in trying to show how they are the building blocks of neurotic character structure, which itself still needs to be taken apart and rebuilt. Nevertheless, her arguments and her practice had prepared the ground for any operationally minded therapist to reject her theory of character structure and work directly on the "shoulds", through a single lumper argument. And this is exactly what Ellis (well trained in the logic of personality theory) did in his turn to Rational Psychotherapy. The explicit emphasis on the upsetting sentences as "shoulds" and "musts" came later, but this is what they already were in practice by 1958.

## Holistic theory of emotion

For his account of emotion, Ellis used lumpers similar to those used by Dewey, not necessarily because he read Dewey, but because such lumpers were still currently available and powerful in psychology. In his 1962 *Reason and Emotion in Psychotherapy* he drew on Magda Arnold's recently published *Emotion and Personality* (1960), whose allegiance to Dewey is made clear in the space given to his theory of emotion, and her very positive evaluation of it. Ellis was struck by the similarity of Arnold's theory to his own: "Dr Arnold's theory of emotion is remarkably close to a view which I evolved in 1954" (Ellis, 1962, p. 44). The ABC model is a splitter, but not obviously so in its incipient form in Ellis (1962), where the letters stand primarily for points in time rather than psychological processes. The tension between this splitter and the lumpers underlying the theory of emotion came later.

The cognitive revolution

In some respects, the so-called "cognitive revolution" in psychology, which was underway during the 1950s, was founded on splitters.[9] It is based on the analogy of mind and computer, and splits the central cognitive processing from input and output processes. Thus, it differs from the lumper arguments of Dewey (1896), or of ecological psychology (Gibson, 1979). Ellis (1962, pp. 106–107) appealed to some cognitive psychologists as authorities to back his own appeal to cognitive and rational processes. They are well-known names, like Piaget, Festinger, and Bruner, and Piaget especially has had an effect on cognitive science (Boden, 1977). However, in the 1950s, these thinkers were still struggling to assimilate the lumper arguments available against stimulus–response theories, and Ellis does not mention the work that was moving more directly towards modern cognitive science, with its arguments that split input and output as cleanly as Clark Hull (1943) had split stimulus and response. Broadbent (1958), Chomsky (1957), and Miller (1956) had an immediate impact in academic psychology, but Ellis was not quick to jump on that particular bandwagon. Yet now he is happy enough to regard himself as a species of "cognitive (or cognitive-behavior) therapist" (and indeed as one of its founders (Ellis, 1994 p. 246)), so how can we reconcile his lumper theory of emotion with the splitter tendencies in the ABC model and the parallel expansion of cognitive science and cognitive therapy since the 1950s?

Perhaps the key question is whether irrational beliefs are construed as acts which select from experience (like self-talk in the form of "sentences") and guide further activity, or as cognitive/computational mediators. In Rational Psychotherapy, they are clearly the former, since the "musts" and "shoulds" still reveal themselves in self-talk. However, the present rhetorical power of cognitive science has pulled theorists towards the latter, leaving Rational Emotive Behavior Therapy (as Rational Psychotherapy has become) as an extremely successful therapy suspended in a theoretical limbo. After 1962, the writings of Ellis and his followers have almost entirely been aimed at fellow therapists, clients and the non-professional public, rather than cognitive psychologists of any persuasion. The ABC model is presented in practice (in many manuals and popular expositions) as an effective device for articulating experience in order to bring about change, rather than as a psychological theory to be placed alongside the information-processing theories of cognitive science.[10] A psychological theory remains, based on Ellis's theory of emotion, and implied by the therapeutic success that has followed treating beliefs as acts, but it has not been spelt out in modern terms. This may be the reason that Rational Emotive Behavior Therapy has had little impact on academic cognitive psychology. Perhaps, in that respect, it belongs alongside Dewey's critique of stimulus–response psychology, and might even offer itself as a candidate for the unit of analysis that Dewey failed to establish.

## Discussion

We have described the origins of Rational Psychotherapy through Albert Ellis's access to a set of contemporary rhetorical resources—arguments on the nature of science and the effects of language, and splitter and lumper arguments about thought and emotion. We have tried to show how Ellis drew on these to construct a persuasive package. This account of the intellectual origins does not differ in principle from any account of a successful endeavour, from advances in theoretical physics to the development of a new messianic sect. In physics, rhetorical possibilities are circumscribed by method and logic, and the solution of legitimate problems. Only by thorough socialisation into the practices and language of physics can the innovator hope to persuade the audience that matters.

Ellis's skills followed a more diffuse socialisation. He was fluent in the tight languages of psychology and psychoanalysis, and in the popular philosophy of General Semantics. He also underwent a tough apprenticeship in persuasion while a literary entrepreneur during the 1930s, and already had success with popular sex manuals. It was when he put these skills together within the framework of his psychoanalytic practice that he began what became his life's work. It is this beginning that we have tried to address in this chapter.

Later the task was different, to establish Rational Psychotherapy nationally and then internationally. This was another rough and tumble, more social than intellectual history, to do with how counselling and brief therapy became accepted and approved, against or alongside the interests of psychoanalysis, clinical psychology, psychiatry, general practice, and social work. This requires the kind of social history exemplified in the work of Nikolas Rose and others (Miller & Rose, 1994), but that is not the main concern of the present book. In the following chapters we look in more detail at the central concepts of REBT, rationality, and deontological words like "ought" and "should", in their historical and contemporary contexts.

## Notes

1. Boring's family trees of "Masters and Pupils" (Boring, 1963, pp. 137–8) shares this assumption with Richard Dawkins on the "meme" (Dawkins, 1976, p. 206).
2. A related, although different, distinction is made by Rorty (1985/1986) between the "texts" of the human sciences and the "lumps" that form the subject matter for the natural sciences. Rorty's pragmatist and epistemological purpose was to reduce the difference between them as objects of knowledge, by treating them as narratives on a continuum rather than as sharply distinct. Whereas we (like the taxonomists referred to by Mayr) are concerned with distinct ways of approaching common objects of knowledge.
3. The concept of unit of analysis is due to the Russian psychologist Vygotsky. During his short career as a psychologist (from 1924 to his death in 1934) he set himself the task of basing a research programme on a "unit of analysis" (rather than an atomistic "element"), which is "a product of analysis which, unlike elements, retains all the basic properties of the whole and which cannot be further divided without losing them" (Vygotsky, 1962, p. 4). Like Dewey, he rejected the stimulus–response connection as a unit. Here we use "unit of analysis" more generally as part of the basis of any research programme.
4. Boring's (1963) family trees apply quite well to these psychologists.
5. Reminiscent of another skilled rhetor, who launched behaviourism in a lecture and paper with the title "Psychology as the behaviorist sees it" (Watson, 1913)—as though this new breed of psychologist was already well established and a threat to tradition.
6. What is true is that "I very much want to do well in the exam" (a preference). But it does not follow from this that "I must do well in the exam"

(a demand). In the discourse of Rational Emotive Behaviour Therapy it does not follow logically (that is, the preference does not entail the demand) or empirically (that is, there is no law saying that since I prefer something I must have it).

7. Admittedly, it failed to meet basic statistical assumptions—the clients were not randomly assigned to treatments (psychoanalyic *vs.* Rational Psychotherapy), and "observations" were not independent (Ellis was therapist for all clients). However, this has been true of most evaluations of psychotherapy, and even the most rigorous outcome studies of psychotherapy have found no way of meeting that most basic requirement in medical tests, the double blind.

8. Discussed further in Chapter Five.

9. Although, as Murray (1995) points out, cognitive psychology has revived many of the preoccupations and concepts of Gestalt psychology, which was based on lumpers. Their famous lumper was "the whole is more than the sum of its parts", so cannot be reduced to parts. Cognitive science, like Hullian S–R theory before it, has generally been concerned to explain how Gestalt phenomena can be understood in terms of organised elementary processes. These phenomena, and the holistic concepts used to explain them, form some of the challenges from which cognitive psychology has taken its starting point. There has often been a lively and fruitful dialectic between lumpers and splitters.

10. Ellis (1994, p. 60) has used Abelson's (1963) computer simulation of hot and cool cognitions to bridge the gap. Abelson's concern, however, was with ways of restoring cognitive imbalance, in the tradition of balance theory (Heider, 1958). He treated this as a computational problem, rather than one of changing verbal acts ("sentences").

# CHAPTER FOUR

# REBT and rationality: philosophical approaches

## Introduction

In this chapter, we develop the argument that philosophical and historical critiques of concepts in psychotherapy are inappropriate unless the context or discursive formation in which they are used is taken into account. In the case of REBT, it is misleading to try to evaluate Ellis's use of "rationality" by matching it with the concept that has developed in the modern philosophy of science. There is no pure essence of rationality that could enable it to be applied normatively in all contexts. The pitfalls of attempting this were touched on in Chapter Two, and are examined further here by analysing two recent attempts to criticise "rationality" in REBT, by Erwin (1997) and by O'Donohue and Vass (1996). We argue that "rationality" in REBT can only be understood by seeing it as part of a network of categories and practices (a "discursive formation", as defined in the Introduction) that has evolved over the last forty-five years.

There are two related arguments, one general, the other specific. The general argument is that philosophical debate can be helpful in the development of psychotherapy (and other human sciences), but it can also be a hindrance. It can be a hindrance if the philosophical critic analyses concepts out of context, without careful consideration of how the terms are being used by the therapist. The therapist may then join the debate defensively, trying to justify his or her use of terms against the apparently rigorous standards brought to bear from another discipline. When that happens, the therapy may be guided by philosophical conventions rather than by therapeutic interactions, inappropriately if the understanding of the terms has been inadequate in the first place. This is especially true when the philosophy is ahistorical, and brings to bear supposedly universal criteria for thinking, notably in scientific thinking; if they are universal, well and good, but if they are not, and only appear so, the result is at best unhelpful. This can be guarded against by examining the use of the terms in their historical context. The specific argument, the subject of this chapter, is that this danger has been present in some of the philosophical critiques of "rationality" in Albert Ellis's Rational Emotive Behavior Therapy.

The general argument has taken many forms in the twentieth century, when it has been directed especially against attempts by philosophers and logicians to reduce verbal meaning to logical rules. Logical positivism in the 1930s assumed that science is the paradigm of all knowledge, and claimed (following David Hume) that meaningful propositions are either analytic and *a priori*, or synthetic and *a posteriori*—*either* matters of logic or mathematics, *or* about verifiable questions of fact. For logical positivists the meaning of a statement was its method of verification. This excluded, as knowledge, most metaphysical, religious, and ethical propositions, as well as much of the human sciences, but this did not unduly worry the more hard-headed young philosophers of the Vienna circle at the time (Ayer, 1936). However, it also excluded itself, since the propositions of logical positivism, that meaningful propositions are either analytic *a priori*, or synthetic *a posteriori*, are themselves neither analytic *a priori* nor synthetic *a posteriori*. For this and other reasons, logical positivism was undermined from within, a victim of its own destructive logic. It was undermined by Wittgenstein, who compared different human activities (including science and religion) to different forms of life, each with its own language game, and invited the investigator to ask, not for the meaning, but for the use of words (Wittgenstein, 1953); by Quine, who questioned the traditional distinction between synthetic and analytic statements upon which logical positivism rested (Quine, 1953); and by Popper, who saw science, not as an expanding system of certain knowledge, but as a method or practice in which nature is investigated through cognitive conjectures, which are put to the test in attempts at refutation (Popper, 1972). Each of these philosophers and their followers became concerned more with what people, whether natural scientists, human scientists, or ordinary language users, actually do, rather than with what they should do.

As a result of such criticisms historians and philosophers of science in the English-speaking world have become more sensitive to the context in which concepts are deployed, and have converged to some extent with the French tradition following Bachelard, discussed in the Introduction. Ideas do not occur, and cannot be understood, in isolation. Given this, the history of science is now seen as less a matter of inexorably stumbling towards the truth about the universe, than of constructing an effective network of concepts and practices which, during a particular epoch, have given rise to a coherently organised way of passing judgement about what is the case, and of planning technological development.

## Discursive formations again

Thus in order to understand the meaning and full force of "rationality" and "irrationality" in REBT, a historical approach is helpful, and perhaps even necessary. There is, we argue, no essential and eternal entity to which the word "rationality" applies; the word comes with no static set of semantic markers that fix its meaning once and for all, in isolation from other words. It is always part of a discursive formation, and each usage has to be understood in terms of the discursive formation to which it belongs. In this chapter, it is argued that rationality is at the core of the REBT system of categories, somewhat as the spinal cord is at the core of the mammalian system. In both cases, full understanding requires a historical analysis; for REBT it is to understand how Ellis's use of the terms "rationality" and "irrationality" form part of a discursive formation that has evolved into the form we find today. The aim is to enquire into what Ellis has actually been trying do in his use of the terms "rationality" and "irrationality", as a prelude to appropriate criticism.

## REBT as a discursive formation

As we have seen, Albert Ellis began to practise and write about his new therapy around 1955, calling it Rational Psychotherapy. He drew on a number of current practices and concepts in order to develop the techniques of the therapy, and to find words to articulate it to clients, other therapists, and the general public. Especially important sources were psychoanalysis, General Semantics, and psychological theories of emotion and cognition. These sources were analysed in detail in the last chapter. But none of them explain a concept which lies at the core of the therapy and the theory underlying it. This concept and its opposite are "rationality" and "irrationality", and the importance of them is reflected in the name of the therapy; "Rational" has remained throughout the changes made by Ellis. Rational Psychotherapy became Rational-Emotive Therapy, perhaps to counter the criticism that the therapy was just about thoughts and failed to do justice to emotions. Finally, "Behaviour" was added in order to take account of the full range of methods actually used in the therapy—not just cognitive methods to change emotions, but also behavioural methods. So we get the current Rational Emotive Behavior Therapy or REBT.

Initially Ellis drew from a philosophy of science that still bore many of the characteristic marks of logical positivism and operationalism (Ellis, 1950, 1956). Like many others, he saw these philosophies as providing criteria for the *scientific* psychotherapy he had failed to find in psychoanalysis; but unlike others, arguments associated with logical positivism also appeared *within* his therapeutic practice. Thus, logical positivism and operationalism appeared in two distinct, although overlapping and easily confused, discursive formations (DFs). First, it appeared in thinking and writing about REBT, and in arguing with practitioners and other colleagues. Second, it appeared in the procedures of therapy. We will refer to these as DF(metatherapy) and DF(REBT).

In DF(REBT), arguments from logical positivism appear in the process of "disputing". Suppose a client is excessively anxious about a forthcoming examination, and finds it difficult to revise or sleep. In REBT, the client is taught to replace irrational beliefs (iB, such as, "I absolutely must pass the exam") with rational equivalents (rB, "I want to pass the exam but I don't absolutely have to"). Clients learn to dispute the irrational belief by testing it against three criteria, and thereby ascertain for themselves that while the rB (the preference) may be true, the iB is not true. The three criteria are: It does not follow logically ("How does it follow logically from my preference that I *must* have what I want?"); nor is it true empirically ("Where is the law of the universe which says that if I do want something it *must* happen?"); nor pragmatically (i.e., on utilitarian grounds—"How does it help me to tell myself that I *must* succeed?"). Structurally, these steps mirror the principles popular with logical positivists at the time that Ellis first formulated his theory. The first dispute, the logical one, is the principle, first stated clearly by Hume, that "ought" does not follow from "is" (see Ayer, 1936). The second (empirical) dispute is like the covering law model of causality (Hempel, 1965). And the third is the utilitarian principle, which has always been associated with both pragmatism and positivism (Ayer, 1968).

Ellis later held a Popperian critical realist or "open society" view, rather than a logical positivist philosophy of science (Ellis, 1991). Falsifiability rather than the possibility of confirmation are the marks of critical realist science. This changed DF(metatherapy), but it did not clearly change DF(REBT), and in 1994 Ellis repeated his recommendation that clients be shown how "to use empirical, logical and utilitarian Disputes [*sic*] to dispute their grandiose *musts*" (Ellis, 1994, p. 147; see Dryden, 1990), thus retaining the disputing drawn from arguments popular with logical positivists.

There is nothing wrong in principle with this apparent conservatism in DF(REBT). The old principles may have proved inadequate as foundations for a logical positivist metaphysics, but their practical usefulness in the right context remains, and may still be valid and effective for therapy. As we show below, there are difficulties in applying the critical realist falsifiability as a criterion for rationality *within* the therapy, that is, within DF(REBT). In addition, we argue that even if Ellis seems to provide a warrant for evaluating his therapy against standards derived from the philosophy of the natural sciences, there are limitations and pitfalls with this approach—what is appropriate for the discursive practices of the natural sciences may be inappropriate for psychotherapy, however scientific it aims to be. This may be seen in the following recent examples.

## Two philosophical critiques of "rationality" and "irrationality" in REBT

Erwin (1997) and O'Donohue and Vass (1996) find much that is unsatisfactory in Ellis's use of "rational" and "irrational", basing their criticism on normative criteria taken from the current philosophy of science. We will see problems in their analyses even when taken on their own terms. In pointing these out we are not in the business of defending the therapy against detractors, but of trying to open the way to a more helpful and (in a sense that we shall elaborate) rational criticism. In addition, in attempting this, we are less interested in arguing point by point, than in bringing out the weakness of their whole approach. Most importantly to us, their ahistorical perspective takes "rationality" out of context, and pays no attention to its function for Ellis as a therapist and writer. Ellis himself may have been in part responsible for this, insofar as he has failed adequately to distinguish between "rationality" as used *within* the therapy, and the idealised scientific rationality he has come to claim for the therapy itself.[1] Ellis tried to use his concept interchangably in two distinct discursive formations, DF(REBT) and DF(metatherapy). His critics have unwittingly followed him in this, and tried to show that the concept used in one discursive formation, DF(REBT), falls short of the requirements in the other, DF(metatherapy). Our task, then, is to demonstrate what is wrong with this approach to criticism, and to differentiate historically between the two discursive formations containing "rationality". In this way, we hope to clarify the meaning and importance of "rationality" for Ellis and for REBT.

## *Erwin's philosophy and psychotherapy: the application of "rigorous philosophical discipline"*

Erwin wrote as a professional philosopher, and his critique occurs in a book claiming in its blurb to be "the first authoritative work to apply rigorous philosophical discipline to therapeutic claims and counterclaims". It is a short book targeting a wide range of therapies, so the treatment of each is necessarily brief, and risks oversimplification. In the case of REBT, he first outlines what he calls "a crucial assumption from the beginning" which is the "ABC model of human disturbance" (Erwin, 1997, p. 104).

However, Erwin is mistaken here—this was not a crucial assumption from the beginning. When Ellis first announced his new therapy, he listed three processes, and he adopted the usual device of labelling them alphabetically, A, B, and C. Only later did he interpret these as Activating Event, Belief, and Consequence, thus turning the ABC into the familiar acronym now used widely in more general cognitive therapy as well as in REBT. This is not a trivial point. It suggests that the ABC theory, however important in practice, is not crucial. What we are looking for is what is essential to REBT, what identifies it and distinguishes it from other therapies. This hinges primarily on Ellis's use of "rational" and "irrational", rather than on the practical ABC model that has proved so helpful in articulating a range of cognitive therapies, and not just REBT.

Erwin draws most of his account of REBT from a single source, Dryden (1991), which is a transcript of conversations with Albert Ellis. From these conversations, Erwin extracts eight principles. These define Ellis's "preferential" RET, which Erwin regards as distinct from an earlier version of the therapy. Before homing in on these eight principles, he begins with "a few preliminary questions … about the earlier theory" (Erwin, 1997, p. 106). We will follow his order of events, although we do not accept any such sharp division between earlier and later theories. Much has changed since 1955, and many of the changes are of great importance, but the central concept of rationality remains, and this is our focus in this chapter.

In his assessment of what he calls the earlier therapy Erwin begins by asking, "What criteria do RET therapists use to separate irrational from rational beliefs?" (Erwin, 1997, p. 106). He then takes examples, which he dismisses one by one with a rapid logical thrust or a *reductio ad absurdum*. What he does not do is try to answer his own question; he does not, so to speak, allow Ellis space to state the criteria used in practice. It is as though in his eagerness to make logical points he has not really stepped back and reflected on what Ellis is trying to do.

## Can human beings be rated?

One of Ellis's examples of irrationality is "[t]he idea that certain people are bad, wicked, or villainous and that they should be severely punished and blamed for their villainy" (Erwin, 1997, p. 106). This is a challenging example from Ellis, and backed up by four pages of detailed justification (in Ellis, 1962, from which the quotation is taken), but instead of considering this, Erwin goes for the kill with another *reductio ad absurdum*: "Supposed [*sic*] that I believed that about some of the most notorious tyrants and serial killers of the twentieth century. Is it impossible that my belief be supported by good reasons? Why must it be irrational?" (Erwin, 1997, p. 106).

If Erwin had studied Ellis's many discussions of this example of irrationality (in Ellis, 1962, and elsewhere), he would have uncovered the quite traditional view that no human is absolutely good or bad, but rather every person is made up of a mixture of good and bad. Human actions may be unequivocally good or bad (or in-between), but judgements of this absolute kind are not applicable to human beings. *If* this is the case then the step from "X's action is bad" to "X is bad" is illogical, and empirically unjustified, as well as unhelpful. Similarly it is rational (although possibly wrong) to believe it preferable that certain actions be severely punished, but irrational, according to Ellis, to believe that they *should* be severely punished, in any absolute sense of "should". There are conditional "shoulds" which are rational, such as, "If he wants to pass the course he should attend the examination", and there is a rational, conditional "should" in the present example—"If you want a peaceful, orderly society, then murder should be severely punished."

However, many people, including some Calvinists and presumably Professor Erwin, do believe that it is appropriate to judge people as "good" or "bad" in themselves. Buddhists and some other Christians believe in judging the sin rather than the sinner. Is this a matter of opinion, or is one view rational and the other irrational? Ellis debated this question in Chapter Eight of the first edition of *Reason and Emotion in Psychotherapy* (1962).

In 1994, in the second edition of *Reason and Emotion in Psychotherapy* Ellis refers to that chapter as "one of the best essays I have ever written because it outlines a theory of personal worth that is one of the most distinctive features of REBT" (Ellis, 1994, p. 188). His therapeutic target was the sense of worthlessness that is a central problem for many clients. As a Rational Psychotherapist confronted with this he seeks to prove that he or she is mistaken, and that they do have worth. He leans towards what he sees as the existentialist view that "a human being is good or worthwhile merely because he exists, because he *is*, and not because of his intrinsic achievements" (Ellis, 1962, p. 148). However, it is hard to prove this, and he reports that in practice he turns the question around by asking patients for evidence that they are worthless. It is then possible to demonstrate that they are only worthless *by definition*, and that if they maintain this definition "they will inevitably bring on disadvantageous neurotic symptoms, especially anxiety, guilt, and depression" (Ellis, 1962, pp. 155–156). It does not follow, even if the client agrees with this, that

> They therefore must be intrinsically worthwhile. Perhaps the best solution to this problem would be for us to realize that, essentially,

there *is* no such thing as intrinsic worth or worthlessness, for these are terms of measurement which can be properly attributed only to extrinsic, external things and events.

(Ellis, 1962, p. 157; emphasis in original)

This is consistent with, but goes significantly beyond, the traditional view that no human is absolutely good or bad, but everyone is made up of a mixture of good and bad.

This tentative conclusion (that human beings are intrinsically non-rateable) in the first edition of *Reason and Emotion in Psychotherapy* is a firm starting point in the second edition, having become a central part of REBT. It is a conceptual decision, but it is not logically necessary, nor is it empirically provable or falsifiable, even if it is an extremely helpful belief with important practical implications. It is, to use Ellis's own phrase in 1962, a matter of how you define human beings, yourself in particular. Thus in the course of exploring and developing his DF(REBT) Ellis developed a distinct ethical position about the nature of human beings. Erwin's rhetorical *reductio ad absurdum* is an appropriate and worthwhile question from another discursive formation, that of traditional ethical theory, and leads, if challenged, to an ethical debate rather than a discussion of rationality in DF(REBT).

## Rationality and happiness

Erwin's second example is from Ellis and Bernard's paper of 1986: "[R]ational beliefs are defined in RET as those thoughts that help people live longer and happier" (Erwin, 1997, p. 106). Ellis and Bernard could be in difficulties here. By the standards of modern logical analysis, "rational thoughts" cannot be logically *defined* as "thoughts that help people live longer and happier"; it is too easy to find counter-examples, and Erwin is right to point this out—he refers to a discussion in Haaga and Davison (1993) and adds (as another apparent *reductio ad absurdum*) that to identify a belief as irrational, "the therapist would have to establish first that for this particular individual the retention of the belief causes unhappiness or shortness of life" (Erwin, 1997, p. 106).

But again, he gives up too easily. This *is* what the REBT therapist tries to establish, but not (as Erwin implies when he writes in the quote above, "establish first that"), as a preliminary to further therapeutic work. "Trying to establish" is already part of the therapy. Typically the client tries out the effect of changing the belief, either through thought experiment ("Rational-emotive imagery", Dryden, 1990, p. 80), or *in vivo*. If a beneficial change is experienced, the next task is not to test further the hypothetical identification of this belief as irrational (the client's goal is therapy, not the establishment of scientific truth), but to practise the techniques learned on other beliefs, and to incorporate them, when they work, more and more thoroughly into everyday life. In doing this the client is not being a scientist, but is thinking in an effective, everyday fashion, forming hypotheses, testing them out, modifying or rejecting them. This has, as Popper recognised when he used the phrase "trial and error" to describe scientific progress, the same logical structure as scientific thinking. The client's rationality consists in his or her search for ways of thinking that will make for (although not guarantee) happiness and longer life. Thus we interpret "those thoughts" in the quotation from Ellis and Bernard as "that way of thinking" which is contained in DF(REBT), rather than as a set of thoughts that can be taken out of context and classified as rational or irrational.

It is true that if we apply canons from the discursive formations of modern philosophical logic to rationality in DF(REBT), then shortcomings will appear. However, the idea that "rational" may be conceptually linked to living a happy life is by no means unprecedented. It was central to Stoic philosophy, which was drawn on by Ellis in the early development of REBT. In Chapter One, we discussed the parallels between Stoic ethics and REBT as discursive formations, and argued that this comparison provides an appropriate and fruitful way of evaluating rationality in REBT.

*REBT and the principle of the must*

But instead of asking why anyone might believe that "rationality" is linked conceptually with happiness and long life, Erwin tries salvaging the therapy with his own definitions. Not surprisingly, he finds these new targets equally flawed, and after thus undermining the earlier theory to his own satisfaction, he concentrates on the eight principles of the "preferential" therapy. The most important, he rightly believes, is number six, "the principle of the must". The first five are less central, and after criticising them, he turns to "the more serious problems with Ellis' theory" (Erwin, 1997, p. 109). Since principle seven "adds nothing" of substance to principle 6" and principle eight "raises the same questions as does principle 6" (Erwin, 1997, p. 110), we confine ourselves to Erwin's evaluation of "the principle of the must". His paraphrase of the principle is:

> Sixth, the "principle of the must": humans have many irrational beliefs, but it is mainly a subset of them that is linked with disturbance and irrationality. The key ones are about absolutist, dogmatic shoulds, oughts, and musts. According to RET, if humans would act on their simple preferences, they would not, by and large, get into emotional trouble. The problems arise when they "transmute" them into "absolute musts". My preference for X becomes "Because I like X very much, I *absolutely must* have it".

> (Erwin, 1997, pp. 105–106; emphasis in original)

Erwin's criticisms are as follows:

1. "How does he know that people who have emotional problems generally have these beliefs about what they absolutely must or should have?" According to Erwin, most therapists do not report such beliefs.[2] He allows that this may be because they are not looking for them and fail to ask the right questions, but counter-attacks with a different criticism: If we do ask the right questions how do we know that we are not suggesting these beliefs to the client? Certainly this is a problem, but one that has been aimed at all therapeutic claims since Mesmer's demonstrations of hypnosis and the beginnings of psychotherapy during the nineteenth century. As such, it concerns more general epistemological problems, to do with psychotherapy itself rather than just REBT, which is the topic of the present chapter.

2. However, this epistemological problem is made worse "because these beliefs about absolute musts are unconscious, according to RET" (Erwin, 1997, p. 110). Erwin's source for this statement is Dryden (1991), where Ellis says

> The philosophy of unconditional musts is often held tacitly, implicitly and unconsciously. Some profound musturbators don't really acknowledge that they have any musts, or else admit them and think they are valid ... the origin of disturbance is often

unconscious in that people don't *see* what they believe implicitly, how strongly they believe it, and how they disturb themselves with their musts.

(Dryden, 1991, pp. 22–23; emphasis in original)

Our reading of this passage differs from Erwin's. Although Ellis uses the word "unconscious", he does not say, as Erwin implies, that such beliefs are always or even usually unconscious, and he does not mean anything like the Freudian repository of repressed material. Ellis's "unconscious" is closer to Freud's "subconscious". This is borne out historically. In the very early days of Rational Psychotherapy, Ellis the psychoanalyst discovered that even after an analysis had uncovered the origins of the client's problems, he or she was not cured, but continued to get upset by self-talk, with "sentences" which often contained the demands which are at the core of the therapy (see Chapter Three). The problems were overcome not by the analysis, but by teaching the client to change the sentences he uttered to him or herself. At that time, the sentences were conscious, although the client was not always alert to their occurrence in self-talk. A little later, when it appeared that some clients upset themselves with irrational demands, even when these were not revealed in self-talk, Ellis began to refer to unconscious "musts" and "shoulds" (Ellis, 1962, pp. 173ff.). Later still, Ellis acknowledged that earlier he had overlooked that "we use several other kinds of thinking, such as symbols and pictures" (Ellis, 1994, p. 206). At the same time he made clear that tacit and non-verbal irrational beliefs (iBs) are not deeply hidden or repressed, but pre-conscious "and can fairly easily be brought to light if one uses REBT theory to look for and reveal them" (Ellis, 1994, p. 204). Using practical techniques derived from theory is common scientific practice, so Erwin is wrong to see a problem here. The epistemological status of the "musts" does not differ from that of any scientific event not open to unaided observation.

3. Erwin's third criticism is that even if we can establish a correlation between iBs and emotional problems, this does not demonstrate a causal connection. Erwin refers back to an earlier chapter of his book where he develops an "Objectivist Epistemology". His principles there of "causal relevance", "differentialness", and "inference to the best explanation" sound like psychology's basic and well-tried research principles of experimental design and statistical inference. Ellis himself has always advocated such research, but however

important in establishing REBT as psychological knowledge, the causal connections observed in therapy are not usually arrived at by statistical inference. The observations generally rely on a principle of causal thinking based on practical *control* rather than statistical inference.[3]

In science and everyday life, a fundamental rule for establishing experimentally that A causes B, is to establish both if A then B, and if not-A then not-B. Recently, one of us found that his wood burning stove was smoking and overheating. When he inserted the throat plate it burned satisfactorily; when the throat plate was removed, it went back to smoking and overheating. Since other relevant conditions (wind, ventilation, and fuel) remained constant, a causal connection was thus established for practical purposes between presence or absence of throat plate and smoking and overheating. By ensuring the throat plate was correctly in place he was able to control the performance of the stove. This basic experimental thinking (forming hypotheses, testing them out, modifying or rejecting them) is widely used in everyday life and in science, especially applied science. It is also, as we saw above, part of the usual thinking of therapists and their clients using REBT. This point is so important that we take it further with another example. Suppose a client is so anxious at the prospect of a forthcoming examination that she cannot sleep and becomes agitated as soon as she starts preparing for it. The therapist, using Socratic methods where possible (Dryden, 1990), will try to uncover the demands that she is making on herself, such as, "I absolutely must pass the exam; life would be unbearable if I failed." This is not done by just observing the occurrence of these demands in self-talk, but by homing in on the causal connection itself. Using a variety of techniques, the client experiments with his or her self-talk. She tries out, for instance, in an imagined situation (using rational-emotive imagery, Dryden, 1990) or *in vivo*, telling herself first that she absolutely must pass the exam, and then switching to saying (and believing) that she doesn't have to pass the exam, that it won't be the end of the world if she fails. In this way, the client herself takes control, and establishes the causal connection for herself and her therapist. Suggestion may play a part from the beginning, and it will be one of the tasks of the therapist to ensure that this, although it could be helpful, is inessential. This is done (as it is with the throat plate, where initial belief could have depended upon the certainty of an expert friend), by enabling the client to test out the connection for herself. It is never established absolutely, beyond doubt, but she has learned a new skill, one which she can practise repeatedly in a variety of circumstances, until her conviction in its efficacy (and the causal connection) becomes built into her everyday life.

The discourse between therapist and client is part of a discursive formation, DF(REBT). The client is socialised into DF(REBT), and causalities are *directly* established which may differ from (but not by falling short of) the causalities *indirectly* established with randomised groups of subjects and statistical inference. We only fall back on statistics when it is impossible to establish causality directly, as has often proved to be the case in psychology, or when we wish to convince others of what we have observed.

Thus, a problem arises when the therapist wishes to establish herself and her therapy by convincing the world of its great merit. Now it is necessary to hitch DF(REBT) onto the public network, DF(metatherapy), in which the full repertoire of scientific rhetoric comes into play. This includes all the trappings of scientific presentation (experimental design and statistical methods, prolific publication, standing firm in public debate, organising your own institute, and educational methods). What Erwin seems to be doing is taking Ellis to task for falling short in one aspect of those trappings: statistical methods. There is some truth in this, and Ellis himself would probably agree,[4] but this is generally true of psychotherapies, compared, for instance, to experimental psychology, or drug trials. Psychotherapy research fits uncomfortably within the discursive formations that have evolved for these disciplines, and it has not yet constructed one of its own that would more effectively serve its needs.

In conclusion, although Erwin raises some important points for discussion, his criticisms do not go deep—they do not, we surmise, stem from deep and wide reading in Ellis's writings, but mostly from seizing on the face value of remarks made during interviews. There is no attempt to understand more deeply by placing the remarks within the discursive formation that makes up REBT.

## O'Donohue and Vass on rationality and irrationality in REBT

O'Donohue and Vass begin by asserting that the ability to carry out the therapy successfully "would appear dependent upon the quality of the account of rationality contained in RET" (O'Donohue & Vass, 1996, p. 304). They do not argue for the point but quote from Mahoney,

Lyddon, and Alford (1989) in support: "A reliance on the therapist's ability to recognize irrational thinking processes and to actively intervene and persuade clients to change their thoughts from irrational to rational is an essential feature of RET" (O'Donohue & Vass, 1996, p. 304). It is important to recognise that the assertion by O'Donohue and Vass does not follow from this quote. The quote is about the discriminative and communicative skills necessary for effective practice, while the assertion is about an ability to give an account (presumably philosophical) of a key concept involved. However, it is a notorious truism that skilled performance does not require an ability to articulate what is going on, and proper use of a concept does not require an ability to analyse it philosophically. The present case is complicated by the fact that part of the skill in being an REBT therapist is explaining the meaning of rationality to the client, but how is the "quality" of the therapist's account to be judged? There is likely to be a conflict between philosophical precision and therapeutic effectiveness, and this may account for some of the confusion we are trying to clear up in this chapter; it is similar to the conflict we have identified between two discursive formations, DF(REBT) and DF(metatherapy). It is not surprising that O'Donohue and Vass find that Ellis's account of rationality falls short of what they believe rationality really is, namely the "pan-critical rationalism" of W. W. Bartley, based on Karl Popper's philosophy of science. But does this matter?

O'Donohue and Vass list twenty-three quotes from Ellis on rationality as a way of characterising his views, and criticise what these reveal on grounds of clarity, consistency, applicability, and accuracy. They give examples, through brief quotes, of lack of clarity and lack of consistency. This is straightforward and useful, although it is hard to think of any philosopher, let alone a therapist (whose success is measured in the hurly-burly of professional practice), who would survive if this ordeal by soundbite were the preferred method of criticism. Their discussions of applicability and accuracy raise more interesting questions.

*Applicability*

They explain their criticism with an example:

> Crawford & Ellis (1989) list "You should treat me fairly and properly" (p. 7) as an irrational belief. How can a spouse actually

apply this criterion to determine if the behavior of his or her partner meets it? What becomes clear is that Ellis offers no decision criteria for applying his criteria for this belief and rendering a decision about the rationality of the belief. Furthermore, no heuristics or other hints on how this might be done are offered. Apparently, this decision process is viewed as unproblematically straightforward.

    ... this problem can have important negative implications for clinical practice. If a goal of RET is to help clients to become independently rational, then it would seem countertherapeutic for clients to be unable to accurately apply criteria to evaluate particular beliefs ... it would appear to be most useful if a systematic method for the decision procedure that takes criteria of rationality and beliefs and renders reliable judgements about the rationality of these beliefs could be developed and explicated.

(O'Donohue & Vass, 1996, p. 308)

There is an initial misunderstanding here. The desired application is to the client, not the spouse. A key move of REBT is to put in abeyance the question of whether or not my spouse is treating me fairly and properly. Whether she is or not, I am upsetting myself by the demand I am making of her. I do not like it if I am treated unfairly, but I only upset myself if I add to this reasonable dislike the *demand* that she should treat me fairly. The step from rationality to irrationality is contained in this, or any comparable vignette.

O'Donohue and Vass are looking for the wrong kind of criteria. There may be no operational definition available, and no algorithmic "decision procedure" but there are, as we have seen, a number of well-tried methods for deciding with the client whether she is upsetting herself by believing "He should treat me fairly and properly". Such methods are described repeatedly throughout the REBT literature, and though we do not find the formal algorithm/heuristic distinction helpful in *this* context (where it echoes the analytic/synthetic distinction), these are presumably examples of what O'Donohue and Vass mean by heuristics. It is hard to know how they could have missed them, when they write "no heuristics or other hints ... are offered".

These procedures are part of the therapeutic discourse of REBT, of DF(REBT). Following a successful course of therapy, client and therapist will have identified what they call the client's irrational beliefs, which lead to inappropriate or unhealthy emotions, and replaced them with rational beliefs, which lead to appropriate or healthy emotions. "Rational" is usually a key term in the discourse, but to be so it is not necessary to draw on any definition which specifies an exact decision procedure. What is important is to use the term consistently within the given discursive formation, and to use the procedures in a flexible manner, sensitive to what works for the client and what does not work. This is not a "quasi-mysterious" (*sic*) or "arbitrary" process, but analogous to any disciplined talk in the arts or sciences, law or medicine. For many centuries now, philosophers and others have craved vainly for "a systematic method for the decision procedure that takes criteria of rationality and beliefs and renders reliable judgements about the rationality of these beliefs". Descartes offered clear and distinct ideas, as an ideal taken from mathematical thinking. O'Donohue and Vass point this out, and reject it, not because it is an attempt to pin down rationality once and for all (our objection) but because it is a justificational or foundational account of rationality. Yet they continue to assume that a systematic decision procedure is possible, as though questions of rationality could in principle be settled, in all contexts, by reference to a decision table. Our view is that rationality involves the use of reason in circumstances (discursive formations) so diverse that no universal algorithm is possible or desirable. So for us the mistake made by O'Donohue and Vass is the same as Descartes' foundationalist belief in a universal algorithm.

### Accuracy

O'Donohue and Vass offer as the presumed basis of their algorithm, Bartley's "pan-critical rationality". This is appealed to in answer to the question of accuracy: "Does the conceptualization of rationality and irrationality utilized in RET actually capture the phenomenon of interest, i.e., rationality and irrationality?" (O'Donohue & Vass, 1996, p. 308). Bartley emphasises an ideal model for rationality in practice. "How can we be rational?" reduces to how can we "arrange our lives and institutions to expose our positions, actions, opinions, beliefs, aims, conjectures, decisions, standards, frameworks, ways of life, policies, traditional practices, etc. to optimum examination, in order to counteract and eliminate as much error as possible" (Bartley, 1988, p. 213, cited in O'Donohue & Vass, 1996, p. 311). This is based on Karl Popper's falsifiability as the mark of scientific thinking, a process expressed, in the title of his one of his books, as "conjectures and refutations" (Popper, 1972).

There are two practical problems with this bracing Popperian liberalism. The first is that it ignores power structures, or, in Lakatos' (1970) quasi-evolutionary terms, the protective belt that successful institutions (or scientific theories, or species) build around themselves to avoid being too dangerously tested. It is like a shell protecting the vulnerable creature inside (see Still, 1986). The Popper/Bartley theory of rationality (as stated by O'Donohue & Vass) may be an ideal to aim for, but it is distant from the practical problems of ensuring that massively wealthy corporations are exposed to the same critical scrutiny as small traders or that the awkward ideas of a novice research student are given the same consideration as a well-entrenched theory whose ramifications are being investigated in a multitude of well-endowed projects. No one has found a transcendent definition of "optimum examination", guaranteed free from the biases of powerful interests. Both Popper and Bartley have been aware of these difficulties, but O'Donohue and Vass do not deal with them.

The second problem touches more nearly on our present concerns. Even if we do accept pan-critical rationality as an ideal to aim for in a healthy, democratic society, O'Donohue and Vass overstep the mark by applying it to specific beliefs, thereby committing the same foundationalist error committed by Descartes: "A belief is rational to the extent that it has been subjected to and survived criticism, especially the best criticism" (O'Donohue & Vass, 1996, p. 311). Descartes' foundationalist error had been to take the old Scholastic and Stoic cultivation of clear and distinct ideas, and turn it into the essence of rationality. This is what O'Donohue and Vass are doing with Bartley's prescription for a rational society.

The O'Donohue and Vass version of Bartley's prescription applies to general scientific beliefs, such as that the earth is flat and fixed, or that it is spherical and in orbit around the sun—the first has not survived criticism, the second has. It applies less well to political and economic beliefs, where it can too easily be appealed to in order to justify present power structures, since they have survived criticism. It applies much less well to personal beliefs and inferences[5] of the kind encountered in psychotherapy. Take an irrationally jealous husband's unwarranted inference that "My wife is having an affair". The opposite inference is that "My wife is faithful to me". The first is like "there are unicorns in South America", almost impossible to falsify. The second is easy to falsify, but since it is impossible to confirm (according to the criterion) the rational policy will be to hire private detectives, and maintain a persistent state of alert suspicion. The obsessively jealous husband who hires detectives to follow his wife is trying to falsify the inference "My wife is faithful", and confirm the inference that she is unfaithful. The husband is like a careful scientist who will not accept the evidence of what he knows about his wife's character, her signs of love for him, her lack of opportunity, etc., so that, if O'Donohue and Vass are right, in this way, and only in this way, will the husband finally have rational grounds for his inference. But what is rational for the scientist is surely irrational in the conduct of intimate relations. The husband's dysfunctional behaviour would be the result of following the O'Donohue and Vass recipe for rational belief and inference.

However, falsifiablity does apply in an interesting way to irrational beliefs in the form of demands. A general cognitive approach to the jealous husband's problem might attempt to encourage the husband to question the inferences being made, that is to change the A in the ABC model by questioning the evidence that "My wife is having an affair". However, in REBT, what Ellis sometimes calls the "elegant" solution to the jealous husband's problem is to focus on the irrational demand that "she must not cheat on me, that would be absolutely awful". The client is taught to dispute this belief as untrue logically (it does not follow from the rational thought that "I do not want my wife to have an affair"), empirically ("There is no law of the universe which says that if I do not want something it must not happen"), and pragmatically ("Does it help?"). However, in this disputing process the client's demand is subjected to the kind of rational criticism that has been lacking in the past. In other words, by shifting the client's intellectual and emotional focus from the belief "My wife is having an affair" (which is hard to falsify), or its complement "My wife is faithful" (which is easy to falsify, but unhelpful to try too hard to do so), to the underlying demand "My wife *must* not have an affair", Ellis has, *from the start of REBT*, been making use of the falsifiablity criterion in the form of an "optimum examination".

The final ground selected for criticism by O'Donohue and Vass was that of accuracy. They ask, "Does the conceptualization of rationality and irrationality utilized in RET actually capture the phenomenon of interest, i.e., rationality and irrationality?" (O'Donohue & Vass, 1996, p. 308). Their answer by the end of the paper is emphatically

"No", based on a "philosophical analysis" which is regarded as especially justified "because Ellis himself regards RET as having an important philosophical dimension" (O'Donohue & Vass, 1996, p. 308), with "roots in philosophic writings of ancient Greek and Roman stoics" (O'Donohue & Vass, 1996, p. 308). However, as we have seen, their critical analysis draws on criteria of rationality taken from a branch of the philosophy of science that has looked to modern physics for its standard, which in turn is part of a tradition traceable back to Descartes, of basing rationality upon the ideals of mathematics and the physical sciences. They do not question that such standards are applicable to the evaluation of practices stemming from very different interests and a different tradition of philosophical thought.

We accept that by parading the philosophical roots of REBT Ellis invites philosophical critique, but believe that true critique starts with a deeper analysis of how Ellis is actually using his concepts of rationality and irrationality. This is not achieved by squeezing meaning from a table of brief quotations, or even a retrospective summary from Ellis himself. Instead, it is important to have an understanding of how the concepts fit into the rest of the discursive formation that makes up REBT.

## Discussion

As a start towards this it is important to distinguish three related uses of "rationality" in Western thought.

*Descriptive.* Rationality is a capacity possessed by human beings. Aristotle defined human beings as rational animals, by which he meant that they can use reason to work out how to achieve goals, rather than instinct. Even if their reasoning is poor, or they act impulsively and apparently without reason, they are still rational animals, by definition.

*Logical ideal.* The second sense of rational is the logical ideal encountered in the work of Erwin and that of O'Donohue and Vass. In this modern form, it is a residue from the Cartesian and logical positivist view that scientific and mathematical thinking form the *sine qua non* of rationality, rather than an impressive application of it.

*Rational living.* Although, as rational animals, human beings are capable of using reason, they do not always do so in trying to achieve their goals. Sometimes they are overcome with passion, and sometimes, for instance, act furiously, without thought, out of anger. Recognising this, Stoic philosophers wrote about ways of countering the threat (as they saw it) to attempts to lead a virtuous life. Of how to act out of reason rather than passion. Their project was not about suppressing emotions or desire, but how to fulfil desires without blind passion, in the service of virtuous living, and Ellis drew on their recommendations in developing REBT. As discussed in Chapter One his rationality is closer to Stoic reason, than to the more formal, mathematical Platonic reason drawn upon by Descartes.

To live like this is to live rationally. Someone living rationally in this sense will certainly apply falsifiability where that is appropriate. In choosing a spouse or buying a house, for instance, he or she will not be bowled over by appearances, but will reserve judgement until the potential mate is better known, or until the surveyor's report comes in. If the results are favourable, he or she will follow desires in making a commitment. Once made, it will no longer be rational to reserve judgement, to continue to have doubts about the house, seeking increasingly detailed reports on it, or about your spouse, questioning his or her motives, etc. In effect, what has gone before is used as confirmatory evidence. However, it is never foolproof. The charming and courageous young man may turn into a womanising alcoholic, and the house may be swallowed up in an earthquake.

Far from being incompatible with Karl Popper's critical realism, this rationality applied to everyday life is the very grassroots from which his theory was drawn—as Popper pointed out, we are like searchlights rather than buckets in finding out about the world (Popper, 1978, Appendix I), using active trial and error rather than passive association. The theory was developed partly as a solution to the traditional problem of induction, as stated by Hume. The problem was that there are no logical grounds for assuming that the regularities observed in the past will apply to the future, as seems demanded if scientific knowledge is to be regarded as valid. Popper's solution was to give up seeking logical grounds for belief in scientific knowledge, and to focus instead on scientific practice, of "conjectures and refutations". With this focus, we cease to worry about the incorrigibililty of scientific knowledge, and celebrate instead the success of the practices. Science therefore is a highly systematic application of everyday rational thinking, of trial and error or our "forming hypotheses, testing them out, modifying or rejecting them", which is present throughout Ellis's writings, and a crucial part of DF(REBT). It is therefore quite inappropriate to take this rationality in its systematic form, and then turn it destructively upon the everyday practices from which it derives.

This defence does not extend to Ellis's attempts to establish the scientific credentials of REBT, where he has tried to meet the rational ideals of DF(metatherapy). There he is open to some of the criticisms considered in this chapter. The failure of the philosophical critiques of REBT considered in this chapter comes from not distinguishing between concepts of rationality from different discursive formations, DF(metatherapy), and DF(REBT), and of not taking into account the context in which the term "rationality" appears. As discussed in Chapter One, the concept of rationality as rational living in DF(REBT) is based on Stoic rather than Platonic reason. In the next chapter, we look at the relationship between rationality and the deontological "shoulds" and "oughts", whose baleful effect is so central to the practice of REBT.

## Notes

1. Evans (1984–1985) made a similar point in detecting a confusion between "hedonisic" and "scientific" views of rationality in Ellis' writings, although not from the historical point of view we adopt in this chapter. In his crisp reply, Ellis (1984–1985) accepted Evans' criticism, and turned the confusion into a distinction.

2. Erwin gives no evidence for this assertion. Carl Rogers certainly had no axe to grind in favour of REBT, but he wrote of his clients in therapy that they: "tend to move away from 'oughts'. The compelling feeling of 'I ought to do or be thus and so' is negatively valued. The client moves away from being what he 'ought to be', no matter who has set that imperative" (Rogers, 1990, p. 182). This suggests that such demands are commonly observed in clients when they first come for therapies other than REBT. See also the chapter "Tyranny of the should" in Horney (1991).

3. Norman Malcolm discusses the different uses of "cause" in Armstrong and Malcolm (1984, pp. 69–74). Following Wittgenstein, he tries to wean us away from the assumption that there must be one essential meaning to the word.

4. In his writings, he has often urged the need for experiments in order to establish aspects of REBT, and has carried out many himself (see Dryden, 1991, p. 23).

5. In REBT, a factual belief based on evidence is usually referred to as an "inference", and is part of the A in the ABC model. The word "belief" is reserved for the irrational demands or rational preferences that make up the B.

# CHAPTER FIVE

# Rationality and the shoulds

## Introduction

We have argued that a central insight into Ellis's early thought was to recognise that diversities in all the intricacies of psychoanalysis converge upon a single invariant, the irrational "shoulds", a pathology he referred to as "musturbation". This was his lumper, and a new unit of analysis for psychology. But not all "shoulds" are irrational and this chapter is about rational and irrational uses of deontological words, such as "should", "ought", and "must", referred to as "the shoulds". Rationality within a discursive formation is taken as a mutual relationship between conceptual schemes and human agency. These are expressed in what Bakhtin (1981, p. 342) referred to as "authoritative discourse" and "internally persuasive discourse". When the conceptual scheme is in place and its authority transparent, and there is interplay between authoritative discourse and internally persuasive discourse, then the shoulds are perceived as rational. When the interplay is disrupted or suppressed the shoulds are seen as irrational. Breakdown occurs in two main ways. First, it occurs when the effective conceptual schemes are hidden, and the origin of the shoulds obscured. We describe some instances of the latter, from philosophy, psychotherapy, and experimental studies of rationality. Second, in technology and science the mutual relationship sometimes breaks down because authoritative discourse is too powerful, and inhibits interplay. After describing these pathologies, we turn to William James, who drew attention to a repair kit for rationality in his detection of the psychologist's fallacy. Describing the work of Dewey and Husserl as elaborations of this, we distinguish two essential aspects of rationality: disciplinary expressed in authoritative discourse, and emancipatory expressed in internally persuasive discourse.

## Functions of deontological words

Deontological words, such as "should", "ought", and "must", will be referred to as "the shoulds" (after Horney, 1991). The shoulds are used in giving reasons of a certain kind, reasons which appeal to the authority of shared conceptual schemes, sometimes drawing on the specialised codes and technical accounts whose use is described by Tilly (2006). They have a coercive force, akin to demands, and are used to decide and persuade, as well as to defend or justify or explain actions when asked for reasons. It will be argued that when the shared conceptual scheme is in place and its authority is transparent to the agent, then the shoulds are perceived as rational. When conceptual schemes are defunct or inaccessible, or when their authority is questionable, the shoulds are likely to seem irrational. But even then they sometimes maintain their coercive force. This is partly because, as Weber pointed out, the authority of traditionalist or charismatic conceptual schemes is maintained through routinisation and rules (Weber, 1946, p. 262), which creates an appearance of rationality. We will be looking at more extreme cases than this, where the coercive force remains in the absence of any pretence of rationality.

Generally the use of the shoulds forms a bridge between a source of knowledge or prescription and the thought or action prescribed by such sources. The source may be practical, like a holy book, a technical handbook, or a guidebook or map that is relied upon; or more abstract, like the structures and interrelations of eternal essences in a Platonic heaven, or the loosely codified norms of a society, or the conceptual schemes of folk wisdom, religious dogma, or scientific knowledge. If they are articulated, the sources tend to be read or heard as what Bakhtin called "Authoritative Discourse" in his essay *Discourse in the Novel* (published in Bakhtin, 1981, pp. 259–422).

> The authoritative word demands that we acknowledge it, that we make it our own; it binds us, quite independent of any power it might have to persuade us internally; we encounter it with its authority already fused to it.
>
> (Bakhtin, 1981, p. 342)

By contrast:

> Internally persuasive discourse—as opposed to one that is externally authoritative—is, as it is affirmed through assimilation, tightly interwoven with "one's own word". In the everyday rounds of our consciousness, the internally persuasive word is half-ours and half-someone else's.
>
> (Bakhtin, 1981, p. 345)[1]

The shoulds, we argue, originate from the demands of authoritative discourse (AD), and potentially infiltrate internally persuasive discourse (IPD). There they can in principle retain their coercive force even when their origin is lost or defunct.

### Rationality and the shoulds

Where is rationality of the shoulds established? Is it in the conceptual schemes whose AD prescribes rational thinking and actions? Or is it in the thinking and actions of human beings, of which IPD is a part, shown in both inner and outer dialogue? Or does it emerge from the interplay between the two, as entailed by a mutualist ontology (Still & Good, 1992, 1998)? Here we elaborate on the latter view, by examining real and hypothetical instances where the interplay has become frozen or distorted in some way. After describing this pathology in the rationality of the shoulds, we turn to William James and the psychologist's fallacy.

To illustrate rational shoulds in everyday action we begin with an example. During the winter of 2004/2005 one of us with two companions set out on a circular walk over the Cheviots in Northumberland, following a well-known guidebook and an Ordnance Survey map, but without a compass. These were the sources of our AD. We left our car near a farm called Nether Hindhope. The weather was good at first and the route was easy to follow. Then it began to rain, followed by a blizzard, for which we were ill-equipped. Our map began to disintegrate.

Nearing the end of the walk, the book referred to a signpost to Nether Hindhope. We came to a signpost with one arm missing, and after some shared IPD about what we should do, we decided this must be the one referred to in the book, and the missing arm had probably pointed to Nether Hindhope, so was the one we must follow. In fact the path took us back in the wrong direction, and we were lost and getting exhausted in the gloom. Just visible in the distance was a road marked on what remained of the map, although it was the other side of the Cheviots from our car, so to head for it meant that though we would probably find a place of safety, we would not return to our car that night. After more IPD, we agreed that we ought to head for the road, and ended up cold and wet in an isolated shepherd's cottage, drinking port and talking about football. Eventually a friend collected us. During the summer of 2006 two of us retraced the walk in fine weather with a good map and compass, and found that there was no signpost to Nether Hindhope, certainly not the one with the missing arm. The book was wrong. We got in touch with the author to point this out, and the next edition was changed. The processes described here are an instance of duality of structures.

## Duality of structures and mutualism

Words do not have a life of their own. Their being is inseparable from the existence of the people using them, who are constrained yet free in the special way that Giddens referred to as the "duality of structures": "Social structures are both constituted by human agency and yet at the same time are the very medium of human agency" (Giddens, 1976, p. 121; Shotter, 1983; Still & Good, 1992). Following the map and guidebook in our example is part of what constitutes the social structures framing hill-walking. In a small way we were able to mould an aspect of the social structures by emailing the author. Thus, on an optimistic liberal reading, human agency is a benign source of variation within social structures, which in turn confirms or sometimes changes, the social structures. In some ways this flexible model of change, as we interpret it here, is analogous to natural selection, although not as it has been construed by neo-Darwinists and adaptationists (Gould & Lewontin, 1979), who have emphasised the moulding of organisms by environment, at the expense of the moulding of environment by organisms. In their criticism of adaptationists, Gould and Lewontin

(1979) drew an analogy between the design of the spandrels of San Marco and evolution by natural selection. In arriving at the design the architect was constrained by public expectations, current architectural practice, and the structures that they had to mesh with. Possible variations were far from random, and Gould and Lewontin argued that similarly weighty constraints apply in biological evolution. This will be referred to as the "spandrel effect".

In his book on the evolution of the earth, Darwin described a mutual process in the way the soil of the Earth is constituted by the activity of worms, yet provides what can be aptly called the very medium of worm activity (Reed, 1982). Human agents do not mould social structures as straightforwardly (and literally) as worms have moulded the earth, but Darwin's account provides a usefully ideal account of duality of structures to measure reality against.

The human agent is embedded in a human environment which includes the physical setting, but also the language and the constructions and the social setting within which he or she exists. If we imagine a diagram in which social structures or conceptual schemes are at the top, and human agency below, then the whole can be sliced for the purposes of analysis vertically but not horizontally. That is, we believe it makes little sense to study human agency or social structures in isolation, but good sense to take an aspect of social structures and examine the interplay between this and a corresponding aspect of human agency. Language lends itself especially well to this form of analysis, and we could substitute AD and IPD for "social structures" and "human agency" in the above formula from Giddens, taking care not to isolate language from social structure. Both AD and IPD are thoroughly embedded in social structures. The hill-walking example above is partly about language. We were irrational to set out ill-equipped on our walk, failing to follow the rational shoulds derived from the AD about winter conditions and equipment in the book and elsewhere. But after setting out, the AD of map and book guided our activity, telling us the paths we should follow. When conditions deteriorated our agency continued to be constrained by them until the AD proved inadequate, and IPD began to take over. We were led astray by these sources of AD, and later took action to reconstitute the instructions in the book. But the process is not just about language, since all of it took place within a culture from which the activity of hill-walking, and the map-reading and guidebooks that go with it, get their meaning.

With an explicit emphasis on language embedded within social structures, Ian Hacking has examined a special aspect of duality of structures which he called "looping", in his book on multiple personality.

> People classified in a certain way tend to conform to or grow into the ways that they are described; but they also evolve in their own ways, so that the classifications and descriptions have to be constantly revised. Multiple personality is an almost too perfect illustration of this feedback effect.
>
> (Hacking, 1995, p. 21)

Hacking used looping to structure the history of the concept of "multiple personality". He does not refer to Giddens or to Bakhtin, but the psychiatric language of diagnosis provides a ready parallel to AD, and the writings and discussions considered by Hacking correspond loosely to IPD.

A version of "duality of structures" has been described for rationality itself by Gigerenzer and Selten.

> ([M]odels of rationality) evolve over time, just as the idea of rationality has a history, a present and a future ... Over the past centuries, models of rationality have changed when they conflicted with actual behaviour, yet, at the same time, they provide prescriptions for behaviour. This double role—to describe and to prescribe—does not map easily onto a sharp divide between descriptive and normative models, which plays down the actual exchange between the psychological and the rational. Herbert Simon's notion of bounded rationality was proposed in the mid-1950's to connect, rather than to oppose, the rational and the psychological.
>
> (Gigerenzer & Selten, 2000, p. 1)

Simon's (1956) bounded rationality was a move away from theorising based on the mathematical ideal of optimisation, and starts from the reality of cognitive abilities on the one hand, and the structure of the environment on the other. As Gigerenzer put it:

> Bounded rationality in economics, cognitive science, and biology is about humans and animals, not about how they compare with demons and Gods.
>
> (Gigerenzer, 2000, p. 40)

Simon and later writers have thus tried to simplify the "actual exchange between the psychological and the rational" by bringing the two together in a single concept, which Gigerenzer has called "Ecological Rationality". This has given rise to a number of studies showing the importance of context in human reasoning, which demonstrate that the mathematical ideal, indifferent to context, is a poor model of human rationality, which works well given the appropriate context. Thus, physicians given relevant a priori and conditional probabilities were asked to estimate the probability of a woman having breast cancer following a positive mammogram. In one study (Eddy, 1982) the Bayesian probability was 7.8 per cent, but most estimates were around 75 per cent, and such studies led to the conclusion that people do not reason according to the rational principles of probability theory.

> The literature of the last 25 years has reiterated again and again the message that people are bad reasoners, neglect base rates most of the time, neglect false positive rates, and are unable to integrate base rate, hit rate, and false positive rate the Bayesian way.
>
> (Gigerenzer, 2000, p. 61)

But when Eddy's study was repeated with natural frequencies rather than probabilities, physicians were correct most of the time. In an example described by Gigerenzer, "Dr Average", the director of a university clinic, was clearly anxious and evasive when confronted with the problem in probability format, but visibly relieved and quick to find the answer with problems in frequency format, which corresponds more closely to his direct experience. Working in a different tradition of research, Lave (1988) made a similar point when she described the sophisticated mathematical skills involved in the budgeting of shoppers, who had little or no knowledge of school mathematics. The reasoning skills in these cases are not mediated through the rational abstractions learned in the classroom. The abstractions of probability and rational choice theory may still provide an accurate formal account of the mathematical side of the process, but the reasoning skills arise directly from the situation.

The "literature of the last 25 years" had assumed that rational problem solvers *should* always follow the prescriptions of probability and rational choice theory, if they are to act rationally, and that this is independent of context. This led to the paradoxical conclusion that professionals like

Dr Average do not really decide rationally at all, since they do badly in the contexts provided. Dr Average was presented with a problem couched in a form inappropriate for his or her practice, drawing on the wrong conceptual scheme (in the wrong words, although logically correct). The smooth interplay between scheme and thought was prevented and the expert was unable to choose rationally. But if anything was irrational it was the "should" implicit in instructing Dr Average to follow the requirements of the experiment.

In this example, the human agents involved (medical experts) failed to mould or be moulded by the conceptual scheme chosen by the experimenters, rational choice theory, and probability theory. The latter did not provide the right medium for human rationality. Ecological rationality has tried to correct this by taking context into account. In this example the pathology appeared as a result of the laboratory setup; the next example is about a duality of structures extending over thousands of years, embedded deeply into the Western way of life, where the supposed failure is due to the decay of an overarching conceptual scheme.

## Alistair MacIntyre and the decay of moral reasoning

In a thought experiment at the start of *After Virtue*, Alistair MacIntyre asked us to imagine a catastrophe which leads to the destruction of the institutions of science, its books, its laboratories, its teaching, and the scientists themselves, leaving only fragments which later generations use to revive the old discipline. The fragments are put together in a simulacrum of scientific talk and practice.

> But many of the beliefs presupposed by the use of these expressions would have been lost and there would appear to be an element of arbitrariness and even of choice in their application which would appear very surprising to us. What appear to be rival and competing premises for which no further argument could be given would abound.
>
> (MacIntyre, 1981, pp. 1–2)

In this imagined future the rationality of science has disappeared, although some of the language, and some of the heated arguments (now unresolvable), remain. The rest of MacIntyre's book attempted to show historically how this dire state of affairs holds, not for science, but for the modern language of morality.

> What we possess are … the fragments of a conceptual scheme, parts of which now lack the contexts from which their significance derived. We possess indeed simulacra of morality, we continue to use many of the key expressions. But we have—very largely, if not entirely—lost our comprehension, both theoretical and practical, of morality.
>
> (MacIntyre, 1981, p. 2)

Without the coherent conceptual scheme that was once provided by Aristotelian virtue ethics, the deontological words, the shoulds, which continue to be used as stridently as ever, have lost their connection with a shared system of beliefs about what a worthwhile and moral life would be, which is a necessary framework for practical rationality.[2] In the absence of such a link, philosophers, starting with Hume, have puzzled over the meaning of such words, and concluded that they may be no more than expressions of feeling, or attempts at persuasion, or imperatives. They are no longer fully rational, but they have retained their coercive power. Is this a bad thing? MacIntyre believed so, and laments the consequences at the end of the book.

> This time … the barbarians are not waiting beyond the frontiers; they have already been governing us for quite some time.
>
> (MacIntyre, 1981, p. 245)

A comparable debilitation of a conceptual scheme has recently been described by Yurchak, in his analysis of the collapse of socialism in Soviet Russia (Yurchak, 2006). In order to understand this collapse, he made use of Bakhtin's distinction between AD and IPD. This distinction enabled Yurchak to find an alternative to the simplistic, dualistic view that the collapse of such regimes is preceded by a simple disbelief in many people, who carry on the old rituals for the sake of form or safety.

Drawing on Austin, Derrida, and other theorists, Yurchak developed the concept of a "performative shift". Speech acts have a constative dimension and a performative dimension, and according to John

Austin, "every genuine speech act is both" (cited in Yurchak, 2006, p. 22). A performative shift occurs when the performative dimension of ritualised speech acts grows in importance (when it is important to participate in the reproduction of these acts at the level of form), while the constative dimension becomes open-ended, indeterminate, or simply irrelevant (Yurchak, 2006, p. 26).

In these ways the shoulds can retain their power in ensuring ritual conformity, while losing meaningful contact with the conceptual scheme that once gave them meaning. The interplay of duality of structures is not a measure of political freedom. At the height of Stalinism, in 1938, there was public discussion of the new constitution, whereas this was absent in 1977.

> The differences between these two discursive events reveal the differences between the models of authoritative language in the two historical periods. The discussions in 1938 included published suggestions and formulations by individual readers and collectives ... and a published metadiscourse that evaluated these suggestions and commented on them in a voice external to this discourse. The 1977 article, by contrast, simply stated that the Soviet people unanimously supported the text of the new constitution, not referring to any metadiscursive critiques or evaluations.
>
> (Yurchak, 2006, pp. 62–63)

By 1977 the conceptual scheme was unable to support the interplay (however restricted) required for the operation of the duality of structures in rational discourse. Such interplay was present in 1938, but although that necessary condition was present, other factors make the ascription of rationality problematic in Stalinist Russia. These dynamics will be returned to later.

## Exclusion of the mentally ill from the space of reasons

A similar absence or debilitation of a conceptual scheme has been observed in individuals with common forms of psychological disturbance. At this individual level, the shoulds have been implicated in psychological disorder ever since the chapter of Horney's book, "The Tyranny of the Should" (Horney, 1991). But before turning to this, it is important to notice that conceptual schemes and the AD they support, do not have to be generally regarded as rational in themselves in order for the reasons or beliefs to be rational, at least in the simplest sense which Newton-Smith (1981, p. 241) referred to as "minirat". Newton-Smith pointed out that at the simplest level it is the giving of reasons itself that is important, not their quality or acceptability. If I believe that action A will bring about goal B, which I seek, then stating this as a reason for doing A will be rational at this simple level, even if my beliefs as to how to attain this goal are generally considered wrong or unscientific, and/or the goal is one that most people would regard as unreasonable. Newton-Smith (1981, p. 241) called this a "minimal rational account" or a "minirat" account (*minimal rational*). Thus, in some Buddhist centres in the West, the food scraps after a meal are put on a plate outside. The reason? To feed the hungry ghosts. Whether we believe in hungry ghosts or not, this is a minirat account. It is not a minirat account because of the form of words, but because there is a duality of structures between conceptual scheme (the belief system) and thought or action. Thus, "To feed the hungry ghosts" is not a minirat account unless there a belief behind it, involving hungry ghosts, either part of the Buddhist culture involving such beliefs, or beliefs personal to the speaker. Likewise, whatever we think of the social and political structures in Soviet Russia in 1938, the shoulds that appeal to the conceptual schemes of those structures are rational in the sense of minirat. Later, in 1977, those conforming to the system out of self-preservation were acting rationally (in the sense of minirat at least) in relation to a conceptual schema of self-preservation, although not in relation to an AD that has lost its constative dimension.

It is the ability to give reasons that has led some writers to place psychological being within the normative "space of reasons" (Brinkmann, 2006) rather than the non-normative, causal space of scientific investigations into the physical and biological worlds.

If there are actions that cannot be given even a minirat account, then

> [i]t is arguable that if we are to find explanations for such irrational actions we have to turn to psychoanalytic theories.
>
> (Newton-Smith, 1981, p. 242)

In the psychoanalytic account the space of reasons is extended to include actions and beliefs whose reasons were previously unconscious.

Bringing into the space of reasons is to bring into consciousness. The patient may come to understand how the pattern of actions which seems irrational can be understood as the continuation of forgotten conceptual schemes that made sense of the "shoulds" in another world, that of childhood.

In a recent paper, Brinkmann (2006) developed the Wittgensteinian view that the normative space of reasons and the non-normative space of causes are distinct, and that the subject-matter of psychology lies in the space of reasons (Winch, 1958).[3] Thus, in the examples taken by Brinkmann, the doctor taps my knee and my leg moves. It just happens—there is no right or wrong—so this is non-normative. If a sad movie makes me cry I may give a reason for this: "When the baby died it was so sad I had to cry." However, this reason can be wrong, Brinkmann argues, since I could have misunderstood the film by missing the irony and the true message. We avoid this by saying "I found it so sad" instead of "it was so sad", but this merely relocates the presumed causal link. In both cases, interpreting the film correctly, as a work of irony, is presumed to lead to a different emotional reaction, whereas the tap on the knee requires no interpretation intervening between tap and knee jerk.

Like Newton-Smith, Brinkmann suggests that some people are at least partially excluded from the space of reasons.

> [W]hat about those instances when the normative orders are more or less suspended in a person's life, so to speak, for example due to madness, neuroses, psychoses and mental illness in general?
>
> (Brinkmann, 2006, p. 12)

What exactly is it that could exile the psychotic or neurotic from this essentially human space? In this chapter, we pursue this question further, treating it as a variation on the problematic relationship between AD and IPD as described by Yurchak. It is a disruption in the interplay between AD and IPD, in which the shoulds retain their power, even though, as in MacIntyre, they have lost touch with the conceptual scheme from which they were originally derived. Such words arise from the normative systems of AD. Because their power is great and their origin is hidden, they have been compared to coercion by "terrorist gangs" (Rosenberg, 1987), agents of a displaced authority that have infiltrated the IPD and constrained its productiveness.

## Karen Horney and the tyranny of the should

Karen Horney described this potent mixture of vacuity and coercion in the use of the shoulds in her theory of neurosis. In one her most influential essays, "The tyranny of the should", published as Chapter Three in *Neurosis and Human Growth*, she wrote of the

> enormous coercive power of the shoulds, as the motor force whipping a person into action in the attempt to actualize the ideal self.
>
> (Horney, 1991, pp. 84–85; first published 1950)

In this way, Horney brought some of the compulsive forces of unreason, stemming from the psychoanalytic unconscious, to the surface. Not in the traditional form of signs and symptoms as grist for the hermeneutic mill, but as words corresponding to the very point at which the energy stemming directly from the Freudian id or indirectly from the constraining power of the superego is transmitted into the urge to action or inaction. In Horney, the shoulds represent the latter, exhortations on behalf of the ideal self, triggered by all too obvious discrepancies between the ideal and actuality. They retain their coercive power even though the conceptual schemes on which they are based are no longer remembered.

Horney was careful to distinguish the dictatorial power of the neurotic's shoulds from what she considered the following of real moral standards and ideals. Indeed, giving in to the dictatorial power of the shoulds is not just irrational, according to Horney, but immoral (Horney, 1991, p. 73).

> The shoulds, therefore, *lack the moral seriousness of genuine ideals.* People in their grip are not striving, for instance, toward approximating a greater degree of honesty but are driven to attain the absolute in honesty ... There is one further quality of the shoulds that distinguished them from genuine moral standards ... That is their *coercive character.* Ideals, too, have an obligating power over our lives. For instance, if among them is the belief in fulfilling responsibilities which we ourselves recognize as such, we try our best to do so even though it may be difficult. To fulfill them is what we ourselves ultimately want, or what we deem right. The wish, the judgment, the decision is ours. And because we are thus at one with ourselves, efforts of this kind give us freedom and strength.
>
> (Horney, 1991, pp. 72–73; original emphasis)

So "I shouldn't have lied to her", could be a rational and moral self-reflection, or part of a lacerating and immature self-damnation. Here Horney made a distinction similar to MacIntyre's, although for her the significant conceptual scheme has not died with the fading of Aristotelian virtue ethics, but is still available to the psychologically healthy. She was thus more optimistic than either MacIntyre or Freud, and she explicitly took issue with Freud on this point.

> It was one of Freud's gravest errors to regard inner dictates ... as constituting morality in general.
>
> (Horney, 1991, pp. 72–73)

MacIntyre might side with Freud here, but only as a symptom of the time, not as a sceptical truth about morality in general. They are pessimistic in different ways, but neither has the outlook of Horney, whose optimism has been a source of criticism (Trilling, 1942) but also of her popularity and influence on psychotherapy after World War II (Quinn, 1988).

As we saw in Chapter Three, this focus on the coerciveness of the shoulds rather than on unconscious content opened the way for Albert Ellis (1958) to launch Rational Psychotherapy, which has evolved into Rational Emotive Behavior Therapy (REBT), alongside the other, more famous cognitive therapy, Aaron Beck's Cognitive Behaviour Therapy (Beck, 1963). Ellis, after a training analysis with Charles Hulbeck at the Horney Institute, became disillusioned with the lengthy hermeneutic side of the business, with its questionable scientific basis, and concentrated directly on expressed demands themselves, in order to find ways of changing them without worrying about the underlying systems of generation. It is these demands, or the belief systems of which they are a part, and not the objects of emotion themselves, that are the cause of dysfunctional emotion. If the shoulds are based on conceptual schemes and their associated AD, these are unconscious or long forgotten; they perhaps correspond to what Beck has referred to as "core schema", which are uncovered during cognitive therapy in order to dispute and change them (Beck, Freeman & Associates, 1990).

Unlike Horney (but like Freud), in his early writings Ellis did not clearly distinguish between the coercive, unhealthy shoulds, and those that arise from a rational moral system. He often wrote as though all shoulds are irrational and did not at first describe the conditions under which the use of "should" can be rational (as we are doing here). Initially his therapy aimed to dispute all shoulds into oblivion. Early in the historical development of the therapy, the disputing became formalised into three questions: Does the demand follow logically from the want or desire?; Is there an empirical law from which the demand can be logically deduced from the want?; and Is it useful (does it achieve your goals) to make it into a demand? The first two are akin to the arguments of Hume against the rationality of moral belief, which had become, according to MacIntyre, exposed to this attack by the atrophy of the framework or conceptual scheme that underwrote their rationality.

But later Ellis made two important distinctions, which correspond to Horney's two senses of "should". First the distinction between conditional and unconditional shoulds. Thus, "I must spend more time revising" may be conditional and rational, and can be expanded into, "If I want to pass the exam I must spend more time revising." This is a constative (it can be true or false), as well as a performative, drawn from the conceptual scheme or AD that guides students through their college career. Second, the distinction between hot and warm cognitions. The student who thinks in lukewarm fashion, "I must spend more time revising" but then happily drifts off to the pub with friends, may have problems as a student, but they are different from those that Ellis was concerned with. For that (and for irrationality) the cognitions must be "hot", and are probably already intertwined with the anxiety the model suggests they cause.

> The theory of REBT holds that "warm" cognitions or evaluations almost always accompany—and partially "cause"—feelings or emotions, while "hot" cognitions or strong evaluations almost always accompany—and partially "cause" strong and sustained feelings. When "hot" cognitions are absolutistic and imperative … such "hot" cognitions tend to go with, significantly contribute to, and partially "cause" self-defeating feeling, or what we often call "emotional disturbance".
>
> (Ellis, 1994, pp. 60–61)

The heat metaphor is connected with the later distinction between the "grandiose *musts*" that lie behind (and presumably give heat to) the "unrealistic and illogical self-defeating beliefs" (Ellis, 1994,

p. xvi; emphasis in original). These often show themselves as what Beck in CBT called ANTS or Automatic Negative Thoughts. But in the case of ANTS, it is their compulsive immediacy, rather than the heat with which they are held, that gives them their irrational power.

For Horney's neurotic, the conceptual scheme which may once have given substance to the shoulds, has disappeared from sight, as with MacIntyre's thought experiment, or his account of the modern language of morality. If we are right, there is a parallel between the philosophical predicament faced by Hume and later philosophers, and that of Horney's neurotic. Like Hume, Ellis's disputing cuts through the vacuity of the shoulds when they are bereft of the conceptual schemes that gave them force. In both cases the shoulds may be linked with strong feeling or persuasive power, but the rational form of words is an illusion (according both to Hume, and to the neurotic who often recognises clearly but to no avail that the demand leading to hand washing or avoidance of a certain event is not rational). The conceptual schemes are defunct or inaccessible, and there is no flow or interplay in the duality of structures, between conceptual scheme and human agency, or AD and IPD. A similar absence of flow or interplay, and consequently a lack of rationality, has been suspected in the heartlands of modern reason, technology and science. But the structure of this source of irrationality is different from that considered so far. In science and technology the conceptual schemes and AD are very much alive and accessible, and the disruption of interplay that brings rationality into question has other causes.

## Authoritative discourse in modern technology

In *Adventures of Ideas*, Whitehead (1933, p. 61) distinguished between a Craft and a Profession, the latter constituting a necessary restriction of freedom in the organisation of modern society. In a profession there is an organised institution which makes it

> An avocation whose activities are subjected to theoretical analysis, and are modified by theoretical conclusion derived from that analysis ... foresight based upon theory, and theory based upon understanding of the nature of things, are essential to a profession ... The antithesis to a profession is an avocation based upon customary activities and modified by the trial and error of individual practice.

Such an avocation is a Craft, or at a lower level of individual skill it is merely a customary direction of muscular labour.

(Whitehead, 1933, p. 61)

In dialogic terms this parallels the contrast between AD and IPD. The shift from craft to professions was closely linked to modern rationality, through the rise of commerce during the Middle Ages and technological advances. However:

European technology was fertilized from another source. The art of clear thinking, of criticism of premises, of speculative assumption, of deductive reasoning—this great art was discovered, at least in embryo, by the Greeks, and was inherited by Europe. Like other inventions it has often been disastrously misused. But its effect on intellectual capacity can only be compared with that of fire and steel for the production of the blades of Damascus and Toledo. Mankind was now armed intellectually as well as physically.

(Whitehead, 1933, p. 87)

Humankind is armed with rationality, and implicit in Whitehead's 1933 account is a contrast between rationality and trial and error.[4] Rationality belongs especially to the professions and to the disciplines on which they depend. These provide the AD to which reason appeals, not just minirat now, but a rationality that makes reference to the belief systems or conceptual schemes themselves. This is therefore a disciplinary rationality, which we shall refer to as "discrat", whose articulation is AD.[5]

Whitehead's distinction is the basis of what Schön (1983, *passim*) called "Technical Rationality".[6] Schön was critical of the positivist bias of Technical Rationality, and optimistically traces its current replacement by Reflection-in-action

When someone reflects-in-action, he becomes a researcher in the practice context. He is not dependent on the categories of established theory and technique, but constructs a new theory of the unique case. His inquiry is not limited to a deliberation about means which depends on a prior agreement about ends. He does not keep means and ends separate, but defines them interactively as frames to a problematic situation. He does not separate thinking from doing, ratiocinating his way to a decision which he must later convert to action.

(Schön, 1983, p. 68)

A sympathetic narrative of reflection-in-action is provided by Baxandall's history of the building of the Forth Bridge, although he does not refer to Schön. Baxandall is an art historian, and his main interest was in the form of the bridge as an aesthetic object. But the form came about through a series of solutions to problems posed by the "charge" to build a bridge, and a "brief", which takes into account the specific circumstances, such as the recent Tay bridge disaster, which emphasised the need for a bridge that could withstand high side winds, the silted bottom of the Forth, and the mile-long crossing. His "triangle of re-enactment" links together the terms of the problem and culture in a description which gives rise to the Forth Bridge. It is

> A representation of reflection or rationality purposefully at work
> on circumstances ... If we "explain" the form of the bridge at all,
> it is only by expounding it as *one* rational way of attaining an
> inferred end.
>
> (Baxandall, 1985, p. 36; emphasis in original)

In this account of the building of the Forth Bridge we can see the mutual interplay of the duality of structures in rational thinking. AD is duly followed, but the complexity of the context means that the details are worked out at the level of IPD. But the rationality may be less transparent than reflection-in-action implies. There are inertial factors which work against unfettered adaptation to circumstances, as the Gould and Lewontin spandrel effect illustrates. Psychologists have studied this at an individual level under the name of "Functional Fixedness" (Duncker, 1945, *passim*). At a social and political level they are the "microtechnologies" that are part of what Michel Foucault (1977, p. 198) called "disciplinary power". In his work on the development of the "power to colonise" in Egypt, Timothy Mitchell used the work of Foucault to distinguish between the traditional view of power as an exterior restriction, and disciplinary power, which

> Works not from the outside but from within, not at the level of
> an entire society but at the level of detail, and not by restricting

individuals and their actions but by producing them ... Power
relations do not simply confront (the modern) individual as a set
of external orders and prohibitions. His or her very individuality,
formed within such institutions, is already the product of those
relations.

(Mitchell, 1991, p. xi)

So it is hard, perhaps impossible, for the agent immersed in these processes to step back and reflect on them, to move outside the hold of disciplinary power. These factors, the spandrel effect, functional fixedness,
and disciplinary power appear as limitations to rationality, especially
if the agent is oblivious of them, which is nearly inevitable if "individuality ... is already the product of those relations". Thus disciplinary
power represents a way in which AD can maintain itself by suppressing
the unwelcome variations in IPD. The agent in the grip of disciplinary
power may seem rational, and the flow or interplay between conceptual schemes and human action fulfils a necessary condition for rationality, as happened in Stalinist Russia in 1938. But the effect of Foucault's
analysis is to subvert this appearance of rationality by showing how it
gives too much weight to AD, too little to IPD. It is as though AD has
infiltrated IPD and controls it, so that the agent's "very individuality"
is constituted by AD.

The results, scrutinised in Mitchell's analysis of the aftermath of the
building of the Aswan dam, may be seen in AD as a triumph of rationality. The reality was messier. Seeking to understand the origins of the
malaria epidemic of 1942, which killed somewhere in the region of
100,000 to 200,000 people, Mitchell showed how technological progress
(the completion of the Aswan Dam, which brought about a new system
of irrigation which depended upon the use of chemical fertilisers), war
shortages (no fertilisers were available during World War II), and other
changes brought about by the war, were factors that led to the spread of
the *Anopheles gambiae*, which carried the malignant form of the malaria
parasite which was responsible for the epidemic. The reality operates
at the level of disciplinary power (the experts and workers in the field)
pitted against the mosquito, and other non-human agents.

If the web of events in wartime Egypt offers a certain resistance
to explanation, part of the reason may be that it includes a variety
of agencies that are not exclusively human ... (that) make possible

a world that somehow seems the outcome of human rationality and programming ... How is it, we need to ask, that forms of rationality, planning, expertise, and profit arise from this effect?

(Mitchell, 2002, p. 30)

Not presumably in the transparent way described by Baxandall in his account of the building of the Forth Bridge. A benign form of disciplinary power is visible there, as the bridge builders drew on the AD of engineering and metallurgy, and adapted them to circumstance, and it is this visibility that gives the appearance of rationality in action. But Foucault had in mind a hidden form of disciplinary power. Like the "shoulds" of Horney's neurotic, the source of the coercions of disciplinary power are not easily opened to inspection, and are not included in the charge and the brief concerned. Discrat is ambivalent in combining the potential irrationality of disciplinary power with disciplinary rationality.

## Authoritative discourse in science

Science has always assumed a special relationship with rationality, and the interplay there between AD and IPD provides a model to which other disciplines aspire. This has made stepping back and reflecting on it a more sensitive business than is the case even with technology. This earlier confidence has been tempered lately, partly since Kuhn (1962) argued, or appeared to argue, that the *development* of science is not entirely a rational process. Apparently irrational intrusions in the steady, rational march of progress are often examples of science at its most impressive, or what Kuhn (1962, *passim*) referred to as "revolutionary science", which coincides with a thorough shake-up of the old AD. Einstein's theories of relativity were an example, which challenged the traditional AD that constrained earlier physicists to think in Newtonian terms. Einstein's painful resistance to this and search for an alternative has been described by Wertheimer (1961). In some ways he overcame an inertia which is functional fixedness at an individual level, the spandrel effect and disciplinary power at a social or political level. In the language of the philosophy of science, these are similar in their effects to the "protective belt" of a science, which ensures that the "hard core" is not put at risk by searching examination (Lakatos, 1970).

As in Gigerenzer and Mitchell, it is a problem that can be resolved by perceiving the context freshly, uncontaminated by the demands of AD: a feat which is hard but not impossible (Michael & Still, 1992).

Thus inertial factors other than rational thinking have seemed to play a part, and examination of these has given rise to a distinct discipline, the sociology of scientific knowledge. The narratives of science that have emerged from this discipline are far from the more triumphalist accounts of science as the selfless search for truth and knowledge. They are more like accounts of the day-to-day activities of lawyers, business people, or builders of bridges, rational enough in their way, but with much else besides. Instead of human frailty and disciplinary power being held in check in the service of the search for knowledge, these are inseparable from the scientific activity itself. Such exposure was seen by some scientists to question the absolute nature of scientific truth, and to undermine pure science at a material level, by threatening the supply of funds for research. This perceived threat to the AD of science gave rise to the science wars of the 1990s (see Chapter Seven for a more detailed account).

The wars were also the result of the kind of process described by Horney and Ellis. An ideal was thought to be under attack and this led to an amplification of the demands on its behalf. There were insulting counter-attacks, and the frequent use during those battles of the epithet "pseudoscience". There is a coercive, irrational quality in this hot use of "pseudoscience", implying exclusion from the debates and privileges that go with being within the system.

An example of this process is provided by the work of Mario Bunge, a distinguished senior philosopher of science, whose *magnum opus* of forty years ago (Bunge, 1967) was an explicitly pedagogical work on scientific research, and the nearest thing available to an AD on the subject. His rhetoric during the science wars, examples of which are given in Chapter Seven, fully justified the military metaphor for the disputes of the 1990s. His main target was postmodernism, and its infiltration into the Humanities, although it is clear from the disputes that led to the war that the main threat was from the sociologists of knowledge, and their presumption in taking a reflective look at science as a practice.

But historically, Bunge's chief villain was Edmund Husserl. Far from being (as had been thought) the difficult but uncompromising writer who tried to stem the rising tide of relativism by returning to Descartes and Hume and attempting to put philosophy on a scientific footing,

Husserl was a kind of academic terrorist. In Bunge's account he appears as a wild phantasist, and the wild parent of a number of anti-scientific barbarians. These include existentialism ("no ordinary garbage: it is unrecyclable rubbish" (Bunge, 1996, p. 97)); phenomenological sociology ("an invitation to sloth" (Bunge, 1996, p. 99)); and Ethnomethodologists (who "invoke the ... declared enemies of science" (Bunge, 1996, p. 99)). His own words condemn him. In his "celebrated attack on the exact and natural sciences" (Bunge, 1996, p. 98) in *Cartesianische Meditationen* (*Cartesian Meditations*), Husserl described his phenomenology as "in utmost opposition to the sciences as they have been conceived up until now, i.e., as objective sciences" (Bunge, 1996, p. 98; Bunge's translation of Husserl).

But as in the rhetoric of the "war on terror" anything goes when "civilization is under threat" (Chapter Seven), and in the heat of battle Bunge's considerable scholarship was left behind. His translation of the German word *Gegensatz* as "opposition" is unusual and misleading here. In the standard translation of the German passage Husserl describes his phenomenology as forming "the *extremest contrast* [not 'opposition'] *to sciences in the hitherto accepted sense*, positive, '*Objective*' sciences" (Husserl, 1973, p. 30; original emphasis). The meaning there is quite different, and "contrast" accords with Husserl's philosophy as a whole, as well as the context in this book. Bunge makes his compelling point by his selective translation of *Gegensatz*. In this perhaps he followed the rules of engagement outlined by Gross and Levitt, who argued that we are obliged to suspend temporarily the canons of scholarly reason to bring about "a renewal of the academy's traditional devotion to canons of reason" (Gross & Levitt, 1994, p. 55). Like MacIntyre, but for different reasons, Bunge believed that the barbarians are not just beyond the frontier, but are already in our midst, although not yet governing us. They threaten the conceptual schemes and AD of science, and, like terrorists, they don't play by the rules, so the war against them may require the suspension of the standards of human dialogue that hold in happier times.

To some extent AD in science and other modern disciplines depends for its power upon its claim to embody rationality, detached from the mutual relation with IPD. Given this, unchecked IPD is potentially a threat, sometimes warranting the drastic rhetoric of Bunge and other warriors of the science wars. But if Foucault is right and modern individuality is constructed through networks of disciplinary power in the service of production, there seems little room for real resistance, and no cause for such fears. The real threat is to the creativity of IPD not to AD. Discussing this, Michael and Still suggested that Ecological Psychology guarantees a source of experience which is available as a source of resistance on the part of IPD (Michael & Still, 1992; Still, 2001, discusses the realism implied by these views). This idea that experience can provide a source of resistance that is beyond the range of AD and disciplinary power stems from William James' "Psychologist's Fallacy" (Reed, 1990).

## Rationality and the psychologist's fallacy

The psychologist of this fallacy was no less a figure than Hermann von Helmholtz. In the nineteenth century Helmholtz stood out as an exemplary man of science and reason, a peak of rationality acknowledged by all scientists. In his *Physiological Optics* of 1867 (von Helmholtz, 1962) he showed the world, as it now seems, how experimental psychology should be done. It is his methods of asking questions and mapping them onto a physical arrangement in order to answer them that have been followed by scientific laboratory psychology, rather than the more descriptive introspective techniques of Wilhelm Wundt.[7] But in addition he was a great physicist, and in his work on Conservation of Energy he mapped the boundaries of reason applied to the physical world. There are no non-material sources of energy, and therefore magic and miracles along with freedom of the will were banished to be the topic of a different, non-scientific and non-rational, discourse, whose objects have no reality, but are the product of fraud or wishful thinking.

Even while the implications of Helmholtz's law were sinking in, powerful movements were beginning that openly flouted the canons he established for rational discourse about the world. Thus soon after the publication of Helmholtz's work in 1847, the Fox sisters began to hear rappings in their house which they attributed to non-material powers (Carroll, 1997). This received far more publicity than the law of Conservation of Energy, and was one of the events that started the spiritualist movement, whose supposition of extra-physical forces in one form or another conflicted with Helmholtz's law.

William James was a trained scientist, but unlike Helmholtz he had no desire to lay down boundaries to the possibilities of objective experience and its rational expression. He fully appreciated the force of Helmholtz's thinking, saying of his *Physiological Optics* that he imagined it to be "one of the four or five greatest monuments of human genius in the scientific line" (James, 1890, vol II, p. 278). But this did not deter him from enthusiastically pursuing his interest in paranormal phenomena represented so dramatically by the rappings heard by the Fox sisters, or from criticising the theoretical part of *Physiological Optics* as "fundamentally vacillating and obscure" (James, 1890, vol. II, p. 278). It is characteristic of James that he was not overawed by the achievements of Helmholtz, or the confident rhetoric of any other scientist, but was always able to stand back and reflect. Perhaps this is because he had discovered a theory of belief that made it a choice, and reduced the moral intensity (the hot cognitions coercing right belief) associated with the AD of both Christian and scientific faith. After being tormented during the 1860s by the impossibility of reconciling by reason the contradiction between scientific determinism and free will, he discovered a way out through reading Renouvier. In 1870 he wrote in his notebook:

> I think that yesterday was a crisis in my life. I finished the first part of Renouvier's second "Essais" and see no reason why his definition of Free Will—"the sustaining of a thought because I choose to when I might have other thoughts"—need be the definition of an illusion. At any rate, I will assume ... that it is no illusion. My first act of free will shall be to believe in free will.
>
> (James, 1926, p. 147)

This famous declaration, with its implicit subversion of Helmholtz's law, might seem to turn away from rationality and empirical science, where belief is not a matter of choice, but of being true to the facts. But later James turned the tables by showing how Helmholtz and other paragons of rationality do much the same, but with less awareness of what they are doing, when they apply their unexamined scientific AD to psychological phenomena. He called this the "psychologist's fallacy", which is defined as.

> The confusion of his own standpoint with that of the mental fact about which he is making his report.
>
> (James, 1890, vol. I, p. 196)

James gave an example of this fallacy in his analysis of the stream of thought. In a thought like "The pack of cards is on the table", philosophers and psychologists had made the assumption that the thought is made up of a number of different ideas, a *"manifold of coexisting ideas"* (James, 1890, vol II, p. 278). Rationalists had supposed that the manifold is synthesised by an ego; associationists believed that parts add together in a process akin to chemistry. Both are guilty of the Psychologist's Fallacy, because they assume, in an unexamined belief drawing on a long tradition, that there *must* be a *"manifold of coexisting ideas"*. James's radical assertion is to deny this in the name of experience:

> [T]he notion of such a thing is a chimera. Whatever things are thought in relation are thought from the outset in a unity, in a single pulse of subjectivity, as single psychosis, feeling or state of mind.
>
> (James, 1890, vol. II, p. 278)

With great skill he first set up the psychologist's fallacious view, as though it is not just a reasonable hypothesis, but an assumption that any rational person would make. Then turning to the facts of experience, he contrasted the assumption with what actually occurs.

For us, James was not primarily attempting to replace a rational scientific system of belief with an alternative system—although he often went on to do that, as in his theory of emotions—and nor was he simply refuting the old theories by turning to the facts. We believe what James was attempting to do with the psychologist's fallacy was identify and practice a different but equally essential aspect of rationality, not embedded in a conceptual scheme, but applicable universally, even, or especially, in the face of failures of the kind identified by MacIntyre. He showed how to resist being overwhelmed by authority, by AD, by stepping back and reflecting in the realm of IPD. This key point was taken up and elaborated by two otherwise very different writers of the first half of the twentieth century, Edmund Husserl (Bunge's *bête noire*) and John Dewey.

Husserl read William James closely (Herzog, 1995), especially the *Principles*, and it is hard to imagine Husserl's *The Phenomenology of Internal Time-Consciousness* (1964) without James's writings on the stream of consciousness. James's attempt to step back and reflect on what is actually there, free of all preconceptions, is akin to Husserl's dictum

"Back to the things themselves!" ("*zu den Sachen selbst!*"). This gave rise to his phenomenological method of suspending judgement or bracketing the world in the *epoché* in order to describe what is essential in experience for our perceptions and intuitions of reality. For Husserl this was not psychology but philosophy as rigorous science (Husserl, 1965, pp. 71–147). It was different from science, but *pace* Bunge he was not against science or the achievements of science, although he was critical of positivism. In his final and sometimes despairing *The Crisis of European Science* (1970) he begins by paying homage to the achievements of physics, to Newton as well as Einstein, but then pointed out how after the Renaissance the positivist narrowing of science had left behind questions about

> Man as a free, self-determining being in his behaviour toward the human and extra-human and free in regard to his capacities for rationally shaping himself and his surrounding world.

> (Husserl, 1970, p. 6)

The Renaissance legacy had enabled science to claim an authority, and to elaborate an AD, with a universality to which it may not be entitled.

John Dewey was not a disciple of William James, but they both considered themselves pragmatists and there was a persisting mutual influence. Dewey's most famous paper (Dewey, 1896) applied James's insight into the psychologist's fallacy, and his critique of the assumed "*manifold of coexisting ideas*" (James, 1890, vol. 1, p. 278), to the manifold of stimulus–response psychology, or what Dewey called, in the title of his paper, the "reflex arc". Throughout his long career Dewey was interested in developing a theory of logic which could do justice to his pragmatic philosophy. This was the logic of enquiry. He struggled to get it taken seriously during his lifetime, but it was increasingly overshadowed by developments in formal logic; Bertrand Russell was a persistent critic, and philosophers were probably deterred by his refusal to take Dewey seriously as a logician. But recently there has been a revival of interest in the logic of enquiry, as some logicians and philosophers linked with developments in cognitive science have turned away from traditional formal logic towards a situational logic akin to that offered by John Dewey (Barwise & Perry, 1983; Burke, 1994). Describing the logic of enquiry from within this new tradition, Burke detects two aspects: a linear movement towards a resolution of a problem (sometimes, especially in science, towards what Dewey referred to as a warranted judgement); and a cyclical movement similar to trial and error.

> The agent observes the results of his/her/its actions, entertains possible courses of action and expected results based on those observations, experiments with more feasible alternatives to test their viability, observes the results of such experimentation, and around it goes—a process of exploring facts of the matter and narrowing the range of possible actions one can take, until, hopefully, a solution to the initial problem is settled on.
>
> (Burke, 1994, p. 160)

Insofar as this is a perceptual process, Burke argued:

> A notion of noncognitive rationality is suggested here, measured by the appropriateness of given habits in given instances. The rationality involved in determining which habits are triggered in a given instance and which are not is a function of the systematicity of the space of constraints and processes which make up the contents of various habits, matched against whatever actions and results are actually occurring in the present situation.
>
> (Burke, 1994, p. 161)

This is not primarily the application of an AD to the situation at hand, but an immersion in the situation itself. The train of thought is not that from a confident definition of the situation to an appropriate solution, but a return to the situation itself armed with a set of "Habits" to try out possible solutions or ways forward. There is an effort to see the situation in a new and more appropriate way, potentially resisting the demands of AD in favour of experience.

The achievement of these writers was very different, but they shared a commitment to a process that James first described in writing of the psychologist's fallacy. This process consisted of three parts. First, a refusal to be carried away by what is assumed to be the case (the AD of the time), often in the name of rationality itself, but also through political or financial necessity. Second, a stepping back to examine and describe what is actually the case. Third, acting or writing based on this new way of seeing the case. If Burke is right, this process is at the heart of the logic of enquiry. It is trial and error as a process of thought.[8] It need not be, as some earlier writers thought, an inferior kind of thinking, below true rationality (identified with discrat), but a necessary part of rationality itself, emancipating from the *irrational* application of discrat in the psychologist's fallacy. It is therefore referred to here as "emanrat". Human rationality is a balance between discrat and emanrat, or between AD and IPD, part of the dynamic mutuality implicit in the duality of structures.

## Conclusions

In this chapter we have described rationality as a relationship between conceptual schemes (or authoritative discourse) and human agency (or internally persuasive discourse), which together make up a discursive formation. Often, as in MacIntyre's account of Aristotelian virtue ethics, and as contained in the hill-walking example, there exists a mutual interplay in this duality of structures. The conceptual schemes are constituted by human agency yet are at the same time the medium of human agency. When this mutual relationship breaks down then rationality is in question. Breakdown occurs in two ways. First, when the effective conceptual schemes or authoritative discourse are invisible, and the origin of the shoulds becomes obscured. We described a number of instances of this, taking our start from the studies described by Gigerenzer. In MacIntyre's *After Virtue* (1981), the current conceptual scheme has lost contact with the context which gave it sense. The same may be true of neurosis, where the core schema or idealisations that arose from forgotten experiences in childhood are no longer appropriate to the world of adulthood. Second, in technology and science the mutual relationship is sometimes strained, not because the conceptual schemes are debilitated, but because the interplay has been suppressed; authoritative discourse has taken over and defined what is rational, suppressing the emancipatory rationality inherent in internally persuasive discourse. The power of authoritative discourse can prevent the open-minded examination of context, and this is realised through the microtechnologies of disciplinary power, as well as the loosely related spandrel effect, functional fixedness, and protective belt. When this occurs the world is increasingly perceived through the medium of authoritative discourse and the conceptual schemes behind it, constraining the free play of internally persuasive discourse.

Although these two sources of irrationality in the space of reasons are very different, the antidote, the empowerment of emancipatory rationality, is the same in all cases. In psychotherapy, Carl Rogers (1974) developed a therapy in which the client is provided with complete acceptance of him or herself as a person. By cultivating unconditional positive regard or acceptance, the therapist suspends judgement and criticism. As a result, clients can become less defensive and able to step back and reflect, especially on the demands they put on themselves, the shoulds, and have the opportunity opened to them to understand what they really want. The clearest form of this has been spelt out by Gendlin (1981, 1997), who has combined in his writings and his psychotherapy the practices of Husserl and Rogers. The result is "focusing", a way of getting in touch with what Gendlin (1981, *passim*) calls the "felt sense", which reflects what is really important to the client and is ordinarily suppressed by the clamour of competing shoulds. In effect, the client goes back to the things themselves and begins to understand more clearly what is important. He or she is restored to the space of reasons.

In the cognitive therapies of Ellis and Beck the client also is invited to step back with the therapist, in order to be able to reflect on dysfunctional patterns of thought and feeling. This is done more explicitly and vigorously than in person-centred therapy. New conceptual schemes are created by articulating the client's goals, and the thinking processes, especially the shoulds, are actively challenged in the name of rationality. Thus, disciplinary rationality is brought to bear on the irrational shoulds, although an essential part of the therapy is the emancipatory rationality of stepping back and reflecting. It cools the hot cognitions, and halts the automaticity of Automatic Negative Thoughts, prior to the application of disciplinary rationality. The stepping back and reflecting has been made explicit through the incorporation of the Buddhist practice of mindfulness as part of cognitive therapy (Kabat-Zinn, 1990; Segal, Williams & Teasdale, 2001).[9]

In technology and science emancipatory rationality also enables the agent to step back from the demands of authoritative discourse, the shoulds, and in principle see and question the irrational sources of these demands. In this way Einstein cut through the spandrel effect and the functional fixedness of his time, into what has been celebrated as a great triumph of rationality. In technology, problems are routinely resolved through emancipatory rationality, by stepping back and reflecting, and through finding novel solutions. This occurs in small-scale projects, but also on a much bigger scale, as Baxandall described in the construction of the Forth Bridge. But scale is crucial here; the larger the scale the greater the opportunity for irrational shoulds to emerge, through the spandrel effect, functional fixedness, and disciplinary power. Gripped by disciplinary power it can be hard for agents to see clearly the irrationality in the midst of apparent rationality, as Mitchell was able to bring out in his retrospective analysis. He described a disaster that could perhaps, with difficulty, have been foreseen at the time, but which is small relative to the disasters and difficulties promised by the human technological contributions to issues that exercise us at present, such as global warming.

In the United States, the opposition between an oppressive authoritative discourse and an emancipatory discourse has a long history, dating back at least to the early nineteenth century and the writings of Ralph Waldo Emerson (1803–1882). This is an important part of the background to Ellis's own focus on the pathological potential of the "shoulds" and "oughts", and is discussed in the next chapter.

## Notes

1. The potential power of this distinction between authoritative discourse and internally persuasive discourse is brought out in the editors' glossary to Bakhtin (1981): Authoritative Discourse "is privileged language that approaches us from without; it is distanced, taboo, and permits no play with its framing context. We recite it. It has great power over us, but while in power; if ever dethroned it immediately becomes a dead thing, a relic. Opposed to it is *internally persuasive discourse,* which is more akin to telling a text in one's own words, with one's own accents, gestures, modifications. Human coming-to-consciousness, in Bakhtin's view, is a constant struggle between these two types of discourse: an attempt to assimilate more into one's own system, and the simultaneous freeing of one's own discourse from the authoritative word, or from previous earlier persuasive words that have ceased to mean" (Bakhtin, 1981, pp. 424–425; emphasis in original).
2. Of course it is not just words that change, or even conceptual schemes. As Danziger pointed out, it is the discursive formations, of which words form a part, which change, since a language "constitutes an integrated world of meanings in which each term articulates with other terms so as to form a coherent framework for representing a kind of knowledge

that is regarded as true and a kind of practice regarded as legitimate" (Danziger, 1997, p. 13). If a conceptual scheme is a part of a discursive formation, then what seems to have happened, according to MacIntyre, is a disruption of the discursive formations of morality, due to loss of the significance of the conceptual scheme that once held them together. The words continue to be used as though they have the old meaning.

3. Others, notably Davidson (1980), have argued that reasons can be causes, but even if this is accepted, the distinction discussed by Brinkmann still applies, although we would label it differently. We agree that reasons are part of the normative order, whether or not they are causes, and following Brinkmann's treatment of normative orders and the space of reasons as more or less interchangeable, we attempt to avoid controversy by relabelling what Brinkmann refers to as the "space of causes" as the "non-normative order", which is similar to Yurchak or Austin's "constative".

4. A craft is an avocation "based upon customary activities and modified ... by trial and error". Whitehead was assuming an accepted contrast between rationality and trial and error, which is probably due to Lloyd Morgan (1894).

5. Although in this chapter we refer to the discrats of technology and science, modern religions and academic disciplines have their own discrats, and Whitehead's historical split between craft and profession could provide a similar narrative for these.

6. Schön cited Moore (1970), who made use of Whitehead's distinction, but in Schön the distinction has become that between an avocation and a profession, which seems to miss Whitehead's historical point. For Whitehead a profession is an avocation drawing on the rationality of the Western intellectual tradition.

7. Detailed traditional accounts of both Helmholtz and Wundt are given in Boring (1960).

8. This is different from both random trial and error and from Karl Popper's conjunction of "Conjectures and Refutations" (the title of Popper, 1972). It is closer to Popper's use, but he made trial and error part of the discrat of science, whereas we are treating it as a source of resistance to the disciplinary power and other sources of inertia emanating from that discrat.

9. The affinities between mindfulness and Husserl's *epoché*, or bracketing the world, are discussed in Chapter Eight. A similar application of emanrat may meet MacIntyre's strictures by restoring rationality to moral discussion. This is addressed in the next chapter.

# CHAPTER SIX

# When did a psychologist last discuss "chagrin"? American psychology's continuing moral project

## Introduction

The starting point of this chapter is Graham Richards' (1995) claim that American academic psychology includes a moral project present even before the discipline got underway as a modern institution. We accept this, but identify a different kind of moral project, stemming from the radical critique of morality by Ralph Waldo Emerson, rather than the moral aims of Noah Porter and James McCosh described by Richards. This leads to a morality based on (but not reducible to) psychological events, and worked out, not in academic psychology, but in the practical disciplines of counselling and psychotherapy. We trace its elaboration from Freud to the writings and practice of Albert Ellis and Carl Rogers. The critique is of a traditional morality of obligation with its discourse of "shoulds" and "oughts". A parallel is drawn with a similar (and contemporaneous) critique in moral philosophy.

Richards was writing as a modern historian psychologist, critical of the traditional grand histories that chart a more or less triumphant progress from the Greeks to the present. According to some of these historians, psychology as we know it is an academic institution that began towards the end of the nineteenth century. At that time, there was a break, as psychologists attempted to move away from the philosophical and moral concerns that had previously been dominant, towards a scientific approach centred on laboratory psychology.

Graham Richards (1995) questioned the sharpness of this break in his study of some of the best-known textbook writers of the older academic psychology. He makes two points, both suggesting unexpected continuities between the old and the new. First, the earlier American "psychologists" of the nineteenth century (specifically Noah Porter and James McCosh) had been much more closely in touch with contemporary scientific developments than was assumed by their successors. Second, their moral project for psychology, which seems so distant from modern laboratory psychology, nevertheless remained on the agenda for many of the new psychologists, notably William James and G. Stanley Hall, and has even continued throughout the twentieth century. This last claim is argued briefly, and less convincingly. It succeeds only by including within this moral project J. B. Watson's "utopian behaviorist polemics" (Richards, 1995, p. 15), the moral rationale of developmental psychology, social psychology's concern with the mass media, prejudice, and racism, and the quest for self-discovery or self-actualisation in humanistic psychology, which Richards observed is intrinsically moral. There is a danger in his argument here of including too much, in making "moral" apply to all concern for others, so that the motivation of the psychologists rather than the content of their psychology is what makes it moral. In this chapter we argue that humanistic psychology has indeed pursued a moral project, but in its most prominent and successful forms it is not the moral project of Noah Porter or James McCosh. It is akin, rather, to the moral project of Ralph Waldo Emerson. To show this we examine the writings of two leading theorists of psychotherapy in the States, Albert Ellis and Carl Rogers. Both have had some university affiliations, but neither has depended on this and their success has little to do with acceptance by academic psychology.[1] Nevertheless, both studied what are generally regarded as psychological processes in applied contexts, and this is our warrant for taking them to represent psychology's continuing moral project. Where they have led is in the market place and the frameworks of psychological help within the social services, where their two apparently contrasting therapies (one directed and problem-solving, the other person-centred and holistic) have proved two of the most popular in the States in the second half of the twentieth century.

Ellis and Rogers are usually contrasted, but here we pick on common features that we take to characterise not just humanistic psychology, but a broader moral shift that can be traced back at least to Emerson. This shift has had a significant effect on moral discourse in extending its arguments beyond those based on traditional religion, social obligations and duties, and utilitarianism. Current discourse includes these arguments as possibilities to be drawn on by a variety of thinkers, including Rogers and Ellis. Thus, we are not expecting modern writers to appeal directly to Emerson, but to draw on a living tradition that is usefully described as Emersonian.

Some writers have pointed out the religious traditions behind Rogers, not just the New England Transcendentalism that grew up around Emerson (Fuller, 1986), but also Calvinism (Yeoman, 1991), against which Emerson developed so much of his thinking. But Rogers' optimism about the essential goodness of human nature and his faith in the power of human striving towards transformation, which seem to provide the material for such historical links,[2] is markedly absent in the work and writings of Albert Ellis, noted for his irreverence and his tough-minded Stoicism. REBT teaches the client ways of correcting the innate tendencies towards the "stinking thinking" which leads to emotional disturbance. But even after correction these tendencies remain, like a modern version of original sin, and the client has to remain vigilant in order to avoid relapse. What then is shared by Rogers and Ellis that could be called Emersonian?

Both Rogers and Ellis were humanist in emphasising individual responsibility, and the possibility of individual change without invoking external power, whether religious, medical, psychoanalytic, or that of social transformation. Critics of humanistic psychology have usually focused on the writings of Rogers, Maslow, and neo-Freudians like Horney and Fromm, and they detect a facile optimism and a diluting of Freud's uncompromising insights. The style of some of these writings appeals to many readers, but makes them easy targets for intellectual demolition (Jacoby, 1975; Richards, 1989). But again, Ellis is a contrast. His literary style is tough and challenging, he is sceptical rather than optimistic about human nature, and he does not offer a watered-down version of Freud's insights. To Ellis these may be interesting, but are largely irrelevant to therapy, especially to that aspect of it that we are presenting in this chapter as the moral pattern at the heart of humanistic therapy. By including him as a humanistic therapist, we bring out this essential aspect, and define the links to Emerson more precisely.

The Emerson we have in mind is not the unworldly mystic or the homely source of uplifting thoughts deplored or patronised by some American intellectuals (Poirier, 1992, gives several examples), but the philosopher of moral experience drawn on by James and Dewey, whose central importance in American thought is now well established (Lentricchia, 1988; Poirier, 1987; Robinson, 1993). This was the Emerson whose insights were admired and used by Nietzsche in his own re-evaluation of morals, and who pronounced the death of God several years before the German's more famous declaration. The key point in this Emersonian tradition is that the individual is capable of moral choice based on essentially moral experiences or ways of being, but not backed up by any external authority or system of rules, with their psychological sanctions of guilt and a sense of sin.[3] William James's "will to believe" shares this,[4] along with Nietzsche's Zarathustra, and Heidegger's characterisation of authenticity.[5] In each of these cases, the potential moral experience is of alternative modes of being, rather than internal sanctions enforcing an imposed system of rules. However, the specifically *psychological* tradition we are concerned with here belongs to Emerson (in his account of the infusion of soul) and William James (especially in his descriptions of the moment of choice that he called the will to believe), rather than Nietzsche and Heidegger, who were less focused on the psychological processes involved.

## Psychology's moral products

In referring to McCosh's list of emotions, which included such neglected items as peevishness, bitterness, and chagrin, Richards asks in parentheses "and when last did a psychologist discuss 'Chagrin'?" (Richards, 1995, p. 12). The word may be archaic nowadays, but as "That which frets or worries the mind" or "Mortification arising from disappointment, thwarting, or failure" (Onians, 1959, p. 287) it refers to the central topic in the writings of Rogers and Ellis, where it is placed within an explicitly moral context in the strongest and most interesting sense. What is this sense? What do we mean by "moral", and what is a "moral project" in psychology? There are several possibilities.

1. Exhortation. The use of psychology to reaffirm the culture's values, and to correct deviancies through education and self-awareness.

Thus, Richards shows how American psychology's moral project originated partly in reaction to student unrest around the beginning of the nineteenth century. And he quotes from Ladd's *Primer of Psychology* of 1894 to illustrate the continuation of the moral project of Noah Porter. Ladd lists as psychology's practical benefits, "the science and art of education, the management of child-life, the instruction of idiots, the improvement of the vicious, criminal, and insane" (cited in Richards, 1995, p. 10).

2. Motivation. If the intention behind a project is to help people and "to do them good", then it may be called a moral project by virtue of its motivation. In this sense, psychotherapists usually have a moral project, as well as Noah Porter, James McCosh, and Ladd.

3. Investigation. Investigating what is conventionally thought of as *moral* thinking or *moral* behaviour. This has been studied largely as a developmental matter (Kohlberg, 1963; Piaget, 1932).

4. Using psychology to describe or criticise the basis of morality. The most familiar example of this is the moral psychology of British empiricism. This *reduces* morality to psychology in a manner that has come to be criticised as psychologism. Thus, the claim that "This is morally bad" means no more than that I have a certain kind of negative feeling about this ("I don't like this"), is an instance of psychologism. Even if, as some recent philosophers have done (e.g., Hare, 1952), I add a command ("I don't like this and don't do it"), it is still a reduction and a partial psychologism, still open to the objection that "This is morally bad" does not in fact *mean* the same as any statement about my feelings.

However, psychology can be included without falling into psychologism. It can do this by following phenomenology and its notion of "constitution", in which certain structures in experience are a necessary condition for morality, but not identifiable with it. Husserl based his massive philosophical output on this distinction between psychologism (the reduction of human realities, morality amongst many others, to psychological processes) and constitution (the essential conditions for the disclosure of human realities).[6] In principle, psychology may follow both paths, reducing morality to psychological approaches on the one hand (psychologism) and searching for the essential conditions in experience for morality, on the other. We will be concerned mainly with the latter possibility.

In this respect, Emerson was a phenomenologist rather than a reductionist. In his essay "The Over-soul" he elaborated on his conception of the "soul" as something which is not simply added to the mind, like a faculty.

> (It) is not an organ, but animates and exercises all the organs; is not a function, like the power of memory, of calculation, of comparison, but uses these as hands and feet; is not a faculty, but a light; is not the intellect or the will, but the master of the intellect and the will; is the background of their being, in which they lie ... A man is the facade of a temple wherein all wisdom and all good abide ... When it (the soul) breathes through his intellect, it is genius; when it breathes through his will, it is virtue; when it flows through his affection, it is love. And the blindness of the intellect begins, when it would be something of itself. The weakness of the will begins; when the individual would be something of himself. All reform aims, in some particular, to let the soul have its way through us; in other words, to engage us to obey.
>
> Of this pure nature every man is at some time sensible ... It is undefinable, unmeasurable, but we know that it pervades and contains us.
>
> (Emerson, n.d., p. 160)

At this stage of his life Emerson's style was still that of a preacher, but the content was psychological. The argument of his essay hinges on psychological observations—especially of moments when we are aware of the meanness of human life, but also of possibilities that belie the apparent inevitability of it. At these moments of insight we are informed by "soul"; our morality is made possible, even defined by such moments, but cannot be reduced to them. "Man is a stream whose source is hidden. Our being is descending into us from we know not whence" (Emerson, n.d., p. 158). The soul is opposed by Emerson to control by rules of intellect, or even rules of morality (the will).

> In my dealing with my child, my Latin and Greek, my accomplishments and my money, stead me nothing; but as much soul as I have avails. If I am wilful, he sets his will against mine, one for one, and leaves me, if I please, the degradation of beating him by my

superiority of strength. But if I renounce my will, and act for the
soul, setting that up as umpire between us two, out of his young
eyes looks the same soul; he reveres and loves with me.

(Emerson, n.d., p. 165)

I may use moral arguments to mask the degradation of beating my son,
but for Emerson this would not be "true" morality. Emerson's intentions
are radical, going back to the psychological origins of morality in order
to shape our conception of morality. He is part of an American tradition
drawing especially on Swedenborg, but also Romantic critics of the
Enlightenment such as Herder (1744–1803) and Coleridge (1772–1834),
and indirectly, partly through such critics, on Kant (1724–1804).
Thus, Emerson combined two traditions, that of non-conformist
preaching, in which worldy pretensions are exposed and the listener
is exhorted to trust in the voice of God; and the Romantic tradition, in
which the source of true knowledge lies in human experience rather
than intellect or God—not experience in general but special (although
not necessarily exceptional or ineffable) experiences possessing "soul",
which gives direct insight into "the moral law". The traditional God
was dispensed with but not the reverence due to Him. As William
James observed:

> Not a deity *in concreto*, not a superhuman person, but the immanent
> divinity in things, the essentially spiritual structure of the universe
> is the object of the transcendentalist cult [i.e., "Emersonianism"].

(James, 1902, pp. 31–32)

It is not this religious sense as such that we are interested in here, but
the possibility that goes with it—that of special experiences or ways of
being as the basis of morality.[7]

Noah Porter's moral project was not that of Emerson. The student
reader of his *The Human Intellect* (1869) was not exhorted to cultivate
moments when human possibilities reveal themselves, but "The person
who habitually scrutinizes his motives and examines his feelings
in the light of the law of duty and of God, cannot but cultivate and
strengthen his intellect by the process" (cited in Richards, 1995, p. 7).
Richards articulates Porter's moral message and shows that his book
was "firmly embedded in a moral matrix" (Richards, 1995, p. 8). It was

not questioning the basis of morality (4) from the list above, but was moral by exhortation (1) and motivation (2). It invited the reader to use psychology to enforce or nurture what is good, but not to examine the nature of traditional morality. Here, by contrast, we are concerned with psychotherapists who have done this, even though this has been incidental to their avowed therapeutic aims.

## The moral impact of counselling and psychotherapy

Counselling and psychotherapy have had an important effect upon Western morality. This is not just on a theoretical level, or in the practice of receptive individuals, but through the social institutions that play such a part in disseminating and reproducing the moral standards of our time. In a classic work, Halmos wrote:

> The counselling literature as well as its popularised casuistry and prescriptions ... have an immediate impact on the rank and file of society. The critical and interpretive work of the professional literature has been reaching and influencing the cultural and moral leadership in society, and it is a trite observation to make that our philosophy, science, and art, have been profoundly affected by most things that have been written on counselling, ever since the time of Sigmund Freud.
>
> But now, through the very counselling activities of the counsellors, through the growth of the practising profession itself, the socio-cultural and moral influence of this ideology gains strength.
>
> (Halmos, 1965, p. 176)

Halmos was writing about counselling in a broad sense to include

> [p]sychiatrists, lay and medical psychotherapists, clinical psychologists, social caseworkers of several kinds, and some others, (who) have all learnt to share the assumptions and values of the new philanthropic expertise of helping through caring-listening-prompting ... I regard them as a new social factor of considerable influence on the cultural and moral changes in twentieth-century society.
>
> (Halmos, 1965, p. 2)

Halmos recognised that at this level of social influence, as well as the more obvious and "literary" level, the impact of psychoanalysis has been crucial, and, more recently, social historians have begun to trace the way in which psychoanalysis has managed to dominate some professional activities that owe no obvious allegiance to psychoanalysis (Miller & Rose, 1994). But if psychoanalysis has been a starting point, there have been plenty of other movements within counselling, some explicitly opposed to psychoanalytic principles—although even there psychoanalysis has, until recently, loomed large as the standard against which the alternative therapy is reacting.

Halmos and other writers on these matters are apt to treat the influence as a one-way process, and one where the direction is from the counsellors and psychotherapists to the clients and the culture, rather than the other way round. However, few clients are passive recipients, forced to accept what is being offered regardless of what it is. This may have sometimes seemed true when "clients" were called "patients", in medicine and psychiatry, and perhaps in the social services, but, in general, the success of psychoanalysis and other systems of therapy has depended partly upon the willing receptiveness of their public. The tradition to which a successful theorist belongs is also that of the population in which the success occurs. Thus, the Emersonian tradition that we are exploring here is not just a tradition of moral writing, but part of the culture to which Rogers and Ellis on the one hand, and their audiences on the other, belong.

However, the claim in this chapter is not the commonplace that counselling and psychotherapy have had a moral impact. The moral psychology we are concerned with is a critique of the basis of morality, and impact alone does not entail that. However, as we shall see, the writings of Ellis and Rogers explore the psychological basis and consequences of the discourse of "should" and "ought" which is the mark of the traditional morality of obligation. Their critique of this, and the discourses they offer instead, are moral psychologies, whose starting point is in Freud as he was read during the 1950s.

## Moral psychology in Freud and after

We will be concerned with events during the 1950s and 1960s and Halmos is representative of the views of that time on the place of counselling in the moral culture. Philip Rieff captured Freud's special contribution in a widely read book published in 1960. He pointed out that Freud's

> Discounting of self-knowledge was due less to the muffled claims of instinct than to the sharp directives of conscience ... [O]nly the super-ego, the moral faculty, is therapeutically accessible. By thus implicitly making the id not available to rational admonishment, Freud's therapy takes on a more anti-moral address than he may have intended.
>
> The aim of reason may be either (1) to introduce or buttress super-ego controls for purposes of efficiency, or (2) to break down rigid and superfluous moral controls. Freud's patients were invariably assigned aims of the second type.
>
> (Rieff, 1960, p. 70)

This sympathetic critic of psychoanalysis concluded that: "Conscience, not passion, emerges as the last enemy of reason" (Rieff, 1960, p. 71). If this means casting doubt on the wisdom of conventional morality, this is as Freud intended.

> [N]o distinction is drawn in the Freudian scheme between natural and moral evil, no room is left for guilt as distinct from ignorance ... Guilt indicates lack of self-understanding, a failure of tolerance toward himself on the part of natural man.
>
> (Rieff, 1960, p. 275)

Guilt is a natural response towards authority, and

> [r]eligion attempts to appease the sense of guilt; at the same time, only by perpetuating it (by such commemorative repetitions of the parricidal act as the Christian communion) does the authority of faith continue. Morality too stands under the sign of guilt. The best behavior of which we are capable is "at bottom" an attempt "to conciliate the injured father through subsequent obedience."... The sense of guilt is thus the pivot for Freud's conception of morality and religion.
>
> (Rieff, 1960, p. 276)

Thus, morality may not be definable in terms of psychological processes, but the motivation underlying morality is an unconscious psychological process.

Rieff was writing shortly after Karen Horney had published her influential essay "The tyranny of the should" (in Horney, 1991; this book was first published in 1950). He refers to her as making a similar point to Freud's, but also as going significantly further, since she finds that, in Rieff's words, "even after analysis … patients may still have feelings of guilt" (Rieff, 1960, p. 275). Her conclusions from this led her to criticise Freud's naturalistic account of religion and morality, because he had failed to distinguish true morality from the coercive power of the shoulds. This criticism was discussed in Chapter Five.

Now Freud did not wish to jettison morality altogether, only to show the painful and sometimes unavoidable conflicts to which it gives rise. So even though we are not exactly responsible for our bad actions and any sense of objective morality is an illusion, guilt is sometimes to be expected and has to be tolerated. However, Horney felt that the residual guilt after analysis was not the stuff of morality at all. Morality is social, but this guilt was personal and neurotic, and had little to do with the requirements of a civilised society. Thus, she rejected Freud's failure to distinguish between "natural and moral evil". This rejection prepared the way for the "Rational Psychotherapy" of Albert Ellis, who came to target guilt as one amongst many unhealthy or inappropriate emotions, and who went further than Horney by rejecting altogether the unconditional shoulds and demands essential to the discourse of imperative ethics.

As we have seen in earlier chapters, during the 1950s Albert Ellis, then a psychoanalyst trained by Charles Hulbeck from the Karen Horney Institute, began to focus on the self-demands implicit in guilt and other negative emotions as the cause of psychological disturbance. For Ellis, what had seemed a residual problem to Horney became the main focus of psychotherapy. He asked, in effect: "If knowledge of origins does not clear up psychological disturbance, then what maintains the disturbance, and do we need this kind of knowledge to remove it?" His answer, worked out through the development of Rational Emotive Behavior Therapy (REBT), was that we do not need such knowledge, since disturbance is maintained by the "absolutist" demands (about self, others, and the world), often expressed in implicit self-talk containing "shoulds" and "musts".

Like Horney, Ellis tried to distinguish between morality and the "shoulds" that give rise to the guilt of neurosis—although Ellis focused on the emotional distress experienced by clients, such as guilt, rather than on a medical category like neurosis. Chapter Seven of his *Reason and Emotion in Psychotherapy* of 1962 is entitled "Sin and Psychotherapy". It begins as a discussion of Mowrer's view that the key to therapy is public acknowledgement of one's wrongdoing as "sin". According to Ellis's reading in 1960,[8] Mowrer had rejected Freudian accounts of mental structure.

> Vigorously condemning the Freudian attitudes regarding the id, ego, and superego, Professor Mowrer has for the last decade upheld the thesis that if the psychotherapist in any way gives his patients the notion that they are not responsible for their sins, he will only encourage them to keep sinning; and that they cannot become emotionally undisturbed, since at bottom disturbance is a moral problem, unless they assume full responsibility for their misdeeds—and, what is more, *stop* their sinning.

> (Ellis, 1962, p. 132)

It follows, as Horney had discovered, that knowledge of the origins of the disturbance will not by itself change it. Ellis emphatically agreed with Mowrer's rejection of Freudianism and with his conclusion "that psychotherapy must largely be concerned with the patient's sense of morality and wrongdoing" (Ellis, 1962, p. 32); that is, with what Rieff, writing at the same time, identified as pervasive in Freud's practice. But equally emphatically he disagreed with Mowrer's introduction of the concept of sin into psychotherapy as

> Highly pernicious and antipsychotherapeutic. The rational therapist holds, on the contrary, that no human being should ever be blamed for anything he does; and it is the therapist's main and most important function to help rid his patients of every possible vestige of their blaming themselves, blaming others, or blaming fate and the universe.

> (Ellis, 1962, p. 133)

This is not to reject moral principles as a guide to behaviour.

I fully accept Hobart Mowrer's implication that there is such a thing as human wrongdoing or immoral behavior. I do not, as a psychologist, believe that we can have any absolute, final, or God-given standards of morals or ethics.

(Ellis, 1962, p. 134)

Morality is necessary for harmonious social living, and whatever an individual's standards, one of the therapist's tasks is to help him or her to live happily in accordance with the standards desired (by the client). This is not best achieved by inculcating a sense of sin or guilt (at oneself) or moral outrage (at others) through the use of "shoulds" and "oughts" in self-talk. Thus, the practical therapist helps the client to choose to avoid moral wrongdoing because he or she wants to, not because of an internalised command enforced by a sense of sin or guilt if defied. As Horney had pointed out: "To fulfill them [genuine moral standards] is what we ourselves ultimately want, or what we deem right." Much of the rest of Ellis's chapter illustrates the harmfulness of guilt—it leads to psychological disturbance, without even providing an effective means of moral control.

Ellis rejected the empty husk of morality, the "shoulds" and the "oughts", and substituted a system of morality akin to the virtues.[10] REBT consists in identifying goals and coming to recognise that the emotional and behavioural excesses of Damning Anger, Procrastination, Morbid Jealousy, and Addiction (or their older equivalents, the sins of Wrath, Sloth, Envy, and Gluttony), are unhelpful in achieving them. Ellis teaches how to change self-talk in order to exercise the kind of moderation that characterises the cardinal virtues of justice, fortitude, prudence, and temperance. In this sense, the behaviour of a "virtuous" person, according to REBT, would be to act according to reason in trying to achieve his or her goals. In outline, this has the same structure as Aristotle's account of the virtues, whose exercise enables the moral person to achieve his or her *telos*, taking *telos* as similar to the modern "goals".[9] But Ellis's actual focus is on the exercise of the virtues themselves as the cause of happiness rather than the fulfilment of a *telos*, and in this he seems closer to the Stoic moralists (especially Seneca), and he acknowledges himself as a follower of "the Stoic principle of long-term rather than short-range hedonism" (Ellis, 1994, p. 292).

"Long-range hedonism" might seem to place his moral psychology less close to Emerson than to another building block of American culture, the Utilitarianism of Benjamin Franklin, were it not for his goal "to help clients make a *profound philosophic change* that will affect their future as well as their present emotions and behaviour" (Ellis, 1994, p. 248; emphasis in original). Long-range hedonism may provide a rational basis for Ellis's morality, and be used to justify the profound philosophic change, but the change itself is psychological. It comes about by letting go of the absolute claims of demands and beliefs, and the aim for such insight and change puts him firmly within the Emersonian tradition. He rejects Freud's view that guilt is in some measure necessary for social living, and Mowrer's view that guilt is healthy and necessary, and accepts Horney's view that it is bad and unnecessary. But, in addition, he describes the insightful shift, the psychological change, which enables a happy and morally satisfactory life.

The work of Carl Rogers led to a different confrontation of psychotherapy with morality. But from the point of view of psychology's moral project the outcome has been similar. For Rogers, any individual has an internal source of valuing, called "experience", which may be at odds with the valuing absorbed from others.

> This fundamental discrepancy between the individual's concepts and what he is actually experiencing, between the intellectual structures of his values and the valuing process going on unrecognised within him—this is a part of the fundamental estrangment of modern man from himself. This is a major problem for a therapist.
>
> (Rogers, 1990/1964, p. 176)

The therapist provides "a climate favorable to the growth of the person" in a relationship "marked by one primary value: namely that this person, this client, has worth" (Rogers, 1990/1964, p. 176). The client

> Can begin ... to sense and to feel what is going on within him, what he is feeling, what he is experiencing, how he is reacting. He uses his experiencing as a direct referent to which he can turn in forming accurate conceptualizations and as a guide to his behavior ...

As his experiencing becomes more and more open to him, as he is able to live more freely in the process of his feelings, then significant changes begin to occur in his approach to values.

(Rogers, 1990/1964, pp. 176–177)

Such clients

Tend to move away from "oughts". The compelling feeling of "I ought to do or be thus and so" is negatively valued. The client moves away from being what he "ought to be", no matter who has set that imperative.

(Rogers, 1990/1964, p. 182)

All too often moral rules, as represented by the "ought" of external authority, take the place (during "education") of guidance by experiencing what is going on within oneself. This may be recovered by setting up the special conditions offered in counselling, where the old pressures and external demands are temporarily relaxed. The client can thereby get in touch again with the realm of "experiences", which has been overshadowed by conventional moral education.

Let us look again at Emerson's example of harsh treatment of a boy in the name of morality. Emerson, Ellis, and Rogers would each offer alternatives which may differ in content, but which share the appeal to psychological processes, not to justify, but to describe and analyse what they take to be a morally more satisfactory way of acting. This would be similar in each case, and involve listening to the boy and working from the limitations of his knowledge and ability. In Emerson, this comes about through the pervasion of "soul", letting it "breathe through the will"; in Ellis, through the letting-go of the demands contained in the self-talk that controls action, and replacing them with a choice based on wants (sometimes conflicting); and in Rogers, by quietening the voice of social pressure, and allowing experience to guide action. If Emerson is the prophet, Ellis and Rogers are the technologists of this psychologically based morality.

So why isn't the moral nature of these psychotherapies more readily acknowledged by their advocates? The answer seems clear. Ever since Freud set out the importance of not *judging* his patient, this has usually been taken as what Rogers called a "core condition" of therapy and counselling, and Ellis has emphasised the importance of the client's own "self-acceptance", as well as acceptance by the therapist. This does not mean that the therapist approves of the client's actions, but that the client remains accepted *as a person*, not being seen as bad or sinful or unvirtuous *per se*. It is within this relationship based on acceptance, free of the self-talk that makes for guilt and anxiety, that clients have the opportunity to become clear about their goals in life, and how their "absolutist" demands have hindered them from moving in the desired direction. Free of these demands they exercise, we have suggested, the virtues, but nowadays the notion of virtue has become thoroughly entangled with more general moral discourse that implies judgements and commands. Such discourse is all too liable to upset the acceptance that is crucial to the relationship between client and therapist, which is why Ellis so vigorously rejected Mowrer's views on sin and guilt. Therefore, it is generally avoided in psychotherapy, and the *moral* nature of the structure of therapeutic theory is obscured. It is one thing to emphasise the moral nature of psychotherapeutic practice, but quite another to probe and adjust the psychological machinery of morality—yet this is pervasive in Ellis, and at least implied in Rogers.

## Psychological and philosophical moral enquiry

In the above discussion we have highlighted a moral pattern expressed in the writings of two modern therapists, and placed it within a tradition of moral psychology stemming from Emerson. In a parallel but unrelated movement, philosophers have questioned the traditional grounding of ethics in moral imperatives like "ought" and "should". Following Anscombe (1958), this tradition of obligation ethics has been questioned as mistaken about the essence of morality (Crisp & Slote, 1997). Like Ellis, Anscombe targeted the language of moral obligation.

> [T]he concepts of morality and duty—*moral* obligation and *moral* duty, that is to say—and of what is *morally* right and wrong, and of the *moral* sense of ought, ought to be jettisoned if this is psychologically possible; because they are survivals, from an earlier conception of ethics which no longer generally survives, and are only harmful without it.

(Anscombe, 1958, p. 1; emphasis in original)

Alasdair MacIntyre accepted this criticism of moral language in his widely discussed *After Virtue* (1981) (introduced in the last chapter), and described the modern practices that have filled the space left by the emptiness of modern ethics. He argued that the power of moral discourse depends upon a framework of cultural presuppositions necessary for the establishment of objective moral standards, and that this framework has been absent in the West since the overthrow of Aristotelian *telos* and the decline of Christianity. In the absence of these, moral discourse is essentially empty, and is reduced to the expression of feelings. Thus "Emotivism", acknowledged or concealed, characterises all modern moral philosophy. Even those philosophers like Hare (1952) who stress the logical difference between, for example, "I disapprove of this" and "This is bad", are still obliged to fall back on a personal choice of basic moral principles, rather than moral rationality. What has been lost is the Kantian insight that

> The difference between a human relationship uninformed by morality and one so informed is precisely the difference between one in which each person treats the other primarily as a means to his or her ends and one in which each treats the other as an end.

> (MacIntyre, 1981, p. 22)

The resulting vacuum has been filled by some unattractive modern characters, including "the manager" and "the therapist".

> The manager represents in his *character* the obliteration of the distinction between manipulative and nonmanipulative social relations; the therapist represents the same obliteration in the sphere of personal life ... [Like the manager] the therapist also treats ends as given, as outside his scope; his concern also is with technique, with effectiveness in transforming neurotic symptoms into directed energy, maladjusted individuals into well-adjusted ones. Neither manager nor therapist, in their roles as manager and therapist, do or are able to engage in moral debate.

> (MacIntyre, 1981, p. 29; emphasis in original)

Such characters mask their own moral vacuity behind "moral fictions" and, in this respect, the therapist is the worst of a bad bunch, as "the most liable of … typical characters of modernity to be deceived" and "not only by moral fictions" (MacIntyre, 1981, p. 71). The moral life can become possible again only by the construction of forms of community which give meaning to the exercise of the virtues within a human *telos*.

In some respects our own investigations accord with MacIntyre's bleak diagnosis of "a moral calamity" (MacIntyre, 1981, p. vii), as well as his recommended treatment. Both Ellis and Rogers are sensitive to the modern-day emptiness of the moral discourse of "shoulds" and "oughts", still powerful in generating emotional distress, but no longer as a guide to virtuous action. Ellis, like MacIntyre, restores the essence of morality to the nature of the action, virtuous or otherwise, rather than to the intellectual judgement and its implied demands. Furthermore, moral "emotivism" entails, for MacIntyre, "the obliteration of any genuine distinction between manipulative and non-manipulative social relations" (MacIntyre, 1981, p. 22); and it is clear in the writings of both Rogers and Ellis that the core condition of acceptance (or "unconditional positive regard") is an attempt to model a non-manipulative social relation, which is not at all confined to the therapeutic relationship. The practice may be taken out of its proper context and used manipulatively, but this is true of the virtues themselves (e.g., both patience and a simulacrum of acceptance may aid seduction or police interrogation). By ignoring the Emersonian tradition, MacIntyre cannot do justice to the possibility of identifying experiences or ways of being that are essentially moral. In this tradition the client substitutes reasoned choice (based on an awareness of conflicting desires and the interests of others) for a sense of compulsion by the demands for immediate gratification or the need to conform to an external system of commands.

## Conclusion

What we have tried to demonstrate in this chapter is that, as Graham Richards (1995) argued, there is an enduring moral project in American psychology, which was underway even before psychology became established as a separate discipline towards the end of the nineteenth century. However, our moral project is not the one Richards writes about, shown in the concerns of the influential textbook writers of the mid-nineteenth century. Instead it stems from Ralph Waldo Emerson, and has tried to show in practice and theory how a moral life can be based on (although not reduced to) the existence of definable experiences and psychological processes. This forms part of what we have called the Emersonian tradition, and, returning to the distinctions of the last chapter, is part of an emancipatory discourse.

The status of this as a morality is shown by its opposition to the universal dictates of an externally imposed moral code, embodied in the moral "shoulds" and "oughts" that nurture guilt if disobeyed. The practical psychological problem is how to bring about conditions for the essential psychological processes to occur. One set of conditions is provided by the social setting and practices of psychotherapy and counselling, and it is here that the moral project in question has been furthered by Albert Ellis and Carl Rogers.

This critique of a morality of "shoulds" and "oughts" is paralleled by the recent critique of obligation ethics in moral philosophy, even though there has been no mutual acknowledgement between these two movements of the last 45 years, both suggesting an ethics of virtue in place of obligation.

However, stressing the moral aspects of modern psychotherapy collides with some of its more public claims, especially, in the case of REBT and other cognitive therapies, its claim to be scientific. Such a claim, which Freud made about psychoanalysis from the beginning, is powerful rhetoric, but it opens the way to the potentially damaging charge of "pseudoscience", which we saw levelled at Ellis's REBT by Wessler in Chapter Two. The next chapter looks at the history and use of the concept of "pseudoscience", treated as part of a conceptual field that has played a significant part in the evolution of modern psychotherapy, as it charted a hazardous path between its inescapable moral origins and the demands of science.

## Notes

1. Thus, we are not taking issue with Richards' thesis, which had to do with academic psychology, but extending and qualifying it by including psychological therapies.
2. Yeoman's (1991) claims are based on the Covenanters' practice of emotionally acknowledging their sinfulness in order to break through their self-doubts. Once these are left behind, they can become happy in their confidence in belonging to the Elect. The link is at the psychological rather than the theological level.

3. Although Emerson makes much of "the moral law", this is not an external authority but directly perceived by the individual, and may not be the same for individuals in different cultures.

4. James refers to "trusting our religious demands" (James, 1956, p. 56), which means "to live in the light of them, and to act as if the invisible world which they suggest were real". In practice, his most famous act of "trust" was in free will: "My first act of free will shall be to believe in free will" (quoted in Perry, 1948, p. 121).

5. Writing about psychotherapy, Guignon interprets Heidegger's authenticity as "providing a basis for understanding our embedded-ness in a wider context of meaning, the role of constraints in genuine freedom, and the fundamental role of moral commitments in our ability to be humans in any meaningful sense" (Guignon, 1993, p. 237).

6. That is, experienced as existing independently of human experience.

7. It is worth anticipating a familiar objection, that psychological cer-tainty is no guarantee of moral *goodness*. However, like Husserl we are not concerned with the conditions for sure knowledge or examining the logic of moral justification, but with examining the psychological processes essential to moral experience or behaviour.

8. The chapter in the 1962 book is based on two papers (Ellis, 1960a, 1960b) from a debate with Mowrer (1960a, 1960b).

9. Even if we do not go as far as the translator of the Penguin *Nicomachean Ethics* who wrote that "Aristotle had the boldness and originality to base ethics on psychology" (Aristotle, 1955, pp. 22–23).

10. An important but different discussion of REBT and virtue ethics is in Sharpe & Mcmahon (1997).

# CHAPTER SEVEN

# The social psychology of "pseudoscience": a brief history

## Introduction

For separating out the sheep from the goats, one of the key words of the twentieth century has been "scientific". Scientific practice is good practice, and unscientific practice is bad practice, and psychotherapy has been uneasily aware of this. Psychoanalysis was suspect from the beginning, and more recent therapies have spent a lot of effort in establishing scientific credentials. Ellis presented Rational Psychotherapy as a scientific contrast to psychoanalysis, and at the same time Carl Rogers was attemping to prove scientifically the desirable outcomes possible with person-centred therapy. But why? Why does it matter? What is it about "science" and its condemned shadow "pseudoscience" that has made the words so important? This chapter is about the social and cultural settings of the word "pseudoscience", an important part of the context that moulded the development of REBT.

Like "paedophile" and "terrorist", "pseudoscience" has an etymologically transparent sense, and during the twentieth century, it was also used with great rhetorical power—in this case to expose publicly a successful activity falsely claiming scientific status. Thus: "The government is using a pseudo-scientific justification of GM to conceal its acquiescence to global, corporate control of key food supplies" (Butterfield, 2004). But from time to time such words have occurred in a more formal, technical sense around a perceived threat to individual and institutional security. It is in the use of "pseudoscience" in these foci of activity that we are interested.

Twenty years ago, the philosopher Larry Laudan (1983) announced "The demise of the demarcation problem". This problem was to demarcate between science and pseudoscience, and Laudan showed that it is impossible to arrive at a definition of science that will distinguish all scientific from all pseudoscientific or non-scientific statements; there is no scientific essence whose presence or absence can make the distinction. If he and others[1] who shared his view were right, then a decline in serious discussions of the problem would be expected. However, the reverse has recently occurred in applied areas of human and biological sciences, such as psychology, psychotherapy, and medicine. However insoluble by philosophical standards, demarcation remains troublesome, generating passion amongst those who speak on the side of science and feel the need to separate it clearly from other activities. There are currently several attempts posted on the internet to list diagnostic criteria for detecting pseudoscience, as though it were a kind of pathology.[2] Recently the label "pseudoscience" has been used to damn new therapies, such as anti-ageing therapies (de Grey et al., 2002), facilitated communication (Jacobson, Mulick & Schwartz, 1995), Eye-movement Desensitization and Reprocessing (EMDR) (Herbert et al., 2000), and even Rational-Emotive Behavior Therapy (Wessler, 1996).

EMDR is an apparently evidence-based therapy for Post Traumatic Stress Disorder; in 15 years it has become popular in the States and elsewhere, and now claims successful treatment for a wide range of psychological problems. The paper by Herbert et al. stands out as heavyweight by any standards, unremitting in its denunciation of the poor evidence, the crude theory, and the dubious use of publicity. The attempts by the supporters of EMDR to explain away negative results cannot merely be dismissed as bad science, to be remedied by the self-correcting processes inherent in science. They are symptoms of pseudoscience, which entails exile from the domain of science. To prove their point, they appealed to the same criteria that had earlier been found wanting by Laudan and other philosophers.

Two of the authors of the paper on EMDR have co-edited a book designed to fight the erosion of the "scientific foundations of clinical psychology" (Lilienfeld, Lynn & Lohr, 2003, p. 1), and a whole issue of *Scientific Review of Mental Health Practice* (Volume 2, Number 2, 2003) has been devoted to the danger of pseudoscientific tendencies. The urgent, combative tone of some of these publications is unmistakable, and a contrast to the detachment of philosophers and sociologists who dominated the discussion around 1980.[3] What has changed? To answer this we will turn to some earlier history of boundaries set up to protect science.

The psychological theory behind our analysis is that derogatory labelling of others often includes an unstated self-definition. Thus, a negative judgement that EMDR is a pseudoscience can serve to fortify the speaker's sense of self as scientist, sharing such judgements with similar scientists. This is the basis of projection and reaction formation, although here we derive it from the theory of mutualism (Still & Good, 1992), in which "[t]he awareness of the world and of one's complementary relations to the world are not separable" (Gibson, 1979, p. 141). A comforting identification with science may or may not be valid. For the purposes of this chapter, it is valid if there really is a distinct class of scientists to which the writer belongs, and the activities of members of this class have a unique value. It can therefore be valid if science is a unity, and has special access to knowledge not shared by pseudoscientists. If it is not valid according to these criteria, use of the word may still bring comfort, derived from the informal sense referred to earlier.

A sociological version of this comfort-seeking, which avoids the question of validity, is that

> The allegation of "pseudo-science" is ... an aspect of the rhetorical and organizational means by which scientists and other sympathetic agents seek to distinguish the domain of science, and to discredit some other activity, in the process of maintaining and extending the status, cognitive authority, funding, autonomy and other interests and values of those associated with science as an enterprise.
>
> (Wallis, 1985, p. 593)

## Prehistory of pseudoscience

The word "pseudoscience" seems first to have occurred in the twentieth century, but reflects a dynamic that is much older. This is the attempt to define science as something distinct from other activities, with a unique importance for generating knowledge. This has been described as a "mapping process" (Gieryn, 1999, *passim*), drawing boundaries to keep science apart from non-science. But it is more than just mapping, since the high status of science means that space allotted to it is not neutral; by granting "epistemic authority" (Gieryn, 1999, p. x), it conveys privilege for any activity established there. Inclusion or exclusion can determine the future of a discipline, and even its survival.

Darnton (1984, p. 189)[4] has described how Diderot and D'Alembert, the philosophers mainly responsible for the eighteenth-century *Encyclopédie*, used two metaphors, the tree of knowledge with its different branches, and a map with boundaries and interconnections. We will be exploring the tension between these two metaphors in writings about science. On the map metaphor, activities excluded from the area reserved from true empirical knowledge are allocated a different space, one that may in principle be just as fertile. On the tree metaphor, there is not only a hierarchy within the tree, but discarded branches are left to wither, expelled from the organic whole that could give them real life in a world that lives on knowledge. Or, less fancifully, they are excluded from the fertile soil of life-giving research grants. Compared to earlier classifications, the *Encylopédie* gave science a new and prominent place at the expense of theology, a process that Darnton described as "Philosophers Trim the Tree of Knowledge" (Darnton, 1984, p. 191). Theology was no longer an essential part of the organic whole, and this paved the way for its severance altogether from the main tree.

## The nineteenth century

During the nineteenth century, there were attempts to uncover what is essential in scientific activity, or that which separates it from non-scientific activities. John Stuart Mill (1843) laid down canons of experimental reasoning, Whewell (1840) proposed "consilience" (Snyder, 2006) to describe scientific thinking, while the more practical John Tyndall publicly campaigned to enhance the prestige of science above mechanics and religion (Gieryn, 1999).

Defending science against popular suspicion, Herbert Spencer reassured his public that "it is simply a higher development of common knowledge" (Spencer, 1860, p. 13), even if something that seemed different from this had emerged. Readers of learned publications did not have to look far to see this in concrete detail, and to form their own view of how different from common knowledge it could be in practice. A striking example was Robert Koch's work that established the germ theory of disease. As well as an important theorist, Koch excelled as a technician, inventing techniques that remain basic to modern bacteriology. Using these new techniques, he described the life cycle of the anthrax bacillus, discovered the tubercle bacillus, and isolated the bacterium that causes cholera (Brock, 1988, p. 3). His discoveries became accepted through the development of styles of argument for establishing causal connections between germs and disease.

> To prove that tuberculosis is caused by the invasion of bacilli, and that it is a parasitic disease primarily caused by the growth and multiplication of bacilli, it is necessary to isolate the bacilli from the body, to grow them in pure culture until they are freed from every disease product of the animal organism, and, by introducing isolated bacilli into animals, to reproduce the same morbid condition that is known to follow from inoculation with spontaneously developed tuberculous material.
>
> (Koch, 1882, p. 87)

This excerpt from a lecture formed the basis of what are now well known as Koch's postulates, and, on finishing, "the audience was left spellbound, and for a time after he had ended the presentation not a word was uttered" (Lechevalier & Solotorovsky, 1974 cited in Koch, 1882, p. xx).

But he was soon obliged to defend himself against failures to confirm his results. He dismissed these with scornful sarcasm, mostly against "the remarkable ... reception of the new theory by American researchers", chiefly "the great microscopist Schmidt" (Koch, 1882, p. 118), and concluded that there had been no research

> That disproves, even in the slightest, my claims about the etiology of tuberculosis. It was not pleasant for me to criticize such an entirely worthless body of literature.
>
> (Koch, 1882, p. 126)

Harsh words for a man who had been closeted for so many years with those paradigms of unpleasantness, the tubercle and anthrax bacilli.

While the scientist Robert Koch was helping to establish the germ theory of disease, William Radam was constructing a different story from his own version of the theory (Young, 1961). Having emigrated from Prussia to Texas, he worked as a nursery gardener, developing his 30 acres in an enterprising, experimental fashion. When he became ill with malaria and sciatica, he took the same approach to this problem that had brought success in horticulture. Microbes that attack the body, he reasoned, are like bugs that attack plants; therefore

> If I could discover any thing that would kill blight, fungi, and microbes on plants without injuring them, I should also be in possession of something that would cure me.

> (Radam, cited in Young, 1961, pp. 145–146)

With a passion fired by the prospect of the loss of his livelihood and early death, he tried many substances before discovering his "Microbe Killer". This appears to have been a mild antiseptic which

> Could be taken in such huge amounts that it would saturate all the tissues and permeate all the blood of the human frame, and this with safety to the person, with destruction to the microbes ...

> (Young, 1961, p. 146)

Radam and his microbe killer gained a local reputation, on which he capitalised by patenting the process and packaging it for a much broader market.

Radam was in a long tradition of patent medicine maufacturers who boast scientific credentials. Fortunes were made, but success attracted the attention of investigative journalists and reforming politicians. There had been laws for some time against false statements about the ingredients of a proprietary medicine, but no obligation to list its composition (Young, 1961, p. 227), even if, as often happened, they included alcohol or opium. Energetic campaigns led to the Pure Food and Drugs Act of 1906. This tightened the law on misinformation, and required manufacturers to declare on the label the presence of dangerous drugs. Regulation has increasingly required the application of scientific method. Chemistry and biological sciences are used in the production and regulation of medicines and food, and experiments drawing on modern statistical techniques are required to support therapeutic and nutritional claims. Nowadays those treated as experts on these matters are popularly referred to as "scientists".

Koch and Radam will serve as two type specimens on which to base our discussion of science and pseudoscience; it is a change from the more usual appeal to physics as the embodiment of science, and more appropriate for understanding the recent alarm about pseudoscientific tendencies in new therapies. Both drew on the current germ theory of disease, but Koch was recognised as an exemplary (although sometimes unlovable) scientist, while Radam was an amiable entrepreneur who used aspects of scientific language and practice to convince himself and his public of the value of his product.

## The rise of pseudoscience: big and little pseudoscience

Writings on pseudoscience[5] during the twentieth century fell into two overlapping traditions, which we will refer to as big and little pseudoscience, respectively.[6] In little pseudoscience the concept was applied to activities centred on claims and ideas that are commonly seen as bizarre and cranky, at least in retrospect, but have a large following for a short period of time. They laughably fail as science, so demarcation is not a serious issue, and calling them "pseudosciences" is usually uncontroversial. Like weeds they are easily identified, but can threaten cultivated plants if the gardener is not vigilant.

In discussions of big pseudoscience, the concept has been linked to the philosophical issue of demarcation, of how science is to be distinguished from other activities. The other activities in question tend to be intellectually challenging and to attract an educated audience. The classic candidate was psychoanalysis, although others have included Marxism, psychometrics, and biological psychiatry. Historically, astrology and phrenology have been big pseudosciences, although their modern residues are little pseudosciences.

## Tales of little pseudoscience

The modern classic in this genre is Martin Gardner's (1957) *Facts and Fallacies in the Name of Science*.[7] There was already a tradition of exposing scientific pretensions, but Gardner's was the prototype of a new popular genre. He described 24 examples, each contained within about

15 pages; they included unidentified flying objects (UFOs), Lysenkoism, orgonomy, dianetics, General Semantics, ESP, food faddists, and "medical quacks". His motive was educational, to immunise the public against the infection of pseudoscience, by helping us to recognise the future carrier when first encountered. There is a problem but not yet dangerous, especially as "most pseudoscientists have a number of characteristics in common" (Gardner, 1952, p. 8); they "work in almost total isolation from their colleagues" (Gardner, 1952, p. 10) and have a tendency towards paranoia.

Later, Young (1961) referred to quack medicine in the nineteenth century as pseudoscience, and Hines (1988) dealt with some of the same material as Gardner in more detail; he also included more big pseudoscience like psychoanalysis. He still put faith in education, although the stakes were higher.

> [T]he witch delusion and the Nazi horrors show the great damage done by uncritical acceptance of pseudoscientific claims. Both might well have been avoided if the public had been educated in critical scientific thinking.
>
> (Hines, 1988, p. 20)

## Big pseudoscience and unity of science

Writings on science during the first half of the twentieth century were dominated by a modern version of the *Encylopédiste's* Tree of Knowledge; the Unity of Science movement, associated with the Vienna Circle during the 1920s and 1930s; and the unfinished *Encyclopedia of Unified Science*. There was no single philosophy behind this doctrine, and those associated with it such as Carnap and Neurath were more cautious than the bold title of their movement suggests (Creath, 1996). A folk belief in some form of unity is, however, reflected in the common use of the term "science" or "scientist", and the Unity of Science movement formalised this implicit belief.

The word "pseudoscience" emerged from the Vienna Circle and the logical positivism associated with it. In English, the prefix "pseudo" was used to demarcate genuinely empirical statements from others. A pseudo-question was one to which there can be no clear answer, such as, "What is the meaning of life?" (Passmore, 1966, p. 373). The intention behind the prefix was not always perjorative.

Wittgenstein (1922, p. 169) referred to the propositions of mathematics as "pseudo-propositions" without wishing to diminish them, and the literary theorist I. A. Richards (1926, Chapter Six, *passim*) called poetic statements "pseudo-statements". This technical use of "pseudo" was the background to the use of "pseudoscience" in work by and about Karl Popper. He started as a philosopher in the early 1920s, and was a member of the Vienna Circle. "Pseudoscience" has been linked especially with his criterion of falsifiability for demarcating science from non-science.

## Popper and demarcation: big pseudoscience as unfalsifiability

Popper's (1976) autobiography has provided the origin myth for big pseudoscience, in the story of his youthful search for a system of thought to contain his intellectual enthusiasms. First, he was converted to communism during the unsettled period in Vienna immediately after World War I. Its all-embracing certainties promised a suitable framework, but he was disenchanted by the violence encouraged by the party. Later he was shocked at having allowed himself to become uncritically involved. He also failed to find what he was looking for in psychoanalysis, which shared with Marxism the immodest claim to explain everything, and seemed able to turn apparent disconfirmations into their opposite.[8]

The climax and resolution of the story came in 1919 when the young Popper encountered one of the most spectacular events in the history of science, which exemplified for him the principle of falsifiability, that *"it must be possible for an empirical scientific system to be refuted by experience"* (Popper, 1968, p. 41; original emphasis). This was the successful test of Einstein's eclipse predictions, which heralded a new theory, a real improvement on Newton (Popper, 1976, p. 37). The triumph was possible because Einstein's theory, giving a precise prediction in conflict with Newton's, had rendered itself so vulnerable to falsification. This was what the young pilgrim sought.

Popper described his principle of falsifiability as solving two problems. One was the ancient puzzle of induction. This arises if it is assumed that scientific knowledge depends on generalising from positive instances, for example, generalising to "the suspect bacillus causes TB" from the observation that exposure to the bacillus was followed in several cases by the onset of the symptoms of TB; or to "the microbe killer cures many ailments" from the finding that after regular dosage of Radam's microbe killer the symptoms disappeared in well-attested instances. Popper's solution was that scientific knowledge does not depend on generalising from positive instances (which could put Koch and Radam on a par), but on a social practice in which theories and generalisations are challenged and put to the test by fellow scientists. They are trained to view theories critically, and to look for ways of falsifying it. We saw that process clearly in the case of Koch, whose colleagues in the United States and elsewhere seized on his claims and tried to discredit them, and its absence was equally clear in the case of Radam, the lone entrepreneur.

For our story of "pseudoscience", the key move was to apply falsifiability to a new problem, which Popper insisted was the most important. This was to provide a criterion to demarcate science from pseudoscience. However, the logical structure of falsifiability will not suffice as a demarcation criterion. Astrology, Marxism, and psychoanalysis make many statements which could in principle be falsified, but in practice (Popper believed) contrary results are assimilated by the theory concerned, and not allowed to act as falsifications. Radam's claims on behalf of his microbe killer were falsified, so must have been falsifiable, but this does not make his work scientific. No one doubted Koch's status as a scientist, yet he justifiably held on to his theory in the face of failures to confirm it.

Again, the social setting became crucial for Popper as he developed his views. He spelt this out in a fiercely ironic attack on the founders of the sociology of knowledge for ignoring the social aspects of science. His targets were Scheler and Mannheim, whose views (Popper believed) derived from the "Marxist doctrine that our opinions, including our moral and scientific opinions, are determined by class interest, and more generally by the social and historical situation of the time"; this is the "social habitat" which determines, in the form of an ideology, "opinions and theories which appear ... unquestionably true or self-evident" (Popper, 1962, p. 213). But they fail to see that their own views too must be equally determined by the social habitat,[9] and basing scientific knowledge upon the "consciousness" (Popper, 1962, p. 217; original quotes) of the individual scientist, they overlook precisely the

> Social aspect of scientific method, with the fact that science and scientific objectivity do not (and cannot) result from the attempts of an

individual scientist to be "objective", but from the co-operation of many scientists.

(Popper, 1962, p. 217; original emphasis)

Scientific objectivity, like liberal democracy, is constituted by free criticism and social institutions.

Only political power, when it is used to suppress free criticism, or when it fails to protect it, can impair the functioning of these institutions, on which all progress, scientific, technological, and political, ultimately depends.

(Popper, 1962, p. 218)

This account of science as falsifiability, demarcating it from pseudoscience, has had lasting appeal to scientists (both Herbert et al., 2000, and Wessler, 1996 appeal to it), but difficulties still remained when the social aspects were made clear. In practice, theories tend to be held on to rather than jetisoned when disconfirmed, and even Popper's mythic paradigm of falsifiability, the testing of Einstein's eclipse predictions, may have been distorted by a "confirmation bias" (Shermer, 2002, p. 301 citing Collins & Pinch, 1993). Popper did recognise that there is a conservatism in science, and that theories can be clung to with great tenacity in the face of apparently falsifying evidence. He made a virtue of it within his theory; conjectures need to be given a chance to strengthen themselves before they are finally refuted in the face of a testing process that will itself gain strength from encountering determined theories. However, the question remained: When is resistance to falsification in the face of disconfirmation consistent with good scientific practice, and when is it the mark of a pseudoscience?

The need to resolve this difficulty was made urgent by the impact of Thomas Kuhn (1962), since he gave the impression to many readers that Popper's principle of falsifiability had little to do with scientific progress. According to Kuhn, science does not advance through a steady process of "Conjectures and Refutations". Instead, normal science is always framed within a set of "paradigms" of theory and practice, and busies itself with solving the problems thrown up by the paradigms. Anomalies are ignored, and theories whose rejection would threaten the paradigm will be held on to even in the face of apparent falsification. However, sometimes anomalies become too glaring, and this crisis may be resolved through a revolution, giving rise to new paradigms, incommensurable with the old. This historical theory seemed to put a distance between nature and scientific practice, and to undermine Popper's principles of demarcation. The apparent threat to science's reputation triggered energetic attempts to reconcile Kuhn and Popper, and to re-establish boundaries between science and pseudoscience.

## Big pseudoscience as degenerating research programme

The best-known attempt was by Imre Lakatos (1970) in his theory of scientific research programmes. According to this theory, the hard core of a science is preserved by a protective belt, created by the negative heuristic that points research away from the hard core, and the positive heuristic that directs progressive work towards new theories and discoveries. In this way, a scientific theory is protected to some extent against falsification; its auxiliary hypotheses, which mediate between theory and experiment, can be adjusted to allow for discrepancies. However, there are limits on the adjustments that can be made. A research programme is progressive if its theories predict new facts, and lead to the actual discovery of new facts. Otherwise, it is degenerating, and "pseudoscientific" (Lakatos, 1970, p. 118). A serious problem arises when it indulges in "pseudoscientific adjustments" with no restraint (Lakatos, 1970, p. 117). The examples taken by Lakatos were from physics, and suggest that his normative vision of progressive and degenerating research programmes was specific to that discipline. But social sciences can take little comfort from Lakatos' delineation of pseudoscience. In the conclusion to his long essay, Lakatos dismissed Marxism and Freudism as pseudosciences, and also "modern social psychology", since they are not progressive. "They do not add up to a genuine research programme and are, on the whole, worthless," he writes, and he

> Wonders whether the function of statistical techniques in the social sciences is not primarily to provide a machinery for producing phoney collaboration and thereby a semblance of "scientific progress" where, in fact, there is nothing but an increase in pseudo-intellectual garbage.

> (Lakatos, 1970, p. 176)

He pursued the garbage metaphor to a Draconian conclusion.

> [T]he methodology of research programmes might help us in devising laws for stemming this intellectual pollution which may destroy our cultural environment even earlier than industrial and traffic pollution destroys our physical environment.
>
> (Lakatos, 1970, p. 176)

Mario Bunge (1967), a physicist as well as a philosopher of science and of mind, was equally severe on pseudosciences, although he did not (at this time) go as far as Lakatos by suggesting legislation to control them. He showed little interest in the niceties of the demarcation problem, but took the existence of pseudoscience for granted, and asked, "What is wrong with pseudoscience?" He answered that it refuses to ground its doctrines in science and to test them by experiment proper; it lacks a self-correction mechanism, and its aim is to influence people rather than to map reality—criteria general enough to include both psychoanalysis and dowsing.

## Big pseudoscience as ideology

Sometimes a scientist may be tempted to maintain a position in the interest of some external power, like the organisation that provides financial support, or the beliefs of a political dictator. A much-cited example of the latter is Lysenkoism, which was supported by Stalin and became the dominant biological theory in the Union of Soviet Socialist Republics (USSR) during the 1930s. Such external control is often called "ideological".[10]

Blum (1978) used 'ideological' in this sense, and considered mental testing (which he called "eugenics/psychometrics" to bring out its perceived racist origins) to be a pseudoscience for this reason. Like Lysenkoism, eugenics/psychometrics has been officially sanctioned; its "domain is an entire nation or group of nations, and the false beliefs are openly professed as valid science by respected authorities in major educational institutions" (Blum, 1978, p. 146). In a review of Blum (1978), Cooter (1980) argued from a neo-Marxist viewpoint that the deployment of "pseudoscience" always acts conservatively because "it legitimates the worldview that is mystified and mediated through science" (Cooter, 1980, p. 259). However, although this may be the primary force of the word, it can also be used in a secondary sense, to make a rhetorical distinction even without any commitment to science. Thus, the power of psychometrics depends on its scientific pretensions; therefore, a successful attack on it as "pseudoscience" would undermine it (and its racist influence) in the eyes of those who accept the worldview that is mediated through science. Thus, it acts conservatively through such eyes, but Blum was making use of this action in the interests of an anti-racist argument. The self-definition of Blum (a sociologist) was of himself as anti-racist, rather than as scientist.

Ross and Pam (1995) argued that biological psychiatry is a pseudoscience because it "is dominated by a reductionist ideology that distorts and represents much of its research" (Ross & Pam, 1995, pp. 1–2). The assumed political origin of the inherent bias was spelt out clearly.

> Human choices and values are negated, and the sociocultural status quo remains intact. Thus, an overly biologized psychiatry becomes an instrument with which to repress alternative psychosocial models of psychopathology.
>
> (Ross & Pam, 1995, p. 3)

They did not pretend to be neutral. Their book was written from within, to promote a psychosocial model by subverting the dominant views stifling it.

## Big pseudoscience as the art of the insoluble

Writing as psychologists, Leahey and Leahey (1983) saw pseudosciences as "psychological movements that have been rejected by established psychology" yet continue to attract many followers and "form a dark, unconscious side to establishment psychology" (Leahey & Leahey, 1983, p. 14). There are no formal demarcation criteria, since boundaries are established by social consensus rather than by the possession of any special access to truth possessed by science. Appealing to Kuhn, they argued that normal science follows its paradigms, and therefore "*is* a collection of subjects approved for research" (Leahey & Leahey, 1983, p. 238; original emphasis) and "content rather than form or method determines which fields are considered to be pseudosciences" (Leahey & Leahey, 1983, p. 239). Science is not a search for ultimate values, and pseudoscience arises from dissatisfaction with this, and a "deeply rooted human need for a universe of meaning, rather than one of mere order" (Leahey & Leahey, 1983, p. 245). Pseudosciences like phrenology, mesmerism, and parapsychology "are not sciences because they try to delve deeper than any science can" (Leahey & Leahey, 1983, p. 245). Although they did not refer to Medawar, they might agree with him that science is the art of the soluble (Medawar, 1969).

Summarising the argument so far, these examples of big pseudo-science show how the uses of the word reflect the critical and scientific interests of the writer. For philosophers as identified with physics as Popper, Lakatos, and Bunge, pseudoscience was no real threat, but only as long as there are secure boundaries; the demarcation problem was therefore of abiding importance (although not problematic in the case of Bunge).

By laying down rules, Lakatos hoped to supplement and enhance the self-correcting processes of science, and to ensure that lapses could be detected more easily. Blum (1978) and Ross and Pam (1995) (targeted a less obvious danger), where self-correction may look healthy, but where external forces are being used, in Popper's words, to "suppress free crit-icism" (Popper, 1962, p. 218). Blum's stance was from outside science, and he used "pseudoscience" to undermine the scientific pretensions of an established sub-discipline, and thereby strengthen the anti-racist position in the IQ debate of the time. Ross and Pam's was a critique by practitioners, using the label in an attempt to revive and secure their own beleagured position as psychosocial theorists. Leahey and Leahey described a less sinister form of "pseudoscience", where the failure lies in selecting the wrong kind of problem, of seeking to uncover secrets that lie beyond the art of the soluble. Their labelling served a cleans-ing process, acknowledging ownership of psychology's shadow side in order to keep it safely in its place, leaving psychology (and themselves as psychologists) secure.

## Breaching the boundaries: sociology of scientific knowledge

The Leaheys followed Kuhn rather than Popper or Lakatos, and were in tune with some of the dominant views around 1980. Essentialism was out of fashion, and philosophers had become lukewarm about the demarcation problem. Sociology of Scientific Knowlege (SSK) was now well underway; if it had been crushed by Popper's attack on Scheler and Mannheim, it had certainly recovered after being established as an empirical and historical discipline by Robert Merton. It had moved on, from Merton as well as Mannheim, in several respects. It tried to study empirically the causes of scientific knowledge and belief; it was self-consciously reflexive, recognising that the same questions about knowledge and belief can be asked of itself; and finally, it assumed symmetry between the causes of true and false beliefs, between science and pseudoscience (Bloor, 1976). As Latour put it, in his third rule of method for studying scientific controversies and their outcomes: "[S]ince the settlement of a controversy is *the cause* of Nature's representation not the consequence, we *can never use the outcome—Nature—to explain how and why a controversy has been settled*" (Latour, 1987, p. 99; original emphasis).

This breakdown of boundaries between science and pseudoscience was no light matter. The simple formula "science has access to truth, pseudoscience does not" no longer held or was deemed unimportant. And in the scientific world at large there was serious unrest. This culminated in the "science wars", an upheaval which formed the background to the most recent revival of "pseudoscience".

*Restoring the boundaries: science wars and the revival of pseudoscience*

The first skirmishes in Britain were triggered by a scientist's attempt to restore science to its privileged position in relation to truth. Lewis Wolpert (1992) wheeled out the old shocker that Eddington had used sixty years earlier.

> [P]hysics teaches us that the greenness of grass, the hardness of stones and the coldness of snow are not the greenness, hardness and coldness that we know in our own experience, but something very different.
>
> (Wolpert, 1992, p. 6)

These compelling experiences are a construction.[11] Only science has direct access to truth and reality.

This attempt to raise the flag for science would probably have had little impact if Wolpert had not also vigorously attacked SSK. The implications for funding were potentially serious, and reactions surfaced angrily at a meeting of the British Association for the Advancement of Science in 1994 (as reported in Phillips, 2000, p. 188). Wolpert dismissed SSK results as "either trivial, obvious or wrong", and accused the perpetrators of being motivated by envy. SSK's spokesperson, Harry Collins, refused to debate with him at such a personal level, but in the same year Durham University's Centre for the History of Human Sciences did get some of the protaganists together, and the proceedings were published in the May 1995 issue of the journal *History of the Human Sciences*.

Gross and Levitt (1994) attacked on a broader front than Wolpert. Their target was "the academic left", infiltrated by a postmodernism with a foothold in the whole range of Arts subjects. They were defending science against a politically motivated rebellion: "Modern science is seen ... to be both a powerful instrument of the reigning order and an ideological guarantor of its legitimacy" (Gross & Levitt, 1994, p. 12). Like Wolpert, they believed that underlying this was envy, due to science's lofty position in the epistemic hierarchy. Unless checked, the rebellion will ultimately threaten the contemporary university, an institution whose "health has become incalculably important for the future of our descendants and, indeed, of our species" (Gross & Levitt, 1994, p. 7). Humanity itself is in danger when postmodernists try to seize possession of the tree of knowledge, and obliterate the distinction between science and pseudoscience.

Their chapter on SSK took on Bruno Latour. The attack was personal, the intellectual equivalent of war. Latour's work "provokes and titillates" (Gross & Levitt, 1994, p. 57); "a rather light-footed style is needed to get away with such stuff" (Gross & Levitt, 1994, p. 58), so he needs all of "his intellectual cunning and his seductive charm" (Gross & Levitt, 1994, p. 59). The "stuff" was Latour's "Third Rule of Method", "which drives more earnest and responsible philosophers of science into paroxysms of disgust" (Gross & Levitt, 1994, p. 58). They refuted the Third Rule with a "homely example", that of people cooped up in a windowless office settling a dispute about whether it is raining by stepping outside. "Insofar as we are disciples of Latour, we can never explain our agreement on this point by the simple fact that it is raining ... Baldly put, this seems ridiculous" (Gross & Levitt, 1994, p. 58). This goes to the heart of the matter: science's epistemic authority had been challenged, and a new urgency arose, leading to a return with Wolpert to fundamentalism about truth in order to restore the demarcation between science and pseudoscience.

In the year that Gross and Levitt's book was published, the New York Academy of Sciences sponsored a conference with the same theme (Gross, Levitt & Lewis, 1996). Not all the contributions were on a war footing, and even the chapter on Bruno Latour was within the bounds of peacetime debate. As we have already seen in Chapter Five, this was not true of Mario Bunge's contribution. If you walk

> From the faculties of science, engineering, medicine or law, towards the faculty of arts ... you will meet another world, one where falsities and lies are tolerated, nay manufactured and taught, in industrial quantities.
>
> (Bunge, 1996, p. 108)

Civilisation is under threat, not from terrorism but from academic charlatans who peddle anti-science and pseudoscience.

> Spare the rod and spoil the charlatan. Spoil the charlatan and put modern culture at risk. Jeopardize modern culture and undermine modern civilization. Debilitate modern civilization and prepare for a new Dark Age.
>
> (Bunge, 1996, p. 110)

Bunge declared a ten-point Charter of Intellectual Academic Rights and Duties, and concluded with a stirring call to "all genuine intellectuals" to

> Join the Truth Squad and help dismantle the "postmodern" Trojan horse stabled in Academia before it destroys them.
>
> (Bunge, 1996, p. 111)

In spite of the famous victory of Sokal's Hoax,[12] the hostilities petered out indecisively when the defence failed to match this level of aggression (Ross, 1996). Gieryn (1999, p. 349) described the science wars as "savage cultural cartography". But it was also tree work, angry pruning, with hurt nostalgia for the days when scientists were universally respected as dedicated servants of the tree of knowledge; and pseudoscientists were laughable pretenders, recognisable by their isolation and their paranoia.

## Aftermath of the science wars: the increasing threat from little pseudoscience

During the 1990s, in the midst of all this distressing activity, writings on little pseudoscience acquired a new urgency. Later books, including several by Gardner himself, continued to stress their educational function. However, his hope for a more enlightened public had not been realised: "Science education in our nation, especially in lower grades is getting worse, not better" (Gardner, 2000, p. 3). Pseudoscientists were no longer isolated cranks, but well organised and with enough popular support to sooth their paranoia.

Sagan (1995) was equally worried about the new threat. As an astronomer, he paid special attention to UFOs and alien abductions. The boundaries are not secure since "a kind of Gresham's Law prevails in popular culture by which bad science drives out good" (Sagan, 1995, p. 6); and being error prone we need training in sceptical thinking (Sagan, 1995, p. 21). However, educational immunisation is not sufficient: the problem goes deeper. Thus the thoroughly educated Professor John Mack, a Harvard University psychiatrist and Pulitzer Prize winner, came to believe the testimony of those who claimed to have experienced alien abduction. Mack proposed "the very dangerous doctrine" that "'the power or intensity with which something is felt' is a guide to whether it is true" (Sagan, 1995, p. 153). The danger is within, and we must learn to question even our strongest feelings.

Michael Shermer (2002) is the director of the Skeptics Society, and founder of the *Skeptic* magazine, which has been warning the world about pseudoscience for several years. The first edition of his book in 1997 ended with a chapter entitled, like the book itself, "Why do people believe weird things?" The second in 2002 added a new chapter, "Why do *smart* people believe weird things?" The confirmation bias that influenced reports of the testing of Einstein's eclipse predictions was a danger for very smart people indeed—Eddington, Einstein, and Popper! Education is not enough. In a note added to the 2002 edition, he brought the urgency up to date; the mass suicide by the Heaven's Gate UFO cult in 1997 proved that weird beliefs are not harmless fun (Shermer, 2002, p. xxvi).

Not only has the nature of the fear changed, but also the target. Pseudoscience, big or little, can no longer be held at a distance. Like terrorism, it is felt as a danger to us all, an internal not an external threat, and not open to ordinary debate. It is these fears that have spilled over into journal articles, the mission of which has been to expel new therapies into the wilderness of "pseudoscience". But there is disagreement about the wisdom of such stern methods. The issue of *Scientific Review of Mental Health Practice* referred to above, was a discussion of a lead article from Richard McNally by a panel that included Mario Bunge and some of the authors of the EMDR article (Herbert et al., 2000). Disagreeing with them, McNally concludes:

> [T]he best way to debunk bunk in clinical psychology is to examine the relevant evidence. Attempts to diagnose pseudoscience are an unnecessary and roundabout way of achieving the same goal.
>
> (McNally, 2003, p. 116)

In the same spirit, Lilienfeld, Lynn, and Lohr (2003), contains careful examinations of intractable difficulties in achieving a scientific psychotherapy. On the one hand, the editors' introductory chapter to the book refers to "the festering problem of pseudoscience *within* clinical psychology" (Lilienfeld, Lynn & Lohr, 2003, p. 10; emphasis added) and offers a list of ten criteria for the detection of pseudoscience, and the book ends with a five-point recommendation for mobilisation ("the battle against pseudoscience is too substantial to be waged on a single front" (Lilienfeld, Lynn & Lohr, 2003, p. 462)). On the other hand, many of the chapters are not about pseudoscience, but address the problems that threaten the scientific security of the best clinical psychology. They bring out the difficulties in scientific regulation of psychotherapy, compared with patent medicines and food.

One problem arises from the distinction between efficacy and effectiveness (Garske & Anderson, 2003; Seligman, 1995). Efficacy is how well the therapy works under controlled conditions; effectiveness is whether it works in practice. Efficacy and effectiveness may not always coincide. And what if pseudoscientific mumbo-jumbo is effective therapy? Is that a case for Bunge's Truth Squad? A second problem is the placebo effect (Walach & Kirsch, 2004). In medical research, the ordinary placebo effect is allowed for by double-blind, randomly controlled, trials. In trials of antidepressant drugs, there is usually a large effect of both the drug and the placebo, with a relatively small difference between them. This relatively small difference could, in principle, be explained by an active placebo effect, in which the side effects of an active drug trigger a placebo response. There is evidence that active placebos are better than inert placebos, so that the apparent drug effect in clinical trials could sometimes be largely a placebo effect, with subsequent therapeutic effectiveness pumped up by the publicity surrounding individual anti-depressants. This is disturbing news, since drug trials are usually regarded as the gold standard to which psychotherapy can only aspire. What happens to the aspirant when the gold turns out to be counterfeit? Does psychotherapy focus attention on the special nature of its own problems (as McNally recommends), or are the anxieties turned outwards in a derogatory labelling of others that includes an unstated self-definition as scientific. The book amply illustrates both answers, as well as the difficulties that trigger the insecurity.

## The disunity of science

The comforting force of an implicit self-definition as scientific rests on an assumed identity with other scientists, and hence on a unity in science. But is there much in common between the struggle to find a way of controlling for placebo effects in psychotherapy, physicists investigating the reality of Quarks during the 1970s (Galison, 1997, pp. 642–643), biological taxonomists classifying a newly discovered species, or metereologists coordinating data to predict tomorrow's weather? Is there really a tree of knowledge whose unity provides security even for its remotest branches?

Suppes (1978) examined the assumptions behind the Unity of Science movement. The potential unity is based on three possibilities: reduction of language, of subject matter, and of method. He argued that none of these is compatible with modern science, and concluded that science is not

An ever closer approximation to a set of eternal truths that hold always and everywhere … (but) … is perpetual problem-solving. No area of experience is totally and completely settled by providing a set of basic truths; but rather, we are continually confronted with new situations and new problems, and we bring to these problems and situations a potpourri of scientific methods, techniques, and concepts, which in many cases we have learned to use with great facility.

(Suppes, 1978, p. 14)

Other writers have followed, philosophically (Dupré, 1983; Rosenberg, 1994), historically (Galison, 1997), and both together in the chapters of Galison and Stump (1996). Kuhn's theory posited discontinuity between different periods of a science, in the form of incommensurability. The synchronic version of this starts from "the extraordinary variety of scientific languages, practices, purposes, and forms of argumentation" (Galison & Stump, 1996, p. 13), not just between the sciences, but within a science such as physics. This might suggest a mapping task, drawing boundaries before looking at the action within each paradigm. But Galison has focused on the areas between the disunified parts of science, the "trading zones" (Galison & Stump, 1996, p. 13). Rather than worrying about paradigms or frameworks that create incommensurability problems, Galison made incommensurability the norm and argued that "the different subcultures of science ... work out local trading zones in which they can coordinate their practices" (Galison & Stump, 1996, p. 14). The study of these trading zones in recent physics has proved a fruitful celebration of disunity (Galison, 1997).

Hacking (1996) has given a clear summary of the issues. He took, as his starting point, Crombie's six styles of scientific reasoning. Whereas Galison had found disunity within a limited time and place, Crombie's six styles were based on his massive history of Western Science since the Greeks, disunity over 2,500 years. There is unity as well, based on science's commitment to argument and evidence, and its belief in rational causality (Crombie, 1994, p. 4), but no methodological essence to shore up the tree of knowledge, or justify the mission implied in "Unity of Science".

## Conclusion: different pseudosciences

We have explored how the technical use of "pseudoscience" is centred on a perceived threat to the security of science, or a sub-culture of science, or an interest threatened by another's scientific pretensions.

The reassurance achieved depends on asserting the accuser's own participation in the unity of science, as a branch of the tree of knowledge. One and the same process prunes the enemy from the tree, grafts the self to it. The threat is likely to be felt most strongly in the branches that are least secure in their status of science, like the least eligible members of a club that confers status on all its members equally. Pseudosciences themselves do not have an obvious unity. If they fall short as science it is in very different ways; there is not much in common between, for instance, psychoanalysis and dowsing, but they acquire a reflected unity by shared exclusion from a unified science.

So what if science is not a unity, if there is no tree of knowledge, and the technical sense of "pseudoscience" has little validity? What if the club is an illusion and the labels "science" and "pseudoscience" are like the badge saying "courage" given by the Wizard of Oz to the cowardly lion (which of course had effect, like a placebo). Each use of the word will then spring from the specific problems and insecurities of the sub-culture in question. We end by viewing pseudoscience from this point of view, and distinguish ten versions, ten aspects of pruning the fantas-tical tree of knowledge.

## False pretension to knowledge

The first pseudoscience is a subtle and disciplined system, often with a passion and an immediate relevance that could tempt the uncommit-ted student away from even the intellectually most exciting parts of science. It is a *Weltanschauung* that poses as an alternative vehicle of empirical knowledge. Marxism and psychoanalysis were the examples taken by Popper. The status of science itself is at stake. This is pruning the tree of knowledge with an axe.

## Degenerating research programme

Here the focus is less on alternative disciplines, than on a potential pathology within science itself, the demarcation "between scientific and pseudoscientific *adjustments*" (Lakatos, 1970, p. 117; emphasis in original). It is not an alien force, or a wilful attempt to gain from boast-ing scientific credentials, but a disease to which any science is prone in the absence of proper vigilance. This is detailed pruning of the tree, using sharp secateurs.

*Ideology*

This draws attention to exceptionally powerful areas of science that refuse to question flawed presuppositions shored up externally, and threaten to stifle progressive alternatives. This is not pruning, but unmasking a false gardener who is nurturing diseased branches.

*Going beyond the soluble*

Going beyond the soluble involves not being content with areas within reach of current scientific psychology, and instead speculating outside the boundaries. A firm but gentle trim is required, like guidance for students of psychology who yearn for something more dramatic.

*Individual cranky theories*

This use of "pseudoscience" fortifies the individual reader's sense of his or her rationality and allegiance to science. It is educational, warning the public that the outlawed branches should not be mistaken for science.

*Organised cranky theories*

This emerges out of "Individual cranky theories". The rejected branches have taken root and are getting out of control, so more drastic clearance is necessary.

*Dangers from within*

Pseudoscientific tendencies are in us all. The tree may itself become diseased, and more than pruning will be required if it is to survive.

*Unregulated medicine*

The label "pseudoscience" draws attention to failures or absence of regulation of patent medicines, and asserts the need for scientific standards against market lawlessness. Such disorder threatens both the public and established manufacturers. This is grafting regulation onto the tree, making it scientific.

## Unregulated therapy and cranky theory

This is the use by Herbert et al. (2000), and their pseudoscience is a mixture of organised cranky theories and unregulated medicine. They attack EMDR both for claiming but not demonstrating success as therapy (a regulation issue) and for the crankiness of their theory (a demarcation issue).

## Suppression of pluralism

Finally, we invent our own pseudoscientific psychology, reflecting our anxieties about the Truth Squad. William James is sometimes seen as the father of modern psychology, but his paternity is paradoxical since he founded no school. That may be because he was self-consciously a pluralist, interested in many psychological topics and tolerant of all (including some now excluded as pseudosciences). Psychology as a discipline, in spite of attempts to unify, has followed James in this respect. Disunity was his legacy. This is the source of psychology's scientific strength rather than a weakness, since the trading zones that follow from disunity are not just places for exchange, but also for fertilisation.[13] In which case a unified psychology, enforced by the Truth Squad, would deserve to be dismissed as a pseudoscience.

## Conclusions

We have looked at the different uses of the word "pseudoscience". We considered its origins in the emblematic tree of knowledge and later the twentieth-century demarcation debate, which attempted to lay down boundaries around a unified science. At the same time, the word was used in popular writings to distance science from cranky theories with scientific pretensions. We viewed the use of "pseudoscience" as an indication of changing anxieties about science and about being a scientist during the course of the twentieth century. The word has asserted the scientific credentials of the user at the same time as it denies these credentials to the pseudoscientist, and it is sometimes used in borderline areas like psychotherapy to crush the pretensions of rival practices. The urgency of this assertion has varied with the varying insecurities of the period and of the user. It dwindled around 1980 when philosophical attempts to find a formal demarcation petered out, and the growth of social constructivism denied science any special access to truth. The reaction to this led to the science wars in the 1990s, when a coalition of science marched to restore its privileges with a fundamentalist view of truth. This ushered in a new urgency in the use of "pseudoscience", especially from the least secure branches.

We argued that the technical use of "pseudoscience" implies a unity of science, a privileged tree of knowledge or space from which the pseudoscience is excluded, and the user's right to belong is asserted. By questioning this unity, recent writings potentially undermine the validity in its use (other than in the everyday rhetorical sense of an activity falsely claiming scientific status), and suggest that the comfort drawn from it is based on an illusion. From this sceptical viewpoint we concluded by summarising the different uses uncovered in this chapter.

In some respects, Ellis's REBT remained untouched by all this. He always acknowledged the scientific weaknesses of REBT, the lack of controlled trials, and the dependence upon a philosophy of demands that frames the model. Potentially, CBT is more vulnerable to the charge "pseudoscience" since its widespread success depends upon its scientific pretensions as a paragon of evidence-based practice. The attacks on EMDR as pseudoscience come from CBT practitioners and focus on the weaknesses of the evidence in published papers of supposedly controlled trials. This eagerness to establish boundaries suggests, according to the argument of this chapter, some insecurity on the part of the accusers. The insecurity is warranted. In this area, the standards for establishing a causal connection are a long way from the scientific foundations set up by Robert Koch over a hundred years ago. Outcome studies of CBT or any psychotherapy cannot even be double blind, since the members of the experimental group have obvious information to tell them which procedure they are undergoing. This is generally acknowledged, but it is argued that it is the best we can do even if it falls short of the gold standard provided by the double blind testing of medical drugs. But what if the standard itself turns out to be worth much less than its weight in the case of psychiatric drugs like anti-depressants? The evidence for an active placebo continues to mount (Kirsch, 2009). However, if the gold standard falls, then those invested in its methodology fall, too. REBT is freed of this risk. Its main investment has been in a different currency, shared with Epictetus, the effectiveness of a shared emancipatory reason common to client and therapist. This moral aspect will remain untouched even if the weaknesses of the methodology of psychiatric outcome studies become more obvious than they are, and bring the whole edifice of evidence-based practice down. The flip side of this lack of vulnerability has been the marginalisation of REBT, which is the topic of Chapter Nine. In the next chapter we look at a recent therapeutic technique that seems to have made itself at home in both discursive formations, the moral and the scientific. This is Kabat-Zinn's (1990) mindfulness, whose moral connections are undeniable, but which has managed to establish itself firmly as evidence-based practice, through outcomes studies using questionnaires backed up with physiological measures.

## Notes

1. "It is in fact pointless to attempt to articulate a principle delimiting the scientific from the non-scientific" (Newton-Smith, 1981, p. 91); "[T]here is no single satisfactory philosophical answer to the question of how to demarcate science from non-science" (Dolby, 1996, p. 162).
2. Typically, the pseudoscience is revealed by the absence of a list of ten qualities derived from Bunge (1984). Science, unlike pseudoscience, admits its own ignorance, advances knowledge by posing and solving new problems, welcomes new hypotheses and methods, has testable theories and hypotheses (always; pseudoscience only sometimes), looks for examples that contradict its beliefs, etc.
3. Hanen, Osler & Weyant (1980); Laudan (1983); Wallis (1979).
4. Discussed in Gieryn (1999).
5. Some writers spell "pseudoscience" with a hyphen: "pseudo-science". We have not pinned down a consistent pattern in this, although the inclusion of the hyphen seems more typical in "little pseudoscience" (e.g., Gardner, 1952; Young, 1961) than "big pseudoscience" (e.g., Blum, 1978; Cioffi, 1998). Time may also be a factor—the hyphen being dropped as the word became more familiar.
6. Blum (1978) called them grand pseudoscience and petit pseudoscience.
7. This was first published by Putnam as *In the Name of Science* (Gardner, 1952), but sold poorly; after being issued by Dover as *Facts and Fallacies in the Name of Science* it became a best-seller (Gardner, 2000, p. 3).
8. Popper did not dismiss such systems altogether (Popper, 1972, p. 37). Many writers who have taken psychoanalysis as a pseudoscience treat it as worthless (Bunge, 1967; van Rillaer, 1991), but there has also

been careful debate that has shed light on both psychoanalysis and demarcation (Cioffi, 1998; Grünbaum, 1984).

9. This was the principle of reflexivity, which was far from ignored by later sociologists of knowledge, discussed below.

10. The term "ideological" has been used by conservative thinkers to berate Marxists and others, but also by Marxists of those who act in the interests of their group or class, but believe they are disinterested (Williams, 1976). So Popper used it of Mannheim, and Mannheim might have cast it back with a different meaning.

11. Susan Stebbing (1944) is generally credited with having exposed the fallacy in Eddington's argument.

12. That is, the acceptance and publication by *Social Text* of scientist Alan Sokal's parody of postmodernist use of scientific language (Sokal & Bricmont, 1998).

13. Good (2000) describes this fertilisation between the two sub-disciplines of social psychology, in Psychology and in Sociology.

# CHAPTER EIGHT

# Historical aspects of mindfulness and self-acceptance in psychotherapy

*Introduction*

In this chapter, we describe some of the historical conditions that made possible Kabat-Zinn's (1990) very successful use of mindfulness in his stress management program and the subsequent extraordinary spread of this practice as it infiltrated psychotherapy in all its forms throughout America and Europe. The ground had been well prepared by the non-judgemental acceptance of people and symptoms by Humanistic psychotherapists, and by the increasing assimilation of Buddhist ideas into Western psychology and psychotherapy. There was little new in it, and in some ways Kabat-Zinn's work has been a brilliant exercise in pure entrepreneurship. He started a bandwagon and other therapists, including Albert Ellis, were quick to jump aboard. This was helped by a useful vagueness in the word. "Mindfulness", as the translation of the Pali *sati*, came to refer to both the manualised practice that provides the evidence for its efficacy in the hands of Kabat-Zinn and others, and the more complex process of clear comprehension and recollection that is described in his more discursive writings, and which is similar to Ellen Langer's use of "mindfulness" in her 1989 book of that name.

At the same time, it retained for many its origin at the heart of Buddhist meditation (Nyanaponika Thera, 1962).

## The present state of "mindfulness"

The English words "mindful" and "mindfulness" have been around in a modest way for over 300 years. They could belong to psychology, psychotherapy, or possibly ethics, but have played no serious part in the official discourse of these disciplines until around 1990, when they began to proliferate remarkably. They appeared vigorously from two directions simultaneously.

In 1989, Ellen Langer's use of "mindfulness" in the title and contents of her book (Langer, 1989) drew on the traditional English meaning of "taking heed or care: being conscious or aware" (Trumble & Stevenson, 2003); this is the dictionary's attempt to capture how the word is used, and Langer's own exploration of mindfulness has added to this by raising its profile within psychology and sharpening our sense of its possibilities. "Mindfulness" has close semantic links with memory and intention (such phrases as "I mind when we arrived" and "I'm minded to tell her" are still in use in some dialects), and is the opposite of mindlessness, of acting unthinkingly. Langer's work is in the mainstream tradition of experiments on thinking. Classical experiments in psychology showed how set or habit in problem solving can lead to a failure to see simple solutions to problems (Duncker, 1945; Luchins, 1942). Langer reported similar experiments, but her interest was more positive: less on the mindlessness that leads to mistakes and more on developing the mindfulness that can guard against such mistakes. The first paragraph of her book captures the spirit of this dramatically, by showing how the involved awareness promoted by mindfulness can actually prolong life:

> [T]he elderly residents of a nursing home were each given a choice of house plants to care for and were asked to make a number of small decisions about their daily routines. A year and a half later, not only were these people more cheerful, active and alert than a similar group in the same institutions who were not give these choices and responsibilities, but many more of them were still alive. In fact, less than half as many of the decision-making, plant-minding residents had died as had those in the other group.

(Langer, 1991, p. 13)

By being given choices and responsibilities, they were stimulated into a more mindful approach to life. This is psychology, but it also places mindfulness firmly within an ethical context, as an Aristotelian requirement for living a good life (Chapter Five), rather than with an emphasis on obeying a moral code.

The second appearance of "mindfulness" was largely through the therapeutic work of Jon Kabat-Zinn (1990); it was for a different audience and in a different style and has been far more dramatic in its impact than the academic research of Langer. During the 1980s Kabat-Zinn took the word "mindfulness" from its specialist use in Western Buddhism, and in his scientific publications he has focused on mindfulness as a practice or technique. He defined it as "paying attention in a particular way: on purpose, in the present moment, and nonjudgmentally" (Kabat-Zinn, 1994, p. 4). With this at the core, he created mindfulness-based stress reduction (MBSR), initially for the treatment of chronic pain. The training includes a body scan, walking meditation, yoga exercises, and awareness in daily life, in which the participant learns to be mindful of everyday activities; these are drawn from a number of sources, including Buddhist practitioners Jack Kornfield, Joseph Goldstein (Goldstein & Kornfield, 1987), and Thich Nhat Hanh (1991; first published 1975). This formed the basis of the stress management program at the University of Massachusetts, with its own specialised training, research, publicity literature, tapes, and workshops throughout the world. Its success has been outstanding. By specifying exactly the techniques used (by "manualising" mindfulness) Kabat-Zinn was able to carry out controlled and replicable outcome studies, sometimes using physiological measures of change, and to put MBSR and therefore mindfulness firmly within the tradition of scientific psychotherapy. Such success is more than a matter of scientific demonstration. There have been comparable demonstrations of the physiological and therapeutic effects of transcendental meditation (Wallace, 1970) and other forms of meditation (West, 1979) but although these have played a part in the popularity of these practices, they have not achieved the widespread acceptance and respectability of MBSR as "evidence-based practice". Nowadays, such success involves a number of other factors, including an energetic and charismatic leader, the presentation and publication of papers addressed to an appropriately critical audience (who are ready to receive the innovation), and endorsement by a powerful academic institution. These factors came together in the 1990s.

As well as establishing MBSR as evidence-based practice, Kabat-Zinn has gone beyond this in many of his publications, which have a discursive, uplifting edge addressed to a wider audience. His scientific work is about the teachable technique of mindfulness and its therapeutic benefits, but his more general writings have also looked towards mindfulness as the lasting state of mind which results from the practice, and at the potential benefits of this at personal, social, and political levels (Kabat-Zinn, 2005).

In MBSR, Kabat-Zinn had thus selected a technique that could apparently be isolated from its context in Buddhist practice, and applied where appropriate. He was open about the origin of the practice in Buddhism, but equally clear that his stress management program was not a part of Buddhism. It stands on its own (although anyone with a knowledge of modern Buddhism would recognise the word "mindfulness"), and this probably made it easier for Marsha Linehan (1993a) to incorporate Kabat-Zinn's mindfulness into her Dialectical Behaviour Therapy. It enabled people with Borderline Personality Disorder to step back and choose, rather than be carried away by powerful thoughts and feelings. She captured this state of "decentering" in a Venn diagram in which "wise mind" emerges from the overlap between "reasonable mind" and "emotional mind" (Linehan, 1993b, p. 109). Later John Teasdale, Zindel Segal, and Mark Williams adapted MBSR to create their "Mindfulness-based Cognitive Therapy" (MBCT) for the treatment of recurrent depression. Their scientific reputation as researchers into the structure and efficacy of Cognitive Behaviour Therapy (CBT) was very solid, and their espousal of Kabat-Zinn's mindfulness has played a big part in making it a widely acceptable part of the clinical psychologist's repertoire of evidence-based practice.

Encountering Marsha Linehan's work, they were struck by the way mindfulness would (on their information-processing model (Teasdale, Segal & Williams, 1995)) interfere with the spiralling cycles between thought and affect, and enable patients to recognise them and take appropriate action as they appeared. In this way, patients liable to bouts of depression should be able to avoid them, even without the application of CBT. Since it can be taught in groups, it is less costly than the one-to-one meetings usual with CBT. They contacted Kabat-Zinn, and have reproduced parts of letters written at the time (Segal et al., 2002, p. 44). They were conscious of the link with Buddhism, but whereas Segal was uneasy with the possible connection with meditation,

Teasdale welcomed Kabat-Zinn's "ability to extract the essence of Buddhist meditation and to translate it into a format that is accessible and clearly very effective in helping the average U.S. Citizen" (Segal et al., 2002, p. 44).

These modern investigators of mindfulness as therapy all report successful outcome studies. They are in the tradition of scientific psychotherapy, which owes allegiance to science and evidence-based practice, and has its origin in the behaviour therapy of the 1960s and the cognitive therapies a few years later. One significant break with this tradition was reported in Segal et al. (2002). At first, following an initial brief visit to Kabat-Zinn's stress management clinic, they achieved only partial success with what they called "attentional control training". Something was missing, and returning to the clinic, they realised that they had under-estimated the importance of instructors having their own mindfulness practice. Participants learn partly through their own practice, but also through the way the instructor is able to embody mindfulness in the class. Taking this on board, they committed themselves to regular mindfulness meditation practice, and moved on to the "Mindfulness-based Cognitive Therapy" (MBCT) which became the theme of their book. This shift seems convincing, and few would dispute this need for personal practice, but it has not been scientifically demonstrated. It was not tested by the exemplary randomised control usual in the work of these researchers, and it is possible that the use of the word "mindfulness" already had a resonance for many people (clients and therapists) that gave the practice a power lacking in "attentional control training". Whatever the reason, this was an important change and personal mindfulness practice is now a routine requirement for trainers in mindfulness.

During the 1980s other writers in this tradition were converging on practices similar to mindfulness. Steven Hayes had already developed techniques for developing awareness and acceptance, acknowledging a general debt to Buddhism (Hayes, 1984; Hayes, Strosahl & Wilson, 1999), but he did not originally use the word "mindfulness". Marlatt (2002) has used mindfulness in his work on addictions, and like Segal et al. (2002) has continued to present this within a CBT framework, although he has been more explicit about the Buddhist connection, and the difference this makes. Adrian Wells (1997, p. 31) was using the term "metacognition" in his studies of anxiety and its treatment. This is drawn from developmental psychology not Buddhism, but as Wells recognised it is similar to mindfulness in its decentering and the calm observation of inner thought processes and feelings.

The methods of all these and more recent writers share one striking feature. Instead of attacking symptoms as essentially negative and undesirable, the emphasis is on a non-judgemental acceptance of symptoms, and a focus on more positive alternatives. A similar pattern, without an emphasis on mindfulness itself, has arisen recently amongst a number of other workers in this tradition of scientific psychological therapy (Davidson, 2002; Gilbert, 2005; Padesky, 2004; Seligman, 2002).

The popularity of mindfulness thus seems to be part of a general movement in scientifically based psychotherapy. The contrast between this work of the last fifteen years and the practices as they were forty years ago is remarkable. At that time, behaviour therapy was still dominant as scientific therapy, and aversion therapy was the therapy of choice for many symptoms. Symptoms were not accepted non-judgementally, but targeted like any medical symptom and eradicated through punishment, or modified through shaping. In one of his earlier papers, John Teasdale (1976) described aversion therapy given to a patient with a compulsive urge to masturbate in public places. In his careful, self-critical discussion, Teasdale acknowledged that the formulation opening the way to this treatment was probably incorrect, since it ignored the social difficulties at the root of the problem; this suggests the beginnings of the shift in thinking towards acceptance of symptoms and adoption of alternative strategies.

In behaviour therapy and early CBT, the roles of therapist and patient were clearly distinct. Unlike the trainer in mindfulness, the aversion therapist was not expected to undergo the electric shocks given to the patient, and cognitive therapists were not usually expected to receive a course of CBT as part of their training. Once the patient's assent was given, the therapist was the expert, the master of ceremonies in charge of therapeutic activities, just as the physician's role is that of expert, dispensing diagnoses and medicine, in order to remove symptoms directly or by changing the underlying cause. The treatments of most psychiatry and scientific psychology were the same in this respect. When Aaron Beck (1963) introduced his version of cognitive therapy (CBT) he offered it as a new psychiatric hypothesis. Previously depression had been described as a disorder of affect, by contrast with schizophrenia, which is a disorder of thinking. Beck's novel suggestion was that depression also is a disorder of thinking, and not primarily of affect. To get rid of the symptoms, therefore, it was necessary to attack the cause, the dysfunctional thinking. The contrast with Ellis (1958) was subtle and blurred but significant (Chapter Nine). For Ellis the causes of unhealthy or inappropriate emotions and actions were irrational beliefs, to which we are all liable, since they are innate (Ellis, 1994). The therapeutic dialogue, therefore, is between fellow sufferers, rather than between the healthy expert and the unhealthy patient.

Contemporary with this hard-nosed scientific psychotherapy of the 1960s and 1970s, there were other emerging approaches with different allegiances. These were part of humanistic psychology, heralded as the third force offering an alternative to the reductionism of either psychoanalysis or behaviour therapies. Humanistic psychology in general was holistic and focused on the creative potential of the client, rather than removal of symptoms due to conditioning or to persisting fixations from childhood. In addition, sometimes allied to or part of a humanistic approach, there were specifically Buddhist influences in psychology and psychotherapy. Both the humanistic and the Buddhist approaches showed the non-judgemental acceptance now playing a part in scientific psychotherapy.[1] Viewing both together, we will see that some of the important ingredients for mindfulness practice were present within a humanistic tradition of psychotherapy. If the practice did not mushroom into what it has become following the work of Kabat-Zinn, that may be partly because the conditions for intellectual credit had not yet been achieved. The new applied psychologist, wishing to make a steady career in the mainstream, needs to be careful in his or her alliances. Behaviour therapy and psychoanalysis were reliable investments at that time, leading to well-defined careers, whereas the progress of a psychologist or psychotherapist committed to a humanistic approach was less certain.

## Precursors of Kabat-Zinn's mindfulness: non-judgemental acceptance in the humanistic tradition

The humanistic movement was a loose alliance between psychologists turned philosopher such as Rollo May (1969) and Abraham Maslow (1971), and psychotherapists. The humanistic psychotherapist looked for personal transformation instead of symptom relief as the end result of successful therapy, which was brought about through awareness and acceptance.

This contrast was expressed clearly by Irvin Yalom, in a comparison of two patients, both middle-aged women whose children had just left home. Each had been looking forward to this event, but now found themselves unexpectedly anxious and empty. For one the treatment results are excellent: "with the help of Valium, supportive psychotherapy, an assertiveness training women's group, several adult education courses, a lover or two, and a part-time volunteer job ... She returns to her 'premorbid' level of comfort and adaptation" (Yalom, 1980, p. 166). The other, through a dream, comes to recognise that: "Time moves on ... and there's no way I can stop it. I didn't want John to grow up. I really treasured those years when he was with us. Yet whether I like it or not, time moves on. It moves on for John and it moves on for me as well. It is a terrible thing to understand, to really understand." Yalom comments: "She had moved into the realm that Heidegger describes as authentic being: she wondered not at the *way* things are but *that* things are. In my judgement, therapy helped the second patient more than the first. It would not be possible to demonstrate this conclusion by standard outcome measures; in fact the second patient probably continued to experience more anxiety than the first" (Yalom, 1980, p. 167; emphasis in original). In the first, there is symptom relief, in the second personal transformation, through acceptance. It is clear that Yalom, as a humanistic psychotherapist, saw more value in the latter.

Carl Rogers was probably the most prominent psychotherapist in the humanistic movement. His core conditions, especially unconditional positive regard, were designed to create a situation of acceptance, in which the client could be free to explore his or her thoughts and feelings without fear of criticism and with the certainty of being listened to and treated as a uniquely important human being. Symptoms were not treated medically by Rogers, but clients were allowed to explore their signficance in relation to the person as a whole, in order to achieve what Maslow had called "self-actualization" (Maslow, 1971, p. 42). The approach was therefore holistic, rather than symptom-oriented like behaviour therapy and early forms of CBT.

One early champion of Rogers' style of therapy was the General Semanticist Hayakawa (1952), whose *Language in Thought and Action* was popular with a wide audience. Korzybski's General Semantics was perhaps the first popular modern movement to explore in detail the way feeling is influenced by words and thinking, and has had an influence on cognitive therapy (see Chapter Three; and Still & Dryden,

1998) which is largely unrecognised, perhaps because his holistic, speculative approach had little appeal to the scientific psychology of the time. Words often contain judgements, and it is negative judgements that lead directly to emotional disorders. This was illustrated in Chapter Three by Hayakawa's example of the judgement involved in "I am only a filling-station attendant". Hayakawa drew on Rogers' theory of self-concepts, as "realistic" or "unrealistic". Therapy consists in self-actualisation through recognising and rejecting unrealistic self-concepts, and building realistic self-concepts to replace them. Rogerian therapy provided the secure, non-judgemental emotional environment in which the client can investigate and change self-concepts, and develop self-acceptance.

Another General Semanticist (and psychologist), Wendell Johnson, developed a treatment for stuttering, which he saw as partly the result of the critical label "stutterer" given to speech hesitations. The child so labelled anxiously struggles to avoid hesitations, and the speech therapists of the time reinforced this self-critical labelling. In Johnson's therapy the stutterer was encouraged to "deliberately imitate his own stuttering", which leads to the development of "a forthright, unhurried, deliberate performance of what would otherwise be done under protest and with tension" (Johnson, 1946, pp. 462–463; see Chapter Three).

This is an early version of what Viktor Frankl, another major humanistic psychotherapist, called "paradoxical intention".

> [P]aradoxical intention … is based on the fact that a certain amount of pathogenesis in phobias and obsessive-compulsive neurosis is due to the increase of anxieties and compulsions caused by the endeavour to avoid or fight them. Paradoxical intention consists in a reversal of the patient's attitude towards his symptom and enables him to detach himself from his neurosis.
>
> (Frankl, 1967, p. 155)

Thus if a patient cannot sleep, Frankl advised the patient to try to stay awake as long as possible. Or a patient whose problem was excessive sweating was advised "to resolve deliberately to show the people whom he confronted at the time just how much he could really sweat" (Frankl, 1967, p. 139)—this entails a form of non-judgemental acceptance of the symptom. Frankl described the spiralling that leads to intense anxiety and other symptoms, and how paradoxical intention breaks the spiral by recruiting the uniquely human capacity for "self-detachment" and humour. It has sometimes been used simply as a weapon against troublesome symptoms, but Frankl viewed it as something deeper, leading to a transformation which he called a "restoration of basic trust in Being" resulting in "existential reorientation" (Frankl, 1967, p. 148). Like Yalom, his thinking derived from existentialism and phenomenology, which "speaks the language of man's prereflective self-understanding rather than interpreting a given phenomenon after preconceived patterns" (Frankl, 1967, p. 14). This echoes the call of Edmund Husserl, the founder of phenomenology, to go "back to the things themselves", in his technique of *epoché* or bracketing the world by suspending judgement, which has interesting affinities with mindfulness (Segall, 2003, p. 80).

Given that *Gestalt* is the German for "whole", it is not surprising that Gestalt Therapy, with its explicit emphasis on creative activity, was firmly within the humanistic tradition. Perls, Hefferline, and Goodman (1951) set out to correct the neglect of the role of the body in psychological disorder (even by Korzybski; Perls, Hefferline & Goodman, 1950, p. xii). The first part of the book described a number of exercises or experiments in self-awareness, designed to bring to consciousness the thoughts and bodily activities which were regarded as setting up unconscious blocks to contact with the social and physical environment. These experiments were designed by Ralph Hefferline, who had been a student of B. F. Skinner. Skinner (1945) had written on how private events can be brought under stimulus control, and Hefferline became well known for his demonstration of how unconscious muscular movements can enter awareness by linking them with a visible or auditory consequence (Hefferline, 1958). This was one of the foundations of biofeedback. In the Gestalt exercises, participants were given a series of instructions, not as tasks or tests to carry out with the risk of failure, but as experiments, to explore and see what happens. The first was:

> Try for a few minutes to make up sentences stating what you are at this moment aware of. Begin each sentence with the words "now" or "at this moment" or "here and now".
>
> (Perls, Hefferline & Goodman, 1972, p. 31)

These and other instructions set up a process akin to mindfulness as defined by Kabat-Zinn (on purpose, in the present moment, non-judgementally), although the deliberately exploratory and investigatory set may differ significantly from the more passive awareness of Kabat-Zinn's mindfulness. The non-judgemental aspect was spelt out clearly a few years later by another Gestalt therapist, Beisser (1972, p. 88), whose "Paradoxical Theory of Change" was

> That change occurs when one becomes what he is, not when he tries to become what he is not ... The person seeking change ... is constantly moving between what he "should be" and what he thinks he "is", never fully identifying with either. The Gestalt therapist asks the person to invest himself fully in his roles, one at a time ... The behaviorist therapist rewards or punishes behaviour in order to modify it. The Gestalt therapist believes in encouraging the patient to enter and become whatever he is experiencing at the moment.

> (Beisser, 1972, pp. 88–89; author's emphasis)

This entails awareness and acceptance, suspending judgement about what you are, your feelings and thoughts, at any moment.

Although he might not have been happy with the label, R.D. Laing belongs here. In a famous passage in *The Divided Self*, he analysed the reported demonstration by Emil Kraepelin of a patient showing the signs of catatonic excitement. Kraepelin wrote that in his replies to questions, the patient *"has not given us a single piece of useful information. His talk was ... only a series of disconnected sentences having no relation whatever to the general situation"* (cited in Laing, 1965, p. 30; Laing's emphasis). Laing pointed out how easily sense can be made of the patient's replies as the outbursts of an extremely distressed eighteen year-old being exhibited as a psychiatric case before a lecture room of students. He drew a famous conclusion: *"Sanity or psychosis is tested by the degree of conjunction or disjunction between two persons where the one is sane by common consent"* (Laing, 1965, p. 36; original emphasis). To understand, we need to understand the whole person in context, to accept what is said and done without judgement in order to understand; and without the preconception that the psychiatrist is sane, the patient mad.

Albert Ellis himself was another precursor (Ellis, 2006), in his advocacy of non-judgemental self-acceptance, which is part of his humanistic view of people

> As holistic goal-directed individuals who have importance in the world just because they are human and alive. It unconditionally accepts them with their limitations, and it particularly focuses

upon their experiences and values, including their self-actualizing potentialities ... Although CBT (like behavior therapy ...) is usually humanistically oriented, it does not have to be, while a humanistic outlook is intrinsic to REBT.

(Ellis, 1994, pp. 248–249)

It is intrinsic because of Ellis's stress on the client's self-acceptance, and the possibility of philosophical change (a form of transformation), which follow from his view of the self as logically impossible to evaluate. There is nothing like this in the early work of CBT, although it is not excluded.

The writers considered in this section differed in many respects, but all advocated, like mindfulness as defined by Kabat-Zinn, an attitude of calm awareness and acceptance towards symptoms, and the development of creative alternatives. This is not the same as resignation, since acceptance is a prelude to change, but it is different from the traditional medical attitude of treating symptoms from the start as ills to be removed. The popularity of this tradition in psychotherapy suggests a receptive audience waiting in the wings for any valid technique incorporating these principles. Most of the humanistic psychotherapists referred to above were familiar with and probably influenced by Buddhist ideas, although this is rarely made explicit in their theory or practice. There were, however, psychologists and psychotherapists whose debt to Buddhism was much clearer.

## Precursors of Kabat-Zinn's mindfulness: Western Buddhism

Buddhism has been spreading in the West for well over 100 years, but after World War II there was an explosion of interest, especially in Zen Buddhism, and especially in the States. This was partly a result of the war itself, as American psychiatrists and others stationed in Japan after the war came back with an interest in aspects of Japanese culture, including Zen (Jacobson & Berenberg, 1952). They were especially interested in the psychotherapy of Shoma Morita.

During the first half of the twentieth century, Morita developed a psychotherapy based on Zen Buddhism that reversed the Western medical approach of attacking the symptoms. His therapy was created to deal with what was seen as a peculiarly Japanese problem, *Shinkeishitsu*. The patient

Is a person with a particularly strong need to lead a full life, perfectionist tendencies, and extreme self-consciousness … This person encounters some unpleasant event that focuses his attention on a particular problem; blushing, headaches, and constipation are typical examples … He becomes caught in a spiral of attention and sensitivity which produces a kind of obsessive self-consciousness. His efforts to overcome the problem directly by his will serve only to exacerbate his fixation.

(Reynolds, 1976, pp. 9–10)

Treatment is based on two principles, which are essentially two aspects of mindfulness as it had evolved in Japan: *arugamama* or acceptance of feelings and of the self as it is experienced; and *muga* or absorption in tasks (Jacobson & Berenberg, 1952). Morita therapy has had little influence, although it has been developed in the States by David Reynolds (1976), and was investigated by Karen Horney as part of her interest in Zen Buddhism and a visit to Japan near the end of her life (Morvay, 1999).

This direct contact between Japanese and Western psychiatrists and therapists was important, but the main impact of Zen Buddhism around 1950 lay in the widespread appeal of its principles and practices to a new public seeking alternative lifestyles (Fields, 1992). Zen offered freedom from suffering by calm acceptance and self-transformation, rather than by changing the world. Many writers in the 1950s and 1960s celebrated this as preferable to the more active Western approach to suffering. One of the most prominent was Alan Watts, whose writings and talks on Zen and Psychotherapy (published in Watts, 1961) and his *The Wisdom of Insecurity* (1951) advocated an acceptance of the present through an "awareness (which) is a view of reality free from ideas and judgments" (Watts, 1951, p. 70). This is mindfulness, like the "choiceless awareness" of another influential champion of Eastern spirituality of the time, Krishnamurti, although neither Watts nor Krishnamurti refers to it as "mindfulness". In his preface to Krishnamurti (1954), Aldous Huxley was fulsome about the radical nature of this reflective practice that withholds judgement.

Where there is judgement, where there is comparison and condemnation, openness of mind is absent; there can be no freedom from the tyranny of symbols and systems, no escape from the past and the environment ... There is a transcendent spontaneity of life, a "creative reality", as Krishnamurti calls it, which reveals itelf as immanent only when the perceiver's mind is in a state of "alert passivity", of "choiceless awareness".

(from Huxley's preface to Krishnamurti, 1954, pp. 16–17)

That is the mindfulness of *arugamama*, or acceptance, but *muga*, absorption in activities, has been even more popular. Eugen Herrigel's *Zen in the Art of Archery* appeared in English in 1953 (Herrigel, 1953), and its title has proved a prolific prototype, from *Zen in the Art of Flower-Arrangement* (Herrigel, 1958), through Robert M. Pirsig's (1974) famous novel, *Zen and the Art of Motorcycle Maintenance*, to the recently published *Zen and the Art of Crossword Puzzles* by Nikki Katz (2006). These and many others each advocate a mindful absorption in the activity of its title.

The interest in Zen Buddhism attracted teachers from Japan, and one of the most important was Shuryu Suzuki, who arrived in the States in 1958. In 1970, his oral teachings were collected in *Zen Mind, Beginner's Mind*. They described the Soto Zen meditation practice of "just sitting" with instructions often to focus loosely on breath, and to notice thoughts and feelings without judgement as they come and go. It is a vivid expression of mindfulness of sitting, although again the word "mindfulness" (unlike "meditation") was not used by Suzuki.

The more general history of the relationship between Buddhism and Western psychology has been described by Rick Fields (1992), where he traces the spread of Zen Buddhism after World War II, then the later popularity of Tibetan Buddhism, and of the Theravadan school, which contained in its scriptures, written in Pali, the most explicit accounts of mindfulness. The Western Buddhist word "mindfulness" was not in common usage in English until the publication in 1962 of Nyanoponika Thera's *The Heart of Buddhist Meditation*; this made many of the best-known Buddhist texts on mindfulness available in English. But even then, it did not achieve much of a life of its own, independent of the more general word "meditation",[2] except amongst Buddhists, until the mid-1970s and the publication of two books: Thich Nhat Hanh's *The Miracle of Mindfulness* (1976), which was a brief and compelling account of mindfulness in everyday life, and Daniel Goleman's *The Varieties of the Meditative Experience* (1977), which was psychological in orientation, but written for and read by a much larger audience, and gave a clear account of the meditation of different schools, with the word "mindfulness" prominent and clearly distinguished from the more general "meditation".

Throughout this period, from 1945 to the present, there were increasing attempts to find common ground between Buddhism and psychology or psychotherapy. Initially these were at a relatively abstract or speculative level (Murphy & Murphy, 1968; Spiegelman & Miyuki, 1985; Suzuki, Fromm & Martino, 1963; Tart, 1969, 1975; Watts, 1961), but later attempts have been by psychotherapists or psychologists who are also seasoned Buddhist practitioners (Brazier, 1995; Claxton, 1986; Crook & Fontana, 1990; Epstein, 1995; Germer, Siegel & Fulton, 2005; Katz, 1983; Safran, 2003; Varela, Thompson & Rosch, 1993). Following the books by Goleman and Thich Nhat Hanh, "mindfulness" has appeared increasingly, often being addressed as a topic in its own right. Mindfulness and psychotherapy were brought together in a brief essay by Deatherage (1980), around the time Kabat-Zinn's more far-reaching use of "mindfulness" began.

It appears from his writings that Kabat Zinn's immediate debt is to Buddhism rather than to these manifestations of mindfulness in the humanistic tradition. He has described his involvement with Buddhist teachers, especially Zen, from the mid-1960s. The influence that we are suggesting, is not so much directly on Kabat-Zinn, but on those many psychologists and psychotherapists trained in a strictly evidence-based tradition, yet tempted by the accepting, nurturing approach offered by the humanistic tradition. It is they, or their successors who have been some of the willing customers of Kabat-Zinn's application of mindfulness.

We have considered two important conditions that made possible Kabat-Zinn's use of mindfulness in MBSR, and then the success of this mindfulness within CBT and other scientifically based therapies. First, there was the development of the alternative humanistic tradition, with its accepting, non-judgemental approach, and its calm attentiveness to the person as a whole, rather than a concentration on presenting symptoms. To some extent, this seems at odds with the scientific symptom-oriented approach, but the approach had a strong appeal to many people drawn to the caring professions, like applied psychology and psychotherapy. There was thus a ready audience receptive for anyone bold enough to bridge the gap, not just in theory, but in carefully worked out practice. Some psychotherapies, such as Steven Hayes' ACT (Hayes, Strosahl & Wilson, 1999), were already bridging the gap between hard-nosed science and humanistic therapy with Buddhism, when Kabat-Zinn captured this possibility in a manualised version of mindfulness.

However, his inspired use of the word and the practice were made possible by a different kind of condition, not just the intellectual influence and the receptive audience, but the selection a century ago of the word "mindfulness" as translation for the Pali word *sati*.

## The translation of "sati" and "sampajanna"

"Mindfulness" is now the commonly accepted translation of the word *sati*, from the Pali, which is the language in which the early Buddhist texts were written down, including the discourses in the *Suttas*. The seventh factor of the Noble Eightfold path is *samma-sati*, translated as "Right Mindfulness", and the practice is described in the discourses on "the Foundations of Mindfulness" or *satipatthana*. However, it was only after some debate around 100 years ago that the word "mindfulness" was chosen as the best rendering. *Sati* is the Pali equivalent of the Sanskrit *smrti*, which is usually translated as "memory". However, *sati* also carries the connotation of attention, and to capture this complex of meanings one of the translators into English of the Buddhist Pali texts, had originally chosen "self-possession" as the best translation in English[3] (Rhys David, 1895–1910). Eventually he settled on "mindfulness" and this carried the day, although in the widely read *Buddhist Bible* (Goddard, 1956, p. 47) the word "attention" was used; Christmas Humphreys (1951, pp. 116–117) used "concentration" and "recollection" in his popular introduction to Buddhism; and the Pali scholar Warder (1974, p. 411) offered "self-possession" as well as "mindfulness" as a translation of *sati*.

To complicate matters, *sati* is frequently linked with *sampajanna* in the Pali Buddhist writings. Sampajanna is sometimes translated as "awareness", so *sati-sampajanna* becomes "mindfulness and awareness", as though awareness is not automatically included as part of mindfulness. Nanavira Thera suggested that if *sati* is to be translated as "mindfulness",

> While it is not different from mindfulness, awareness is rather more specialized in meaning. Mindfulness is general recollectedness, not being scatter-brained; whereas awareness is more precisely *keeping oneself under constant observation*, not letting one's actions (or thoughts, or feelings, etc.) pass unnoticed.

> (Nanavira Thera, 1987, p. 155; original emphasis)

This sense of mindfulness (not being scatter-brained, general recollectedness) is close to that of Ellen Langer, and includes the meanings looked for in the early debate, especially self-possession. In practice, it seems that both these (recollectedness and self-observation) are referred to by "mindfulness" in the Buddhist literature in English.

Nyanaponika Thera[4] construed these Pali words in a rather different way in his *The Heart of Buddhist Meditation*, which is the major source for English translations of the Buddhist discourses on mindfulness. He translated *sati* as "mindfulness", and sometimes as "bare attention", a phrase that he introduced. But clearly the *state of mind* described in the *suttas* is more than bare attention. The mindfulness state of mind includes "clear comprehension" (which is his translation of *sampajanna*), which applies to everyday activities. His respective translations of *sati* and *sampajanna* are therefore almost the reverse of Nanavira Thera. In practice, he used "mindfulness" to refer both to what he sometimes referred to as "bare attention", and to the more general clear comprehension. Bare attention "provides the key to the distinctive method of *Satipatthana*, and accompanies the systematic practice of it, from its very beginning to the achievement of its highest goal" (Nyanoponika Thera, 1962, p. 30). This equation of the two accords with the modern Burmese method of meditation, which was taught in Sri Lanka where Nyanaponika Thera took up residence, rather than with the *suttas* themselves. It has made it possible for Kabat-Zinn to use the same word both for his manualised practice, and for the much more general process of knowing the self and the world, described in his discursive writings.

It is what Teasdale referred to as the "essence" of Buddhist meditation. However, in itself it is not the same as the Pali *sati* seen through the eyes of Rhys David 100 years ago, or Nanaviri Thera and others more recently. That (and Kabat-Zinn's more general process of knowing) may be closer to the mindfulness of Ellen Langer.

*Technological progress and the search for wisdom*

In a recent book, Kabat-Zinn quotes William James at the head of a chapter on the power of attention, arranging the lines to turn James's flowing prose into a poem.

> *The faculty of voluntarily bringing back a wandering attention,*
> *over and over again, is the very root of judgment, character and will.*
> *No one is* compos sui *if he have it not.*
> *An education which should improve this faculty*
> *would be the education par excellence.*
> *But it is easier to define this ideal*
> *than to give practical instruction for bringing it about.*

(Kabat-Zinn, 2005, p. 115)

He comments:

> William James obviously didn't know about the practice of mind-fulness when he penned the passage on the preceding page, but I am sure he would have been delighted to have discovered that there was indeed an education for improving the faculty of voluntarily bringing back a wandering attention over and over again.

(Kabat-Zinn, 2005, p. 118)

But James read widely and it is risky to claim that he "obviously didn't know" or is at a loss about something. The quote is from his chapter on attention in *The Principles of Psychology*. He would certainly have been interested, but would have wanted evidence that the specific training offered by Kabat-Zinn is not only, as the Buddha urged, the sole way to *nirvana*, or, as Kabat-Zinn and others have shown, an effective technique for stress management, but also a better way to academic success than James's own suggestion for improving the faculty of attention, which was to

> [i]nduct [the pupil] ... in such a way as to knit each new thing on to some acquisition already there; and if possible awaken curiosity, so that the new thing shall seem to come as an answer, or part of an answer to a question pre-existing in his mind.

(James, 1890, p. 424)

This was James's suggestion for producing a state that is close to the mindfulness Langer had in mind:

> Focalization, concentration, of consciousness are of its essence. It implies withdrawal from some things in order to deal effectively with others, and is a condition which has a real opposite in the confused, dazed, scatterbrained state which in French is called *distraction*, and *Zerstreutheit* in German.
>
> (James, 1890, p. 404; emphasis in original)

James was also aware of Buddhism[5] and more generally of meditation. In *Talks to Teachers on Psychology*, he recalled visitors from India ("Hindoos") at Harvard.

> More than one of them has confided to me that the sight of our faces, all contracted as they are with the habitual American over-intensity and anxiety of expression, and our ungraceful and distorted attitudes when sitting, made on him a very painful impression. "I do not see," said one, "how it is possible for you to live as you do, without a single minute in your day deliberately given to tranquility and meditation. It is an invariable part of our Hindoo life to retire for at least half an hour daily into silence, to relax our muscles, govern our breathing, and meditate on eternal things. Every Hindoo child is trained to this from a very early age" ... I felt that my countrymen were depriving themselves of an essential grace of character ... from its reflex influence on the inner mental states, this ceaseless over-tension, over-motion, and over-expression are working on us grievous national harm.
>
> (James, 1899, pp. 74–75)

James's audience would not have been surprised at this appeal to the culture of the East in the search for a different, less frenzied, and wiser way of life. The argument was already familiar from the writings of German Romantic thinkers, beginning with Herder, the Schlegels (who translated some of the Sanskrit texts), and Schelling (Sedlar, 1982) and the American Transcendentalists, starting with Emerson and Thoreau (Fields, 1992). His education and his interests linked James closely to both traditions, which looked for the essence of spirituality within individual experience. But it was not just a search for peace, a more relaxed lifestyle, or a cure for stress, but for a different way of knowing, more harmonious with nature than the masterful manner of science and technology. In different ways, they looked to know reality more directly than through the dogmas of Christianity and its institutions, or latterly of science. They were unhappy with the implications of the Cartesian view of the world as a physical machine, which had set philosophers and psychologists endless employment on the problem of translating between the language of physics and the language of mind and human morality. James himself made an important break with the Cartesian tradition when he defined sensations and their physical correlates as having a structure that is not part of their physical description (Reed, 1997), and this was taken further by Husserl and Heidegger, and by Dewey in his theory of enquiry and knowing (Still & Good, 1998). This tradition was drawn on by the humanistic psychologists and psycho-therapists in their attempts to undermine the restrictive definitions of self and world that block the individual's self-actualisation. The poten-tial result is a different kind of knowing.

Kabat-Zinn's mindfulness too is not just about stress management, but about a different way of knowing, and in his more recent writings he goes further and makes it embrace all-knowing in its direct contact with things as they actually are.

> There are many ways of knowing. Mindfulness subsumes and includes them all ... Mindfulness is valued, perhaps not by that name, but by its qualities, in virtually all contemporary and ancient cultures. Indeed, one might say that our lives and our very pres-ence here have depended on the clarity of mind as mirror and its refined capacity to reflect, contain, encounter, and know with great fidelity things as they actually are.
>
> (Kabat-Zinn, 2005, p. 111)

He took the mirror metaphor from a Western Buddhist teacher, Joseph Goldstein, and it is a common image, especially in Zen. But it is also familiar as a metaphor for knowing in Western metaphysics, where it has different associations. It is part of representational realism, where knowing is not direct but based on a construction from inputs described in the language of physics. The difficulties with this metaphysical framework, and the mirror metaphor that goes with it, are discussed in Rorty (1980).

So whatever the value of Kabat-Zinn's insights about mindfulness, problems can arise when he tries to express them in words that are tangled in the thicket of Western metaphysics. A much earlier writer, who was well aware of these difficulties, and who had read closely both Emerson, and the Buddhist translations available to him, wrote:

> Learning to *see*—habituating the eye to repose, to patience, to letting things come to it; learning to defer judgement, to investigate and comprehend the individual case in all its aspects. This is the *first* preliminary schooling in spirituality: *not* to react immediately to a stimulus, but to have the restraining, stock-taking instincts in one's control. Learning to *see*, as I understand it, is almost what is called in unphilosophical language, "strong will-power"; the essence of it is precisely *not* to "will", the *ability* to defer decision. All unspirituality, all vulgarity, is due to the incapacity to resist a stimulus—one *has* to react, one obeys every impulse.
>
> (Nietzsche, 1968, p. 65; original emphasis. The German version was first published in 1889)[6]

This is not bare attention, nor is it the mindfulness technique manualised by Kabat-Zinn and others, but it includes these and captures mindfulness as a way of knowing that differs from the more active controlling and socially organised way characteristic of science. This is not to say that it does not occur in science, or indeed in war, as Langer illustrated with her comparison of the patient mindfulness of the old Russian general Kutuzov pitted against the mindlessness of Napoleon, stuck with his idea of conquest and attack and drawn into defeat by the Russian winter (Langer, 1989, pp. 71–72; this is based on Tolstoy's (1983) account in *War and Peace*).

## Conclusion

In this chapter, we have explored the conditions that opened the way for the spectacular success of Kabat-Zinn's use of mindfulness to describe the meditational practices within his stress management program. These conditions were of different kinds. Two related, relatively short-term conditions, were the existence of a thriving but marginalised humanistic movement in Western psychology and psychotherapy; and the assimilation of Buddhist practices and theory. Both tended towards treating feelings and thoughts with non-judgemental awareness, in ways akin to Kabat-Zinn's version of mindfulness.

This version of mindfulness was derived from Kabat-Zinn's own encounters with Buddhist schools in the States. Originally a popular part of the counter culture, in the late twentieth century Buddhism was increasingly being treated as a source of psychological ideas, in works comparing Buddhist and Western psychology. At the same time, there was an emphasis in humanistic psychotherapy on acceptance of symptoms, and a willing audience for any therapeutic practice of this kind that could be shown to be effective. Meditation had had some success, but the word "meditation" itself was probably too openly associated with Eastern religions to be wholly acceptable to established scientific psychotherapy. This caution is expressed in the letter from Segal to Teasdale referred to above—Teasdale appeared to discount this by recognising that in his mindfulness practice Kabat-Zinn has successfully extracted what is important, and presumably left behind the suspect associations.

As defined by Nyonaponika, mindfulness was bare attention, which Kabat-Zinn has shown can be manualised to become evidence-based practice; but it was also something else, being in the world with clear comprehension, similar to Langer's account of mindfulness, and elaborated by Kabat-Zinn in his books. Thus all buyers can be satisfied— the humanistic, since here was a reputable practice, making much of non-judgemental acceptance and shorn of its religious links; the scientific because there was a good evidence base, added to by the work of Linehan (1993a), Segal et al. (2001), and others. And the Buddhist, because this hugely important part of Buddhist practice was becoming much more widely available.

These historical convergences and divergences have a structure that itself has a history linked with the development of science and technology. The reaction to this has been a search for alternatives, and has been found in Western culture in the supposed meditative calm and wisdom of the East, in Buddhism and other religions. But it is not just a search for calm, it is also a search for knowledge of a kind different from scientific knowledge, a knowledge that is less verbal and is tolerant of uncertainty, as expressed in the title of Alan Watts' book

*The Wisdom of Insecurity*, and captured in the famous phrase of a much earlier romantic, "negative capability" (John Keats; the origin of the phrase is discussed in Bate, 1979, ch. x).

What remains to be seen is whether "mindfulness", as used by Kabat-Zinn and others, is really the same as "mindfulness" offered by Rhys Davids as the translation of the Pali *sati*. And whether it is possible, as Teasdale suggested in his letter to Kabat-Zinn, to extract the essence of Buddhist meditation from its context in a framework of *karma* and rebirth which was part of an Indian culture 2,600 years ago, and insert it without change in the very different culture of the United States and Europe of the twenty-first century. As Danziger (1997) has pointed out, and as discussed in the Introduction, it may be a mistake to assume that a concept from one language is the same as the apparent equivalent from another, since their meaning depends on the network of concepts and practices that makes up the different discursive formations through which reality is understood. Ignoring this may have little bearing on whether or not the practice works, but it will certainly affect the way we think about it.

## Notes

1. Psychoanalysis has often shown a similar acceptance, based on Freud's recommendation of "evenly suspended attention", and the variations of this in Karen Horney, Bion, and Winnicott (Epstein, 1995, *passim*). This is certainly more than the moral non-judgemental acceptance that is part of the medical approach of many therapists, but if it is mindfulness, it is by the therapist rather than the client. Free association also involves a non-judgemental acceptance, in this case on the part of the client, and bears some resemblance to mindfulness. But the acceptance of symptoms we are referring to is more characteristic of Jung than of Freudians, with his active acceptance of the shadow aspects of the psyche. Another breakaway psychoanalyst, Otto Rank, is one of the precursors of the humanistic movement, and had a well-documented influence on Carl Rogers and the core condition of unconditional positive regard (DeCarvalho, 1991; also Chapter Four). There is also an interesting but diffuse Christian impact (Cooper 2003; see also Chapter One).

2. Theravadan Buddhist meditation was often divided into two kinds, *samatha* or concentration, one-pointed focus on an object, and *vipassana*, or insight meditation. The latter, which seems to have been the Buddha's discovery, involves a looser focus, often on the breath,

allowing thoughts and feelings to come and go without judgement or clinging. This is similar to what is often now referred to as mindfulness meditation. The goal is insight into impermanence (*anicca*), emptiness of self (*anatta*), and suffering (*dukha*).

3. "[[S]*ati*] is one of the most difficult words ... in the whole Buddhist system of ethical psychology to translate. Hardy renders 'conscience,' which is certainly wrong; and Gogerly ... has 'meditation', which is equally wide of the mark. I have sometimes rendered it self-possession. It means that activity of mind, constant presence of mind, wakefulness of heart, which is the foe of carelessness, inadvertance, self-forgetfulness" (Rhys Davids, 1895–1910, p. 58).

4. Nyanaponika Thera and Nanavira Thera were Europeans who became monks in Sri Lanka, and inevitably took with them philosophical preconceptions, which affected their understanding of Pali concepts. Nyanoponika Thera was German, and his notion of bare attention and occasional use of "sense-data" suggest a traditional representational realist approach, in which the mind forms representations that are a mirror of the world. Nanavira Thera was an English mathematician, but drew on phenomenolgy and existentialism (especially Sartre and Heidegger) in his construal of Buddhist philosophy, which led to a less dualist metaphysics. The implications for psychology of these metaphysics have been discussed in Still and Good (1998). The implications for our understanding of Buddhism remain to be considered.

5. And later even lectured on Buddhism (Taylor, 1996, p. 147).

6. To highlight their similarity, Morrison (1997, p. 211) juxtaposed this passage with an account of mindfulness and clear comprehension from the Pali suttas.

# CHAPTER NINE

# Marginalisation is not unbearable; is it even undesirable?

## Introduction

In some respects, REBT is a marginalised movement. This is not wholly a bad thing. Marginalised movements in psychology and psychotherapy tend to retain their identity, and the writings of their founders continue to exercise an influence. Once absorbed into the mainstream the identity is lost, and the founders are relegated to a past that has been left behind. Movements are kept marginalised when they are at odds with the central, untested assumptions (the hard core) of the mainstream. Many of REBT's insights have already been assimilated by the mainstream, which is currently an alliance between experimental psychology and CBT. But the mechanistic hard core of the mainstream is at odds with normative assumptions about self-worth held by REBT. As long as that continues REBT is likely to remain marginalised, but will keep its most significant insights.

## What is marginalisation?

As a word, "marginalisation" reflects a metaphor twice removed from its source. Margins are edges, away from the centre, and "marginal" has an established use within economics. A marginal group is one that does not share in economic growth, like people on fixed incomes during a time of inflation. Drawing on this usage, marginalisation has a semi-popular application to any movement, group, or individual whose intellectual contributions have little impact on the centre or mainstream.

Marginalisation involves a *relative* lack of power and influence. A person or movement with no pretension to power cannot be marginalised. Thus, it is not simply lack of power. Phrenology has no power nowadays, but is not a marginalised movement. It has become discredited, and its influence is purely historical. In the usage here, a typical marginalised movement has the organisation and energy characteristic of mainstream power, but fails to exercise such power. It has muscle, but not power, and if we desired a measure of marginalisation it would be

$$\text{marginalisation index} = (S{-}P)/S$$

where S is strength of muscle, P is amount of power, and S>P. Marginalisation will be zero if S = P (the power wielded is the same as the muscle available), and it will be 1 if P = 0 (the movement wields no power at all). Notice that muscle and marginalisation are only partly correlated. Thus, systems theory has a powerful niche in family therapy, but its muscle (in terms of number of practitioners, size of organisation, intellectual dissemination, financial turnover, etc.) is less than that of REBT. It is therefore less marginalised. Psychoanalysis, on the other hand, which also has low marginalisation, is still both muscular and powerful.

## The marginalisation of REBT

REBT's power and influence is less now than might be expected from the muscle it has shown over the last forty-five years. In the States, it remains a popular choice, and in Britain, where it has never been widely used, it is probably gaining ground. It has muscle, but not much power. It continues to advance, but it has been outstripped dramatically, not by rivals like psychoanalysis or person-centred therapy, but by its close allies, Beck's Cognitive Therapy and the more recent Cognitive Behavioural Therapy. In the last twenty years, CBT has yoked itself effectively to the methodology and theory of experimental psychology. In their earlier work both Beck and Ellis presented their work as scientific and they published studies designed to demonstrate the effectiveness of their therapies. At the same time, Beck especially made explicit reference to areas of research in cognitive psychology, for instance, emotional bias in information processing (Beck, Rush, Shaw & Emery, 1979). This has led to a programme of research in the States and Britain, carried out by workers with thorough training in experimental psychology and some experience of therapy.

The extent of this was brought home to one of us at a recent annual meeting of the British Association for Behavioural and Cognitive Psychotherapies. There were lively symposia on current research on CBT by researchers with academic affiliations, but there was scarcely any mention of REBT, except in a solitary paper explaining the difference between REBT and CBT. Even though the practice and influence of REBT in Britain is much less than in the States, it was still surprisingly absent. Most of the research reported was couched within a framework first clearly articulated in Britain by Donald Broadbent (1958) during the 1950s. This was established experimental psychology brought to bear upon a particular kind of therapy, and giving it all the power and confidence belonging to mainstream status. It was different from the gathering momentum of "evidence-based practice"—not just research on what works for whom, but a detailed analysis of why it does. It was in the spirit of laboratory rather than applied psychology, and the leading researchers at this conference are as likely to publish in prestigious academic journals in Britain and the States as in specialist cognitive therapy journals. There is nothing comparable for REBT to this convergence of laboratory psychology and therapy. Good research is being carried out (Bond & Dryden, 2000; Dryden, Ferguson & Clark, 1989), but it is in its own terms, rather than within the politically and economically powerful framework of mainstream experimental cognitive psychology.

What was witnessed at this conference was a blossoming of the trend already recognised over twenty years ago by Dryden (1984). He pointed out that unlike Ellis, Beck has remained firmly within the academic arena, and that whereas Ellis's theory has developed as a broad and often sweeping account of all emotional disorders, Beck's has proceeded step-by-step in the cautious tradition of experimental investigation. "Beck and his colleagues ... have spent much of their time and attention studying the psychological processes of the depressive disorders and ... are now adopting a similar approach to the study of anxiety disorders" (Dryden, 1984, p. 247). A recent book mainly by British authors shows how each of the anxiety disorders are now seen as well under control, and CBT has been carefully extended to eating disorders, sexual problems, and attempted suicide (Clark & Fairburn, 1997). Beside this mainstream scientific bonanza, the value of REBT's marginalisation index is distinctly high.

## The ambivalence of marginalisation

In this chapter, we consider the strategic complexities of such marginalisation. Is it simply undesirable, a sign of imminent defeat, or are there advantages in marginalisation amongst the long-term struggles that make up the history of science? Recently, working as a journal editor, one of us sent a historical paper on Freud to a distinguished practising psychoanalyst for review. He replied that Freud was not (or is not) a psychoanalyst, so his own expertise did not qualify him to referee the paper.

In Britain, at least, psychoanalysis is not a marginalised movement. Its conduits of power are not straightforwardly through academic psychology or the National Health Service (NHS), but are none the less real and effective through "the formation of networks of association, the stabilization of connections between problems, the forging of links between different centres of expertise and sites of application, the invention of transferable codes and techniques" (Miller & Rose, 1994, p. 59). What does this tell us about the different relationships between any prominent thinker and the movement generally accepted as founded by him or her? At least in the early days of psychoanalysis, when it was still marginalised, Freud was acknowledged by all, not just as the heroic founder but also as the intellectual leader of the movement.

## Life and death in the mainstream

This blanking out of an accepted founder turns out to be typical of mainstream movements. The originators are not forgotten, but what they actually said or wrote is buried in a distant past. It is regarded as remote and irrelevant to the present, or it is drawn on selectively in order to provide rhetorical support for current thought. They become monumental founding fathers, who often turn out, when historians dig them up again, to be very different from what the textbooks say.

Wilhelm Wundt is a good example of this process. Traditionally taken as the founder of experimental psychology in the nineteenth century, few thinkers, least of all practising experimentalists, would think it worthwhile to look up what he actually wrote. If they did they would be surprised to find that he made experimental psychology subordinate to social psychology (Farr, 1983), and that the experiments he did had a quite different structure from the methodology that has evolved in the States.

A similar distortion has occurred in our memories of the great figures of S–R behaviourism during the first half of the twentieth century, J. B. Watson and Clark Hull. They are seen now as the founders of a discredited movement, buried by the cognitive revolution. But if we go back to their writings we see that their main ideas were absorbed into the mainstream and continue to dominate our thinking. Thus, the objective methods pioneered by Watson and developed within behaviourism remain the cornerstone of scientific psychology, with input–processing–output replacing stimulus–organism–response. What changed was the language, facilitated by the rise of information theory and computers. This has made possible theories that are far more flexible and powerful than Hull's could ever have been. But his original programme of setting up hypothetical mechanisms and testing predictions remains as he refined it during the 1930s.

## Life at the margin

The fate of B. F. Skinner has been quite different. He founded radical behaviourism and his name and his thinking remain firmly stamped upon it, even after his death. His early papers were precise reformulations of old terms like "stimulus" and "response", and new terms like "operant" and "stimulus control", and Skinnerians still return to these in order to clarify current usage of these terms, and to formulate more exactly the distinctive features of radical behaviourism. In the 1950s, radical behaviourism appeared to be on the ascendant, and even developing as a rival mainstream discipline within psychology, with its own journal and national bodies, a distinct language, and an incestuous reference pattern (Krantz, 1972). Since then it has continued to be self-sufficient and muscular, but has become marginalised. It is this, we are arguing, that has enabled it to preserve its identity. The same is true of J. J. Gibson and ecological psychology (Reed, 1988). This movement too is relatively self-contained with its own journals and conferences, and the writings of Gibson himself continue to have special authority twenty years after his death.

We find similar relations between founder and movement in psychotherapy. Post-Jungians make clear how far they have moved from Jung himself, yet return to Jung again and again to start a train of thought or to clinch an argument (e.g., Samuels, 1989).[1] Respectable modern Gestalt therapists often distance themselves from Fritz Perls, although the book *Gestalt Therapy* is still referred to, and not just to the parts written by Ralph Hefferline or Paul Goodman (Perls, Hefferline & Goodman, 1951). Eric Berne's *Games People Play* (1964) is still preliminary reading for students of transactional analysis.

All these movements are marginalised, with varying degrees of muscle. The healthy and open survival of so many marginal movements no doubt depends on a society that is large, wealthy, and committed to pluralism and tolerance. It is thus understandable that radical behaviourism and ecological psychology (and REBT itself) have always had a less secure foothold in Britain than in the States.

In summary, these marginalised groups share certain characteristics. They have a distinct identity, are well organised and well publicised, and always critical of the mainstream. The founders are honoured, and not just as figureheads—their writings are constantly referred to, and still taken seriously as defining the intellectual substance of the movement. In practice, however, there is a tension between keeping to the basic principles of the movement, and presenting work to a more general audience in prestigious journals or conferences. Although the marginalised movement always has its own specialist journal in which only members publish, this is not usually enough to maintain an individual's professional position, especially within universities. So they often compromise by adopting the mainstream style, and getting published in its journals.

## Hard cores and protective belts

Lakatos' "Falsification and the methodology of scientific research programmes" (1970) can throw light on this process of marginalisation. Lakatos' work is a detailed account of how the mainstream's "positive heuristic" enables it to concentrate on research which generates a series of soluble problems, while its "negative heuristic" ensures that its vulnerable parts, its anomalies, and its metaphysical assumptions, remain untested and unquestioned. A "protective belt" is thus set up around the "hard core" of the programme. It serves to police the unquestionable norms of the programme, and prevent them from being seriously challenged.

Lakatos dealt with mainstream rather than marginalised programmes, but his model can be used to articulate the latter's role. Instead of protecting their hard core, marginalised programmes display it unashamedly, and present it as a challenge to the hard core of the mainstream programme. This is anathema, and the mainstream's protective belt ensures that these would-be revolutionaries are held in check. They are marginalised, allowed enough scope and power to express themselves but not enough to pose a real threat. If this happens, the marginalised group may be absorbed into the mainstream, which strives to accommodate to its new internal critics without making any fundamental change (Still, 1986).

Thus, Skinner's project involved an alternative to the principle (made precise by Hull) that scientific psychology requires a programme of testing hypothetico–deductive models within a stimulus–response or input–output framework. Apart from his own alternative methodology he and his followers spent a lot of energy attacking this hard core of the mainstream programme, both before (Skinner, 1950) and after (Skinner 1977) the jetisoning of S–R behaviourism by the mainstream. Similarly, Gibson (1959, 1979) throughout his career was at pains to articulate his own account of perception as an exploratory activity over time, against the received view of a constructive process imposed upon transitory sensory input.

As noted earlier, a peculiarity of a marginalised movement is that its untestable hard core (in Lakatos's sense) is displayed unashamedly. The hard core in Skinner was the circular connection between operant, reinforcement, and stimulus control and a methodology of empirical law rather than mechanism. In Gibson it was that information in the ambient array, necessarily picked up over time, specifies its sources. The protective belt in action against such challenges shows itself in characteristic ways. On the one hand, the assumptions and criticisms of the marginalised movement are ferociously attacked in a sometimes *ad hominem* fashion (Chomsky, 1959, 1971, on Skinner; Fodor & Pylyshyn, 1981, on Gibson). On the other hand, the actual procedures and findings of the movement are often accepted enthusiastically. The Skinner box and many of his methods are widely used, Gibson's perceptual demonstrations have become a familiar part of the visual psychologist's teaching and research repertoire, and both these leaders were much honoured by established organisations during their lifetimes.

## The hard core of REBT

Angry dismissals, combined with some public honour, is a tension familiar to Ellis and REBT. So too is the gradual assimilation into the mainstream of many of the insights and practices of the marginalised movement. The contributions of REBT are thus acknowledged, and there is implicit an inducement to go further, to give up the obstinate insistence on principles that are so dangerously at odds with the mainstream's hard core. This has been resisted, and REBT remains marginalised.

What is this hard-core assumption of CBT that is essential to its mainstream status (yoked to experimental psychology) and is not shared by REBT? Hard cores are protected and often hard to put into words and unacknowledged, but one answer is that it lies in the mechanistic assumptions that allow it to become part of the theoretical and empirical work of experimental psychology. This is what is described above as the programme of testing hypothetico–deductive models within a stimulus–response or input–output model. As Johnson-Laird (1983) defined it, an experimental psychology requires testable theories, and a prerequisite of testable theories is that they can be stated in terms of "effective procedures". However, effective procedures are by definition computable, so

> [i]n so far as there can be a science of the mind it will almost certainly be restricted to accounts that can be formulated as computer programs. To abandon this criterion is to allow that scientific theories can be vague, confused, and, like mystical doctrines, only properly understood by their proponents.
>
> (Johnson-Laird, 1983, p. 8)

Whether or not you agree with this criterion, it undoubtedly captures well part of the hard core of the programme of experimental psychology. The human being is treated as a black box, a closed system subject to inputs and generating outputs. The performance of such a mechanism is in principle measurable, and can therefore be rated. However, to rate the actual or theoretical performance is to rate the machine itself. The value of a machine is inseparable from its performance.[2]

It is this that conflicts with the hard core of REBT. A frequently emphasised part of the practice and theory of REBT is the idea that a human being cannot be rated as a whole. Human beings may act well or badly, but they are not good or bad as such. This is closely linked to the emphasis on self-acceptance and also, although less directly, to the goal of philosophical change, and the idea of an elegant solution in REBT. These essential aspects of REBT are frequently argued for on pragmatic grounds (e.g., Ellis, 1994, p. 191), but also philosophically, and this distances REBT from CBT.

> Various kinds of CBT teach rational coping statements ... But they give no philosophical rationale for holding the belief "I am neither good nor bad, nor can I legitimately rate myself as a total person at all, even though some of my traits are good (efficient) and bad (inefficient) for some of my main purposes." This therapeutic philosophy can probably not be shown to clients without a fairly sophisticated analysis and Socratic dialogue that is especially promoted in REBT.
>
> (Ellis, 1994, p. 250)

Thus, these propositions about self-worth and self-rating at the core of REBT are at least partly normative or philosophical propositions about the nature of human beings. Philosophically they are akin to Buddhism and existentialism, and perhaps influenced by these sources (Ellis, 1994, pp. 48, 53). Therefore, it is not surprising that REBT has been marginalised with respect to a mainstream CBT yoked to experimental psychology and cognitive science. The model of human beings espoused there is the one described by Johnson-Laird as based on effective procedures, and the assertion that human beings cannot be rated makes no sense in this context. This does not mean that card-carrying experimental psychologists must disagree with Ellis on self-worth. As human beings, outside the laboratory, they may well agree wholeheartedly (and sometimes do), while still holding (as psychologists) that REBT's propositions on self-worth, however important as moral guides for living, are beyond the range of a cognitive psychology which presupposes a mechanistic model of human beings.

The REBT concept of self-worth is part of its hard core, and not an isolated quirk that could be left out without great loss in order to bring the movement into the mainstream. If life is a competitive struggle centred on achieving an eternal mark out of 100 for our individual being, and that is its very meaning, then the full range of musturbatory demands naturally follows. This is where the contrast with CBT is sharpest. Consider, for instance, Ellis on depression, where he is illustrating his differences from Beck.

> [W]e can see that when people resort to Beck's triad and view themselves, their environment, and their future negatively, they will almost certainly make themselves seriously disappointed, sad, sorrowful, frustrated, and hopeless. But they will still often not become depressed unless they add to their negative views the grandiose absolutistic *demands* and *commands* that their bad traits, poor environment, and negative future *must* not exist. In RET terms, they make a magical or theological jump from *describing* present and future reality quite negatively to *refusing to accept* it the way it is and, instead, dogmatically *insisting* that it be (and continue to be) better than it actually is.
>
> (Ellis, 1987, p. 126; emphasis in original)

In reply to this, Brown and Beck (1989) pointed out that Beck too had written on the role of "shoulds" and "necessitous thinking", and reported a study designed to test whether it is specific to depression, or a more general feature of psychopathology. They used their *Shoulds Scale*, and concluded that necessitious thinking occurs in a range of disorders, not just depression.

This does not really address Ellis's theory of depression. First Ellis himself certainly has not claimed that shoulds are specific to depression, but that Beck's triad, while it may be a necessary condition, leaves out the shoulds that could make it a sufficient condition. But second, and most important for the argument of this chapter. Ellis's shoulds are not the rather lacklustre variety listed in the *Shoulds Scale*, but are "grandiose absolutistic *demands* and *commands*" involving a "magical or theological jump" from ordinary negative thinking (Ellis, 1987, p. 126). Such demands are right off the end of the *Shoulds Scale*.

## Conclusions

If this argument is correct, the key difference that enables CBT to flow with the mainstream while REBT is marginalised is the latter's insistence on its hard-core philosophy of self-worth and self-rating. Not just an insistence for Ellis personally, but an essential part of the therapy, so essential that it cannot simply be left behind when REBT enters the laboratory. Of course, we can still proceed empirically, and test the outcome effectiveness of teaching the REBT view on self-worth. It may even be possible to produce a model couched as effective procedures to explain why it works. A block diagram, for instance, could show the *self* block being compared (computationally) with the *ideal actual self* block. Arousal and excessive vigilance (hence anxiety) occurs if the value of (*ideal actual self–self*) is above a criterion which will vary between individuals. REBT aims to eliminate this by eliminating altogether the comparisons, not just by raising the criterion (as in positive thinking). But although Ellis does write and say that it would be therapeutically helpful to cut out self-rating, he is not just saying this. As we have seen, REBT offers a philosophical rationale, which can be shown to clients (Ellis, 1994, p. 250).

At this point REBT might make a bold bid for the mainstream, by giving up the philosophical underpinnings of its core, and treating it as a purely empirical issue. Set up the above model and examine the therapeutic effect of rating *vs.* not rating. Suppose there is no difference, or even an outcome in favour of rating. Could the REBT therapist remain neutral and simply give up his or her commitment to the principle of not rating? Or is this truly a philosophically based belief, part of the hard core of REBT, which cannot be relinquished? In the first case REBT will join the mainstream and lose its identity in the melding together of the overlapping principles of REBT and CBT; and Ellis will be remembered (but not read) in fifty years' time as one of the more eccentric founders of CBT. In the second, it will retain its identity and remain marginalised; Ellis will still be read and the mainstream will continue to be confronted with an irritating and potentially dangerous gadfly, whose ultimate commitment is to Stoic reason in the client–therapist relationship, rather than to evidence-based practice.

## Notes

1. Of course, this is sometimes true of Freud and modern psychoanalysts. The example of the correspondent's forceful dismissal of Freud suggests a possibility rather than an inevitability—the founder of a mainstream movement can be thoroughly erased, but this would risk destroying the identity of a marginalised movement.
2. Machines can have value as proud possessions, art works, or museum pieces, but this is secondary to their intrinsic quality.

# CONCLUSIONS

In this book we have looked at some of ways in which Epictetus and Stoicism have influenced Albert Ellis and modern cognitive psychotherapy. It was partly through his reading of Epictetus and later Stoics, that Ellis settled on the cornerstone of his therapy, that we are responsible for our emotions as well as our actions. There are also less direct homologies, based on the implicit Stoicism in the cultural background of twentieth-century America. To some extent, this also conditioned Ellis's thinking and helped provide the receptive audience necessary for his success.

The beginnings of this covert Stoicism were outlined in the Introduction. There we set out the case for the influence of Stoicism on early Christian thought about responsibility and self-control. This formed a background to later moral thinking in the West, which was reinforced by the widespread availability of classical texts after the Renaissance, when Stoic ethics became popular as a personal guide to conduct. In addition, Christianity had lost some of its moral authority by the end of the seventeenth century and philosophers, including Christian philosophers, were turning to human sociality as a basis for morality and political organisation. Stoicism provided a fruitful source for this. The legacy of Epictetus was prominent during both stages, and the

Stoics were drawn on again in the American philosophy of self-reliance, notably by Franklin and Emerson. It was against this background, when authoritarian Christianity gave place to popular self-help gurus as a guide for action and personal development, that the assumptions of psychotherapy arose as a modern ethics (Chapters Five and Six). In this context, the word "Rational" in Ellis's "Rational Psychotherapy" marks a moral allegiance, a commitment to the emancipatory reason that was so central to Stoic ethics.

In Chapters One and Two of this book we set out the specific homologies between the Stoicism of Epictetus, and the cognitive psychotherapy of Albert Ellis, treating each as representative of broader movements to which they belong. We then went on, in Chapter Three, to look at the contributions to the origins of REBT by other twentieth-century movements that bear little obvious relation to Stoicism. Our conclusion from these chapters is that Ellis took from Epictetus and other philosophers his conviction that we are responsible through thoughts for our psychological upsets, and therefore can resolve them, on our own or with the help of a psychotherapist.

But the role of thinking was already present in the many publications of the self-help movement, and in Chapter Three we describe how some of the important details of REBT, especially the controlling role of language through self-judgement and the shoulds, comes from twentieth-century movements rather than Epictetus. During the first part of the century academic linguists such as Whorf (Carroll, 1956) favoured a form of linguistic determinism, in which perception and thinking are constrained by language. This was given a practical and therapeutic form in General Semantics, and Ellis read and was influenced by this work. Out of this background, Ellis and others developed in REBT an extraordinary and original precision in describing and unravelling the self-coercive power of language, that made of REBT such a successful psychotherapy. Another important difference from Epictetus is that Ellis worked as a psychotherapist throughout most of his career, and the modern relationship between client and psychotherapist, and therefore in part the meaning of what goes on within that relationship, especially the medical notion of therapy itself, had no clear counterpart at the time of Epictetus. They inhabited different discursive formations. Yet Ellis was not typical of his time in some respects. He deliberately tried to make of the relationship a dialogue, a cooperative effort rather than the decision of an expert as in the doctor–patient relationship, and in Chapter Two it was argued that this may have been influenced by the dialogic nature of Epictetus' practice. Unlike Seneca or Marcus Aurelius, Epictetus was a public teacher and his thinking arose out of dialogue with his listeners, and the written record of these dialogues, as well as his sayings in the Enchiridion, were read by Ellis during his formative years.

Central to the therapeutic discourse constructed by Ellis were words with a fraught philosophical history, "rational" and the moral or deon-tological words, "should" and "ought". "Rational" appears in different discursive formations, and Chapter Four looked at the muddle that can arise when the differences are not recognised. Ellis's Stoic concept of reason gets confused with the more Platonic notion applied to math-ematical and scientific reason. This more formal notion has been popu-lar in psychology and economics, where its limitations are becoming increasingly obvious. They are even more obvious when applied to the struggling human mind, but Ellis never made this mistake, and retained his commitment to the Stoic reason that was part of Rational Psycho-therapy from the beginning. This Stoic reason is the "emancipatory rea-son" introduced in Chapter Four. It is ethical, a guide to conduct, and Chapters Five and Six looked at its relationship to the role of deonto-logical words, which is the respectful term for what became the lethal "musts" and "shoulds" of REBT. Ellis recognised the need for people to live by a moral system, but the old deontological words have lost the rational basis they might have had within the kind of Christian or Aristotelian virtue ethics described by Alistair MacIntyre (1981). They have retained their inner coercive force but it is now irrational, unless conditional on some modern version of virtue ethics or set of secular goals which gives their use an appropriate harmony. Ellis himself might have taken issue with this historical account, since he speculated that the pathological demands represented by the "shoulds" and the "oughts" used by his clients had a biological origin. But he separated the patho-logical demands from mere use of the words, by postulating that such demands contain "hot cognitions", and it is these that reflect the evolu-tionary advantage Ellis seems to have had in mind.

Chapters Seven to Nine looked at some of the contemporary move-ments and controversies that affected the course of REBT as Ellis positioned himself in relation to them, either in alliance or in reac-tion. During the early days, Ellis was confronted with the rhetoric of humanist psychology, the third way between psychoanalysis and a psychology based on laboratory science. The humanist movement emphasised the moral aspect of psychology that had disappeared from laboratory psychology. Carl Rogers was the humanist's chosen psycho-therapist, and Ellis's confrontational style was in marked contrast with the more passive listening of Rogerian person-centred therapy. In spite of this, he took pains to align REBT with humanism, by showing their compatibility. This was not hard to do, since from the beginning Ellis and REBT took the client's viewpoint and made therapy a cooperative effort, by sharing with the client the rationale behind the techniques used, something not usually done in psychoanalysis or experimental psychology, or even in person-centred therapy. In addition, there is the moral aspect of REBT brought out in Chapter Five, which lies in its use of Stoic emancipatory reason as a way of undermining the lingering coercive power of the "shoulds" and "oughts" of a now empty moral framework.

But Ellis did not stress these moral aspects of REBT. He did not deny them, but they can sit uneasily with scientific claims, and from the beginning of his work as a Rational Psychotherapist Ellis was confronted with the need to establish its scientific credentials. At this time, psychoanalysis was coming under increasing attack for trading under a false label, "science", and became one of the prime candidates for a new label, "pseudoscience". Once the division between science and pseudoscience was articulated, it became a matter of urgency to satisfy whatever criteria were available for policing the border (Chapter Seven). Ellis had himself been one of the critics of the scientific pretensions of psychoanalysis, so there was pressure to make the grade. Of course, he didn't musturbate about this, and unlike the followers of CBT he didn't bother too much with the rituals of control groups and null hypothesis testing. REBT relied upon its effectiveness rather than efficacy, through its commitment to a distinct philosophy based on self-acceptance and the avoidance of irrational demands, and the human (Stoic) reason that comes into play between client and therapist. CBT has been more pragmatic, willing to be led by the promise of evidence-based practice, rather than the practical exercise of a philosophy, in order to secure a place on the safe side of the boundary between science and pseudoscience.

This difference was apparent during the 1990s in different reactions to the egregious rise of mindfulness as a therapeutic practice (Chapter Eight). As a technique for calmly reflecting on feelings and thoughts, it is central to any serious morality, and yet Kabat-Zinn (1990) made a convincing case for its scientific status. The spokespersons of a variety of therapeutic models have felt obliged to make clear their relationship to mindfulness. CBT accommodated it by welcoming it into its repertoire and developing it as another evidence-based practice. REBT, on the other hand, assimilated it by showing its compatibility with its philosophy. This commitment to a philosophy rather than evidence-based practice has been one of the factors that has marginalised REBT (Chapter Nine), rather like a country that stands aloof from globalisation. It misses the benefits, but also the vulnerability should the economic system collapse. The metaphorical equivalent of this system is the methodology of evidence-based practice, and we have touched on some of the weaknesses of this whose fuller exposure could seriously undermine any therapy that has relied upon it so thoroughly for its medical and popular acceptance. The gold standard for this methodology of testing for outcome is the medical testing of drugs, and this is coming under increasing attack, especially for its failure to allow for the active placebo effect in psychiatric drugs (Kirsch, 2009). The collapse of the system based on this methodology is no doubt unlikely, but even if it were to occur, it would leave REBT relatively unscathed, since it depends upon effectiveness rather than efficacy, through the rational appeal of its philosophy and practice, rather than any empirical methodology. It is analogous to what Epictetus depended upon when he set up his school in Nicopolis.

In spite of this final closeness to Epictetus, there has been little contact between REBT and another discourse, that of classical scholarship, where there has been a striking revival of interest in Epictetus (Long, 2002; Sorabji, 2000; Stockdale, 1995). The classicists who heard Stockdale's report of his use of Epictetus to survive in a prisoner of war camp found that it threw light on their understanding of the philosopher. The influence therefore was mutual, Stockdale's practice and self-understanding were changed by Epictetus, and this in turn changed his understanding of Epictetus, which he was able to communicate to fellow classicists. However, in spite of this focus on the modern relevance of Epictetus, there seems to have been no reference to the impact of his legacy on Albert Ellis and REBT or CBT, and of what this can add to our understanding of Epictetus. Perhaps this book, alongside the detailed analogies traced by Robertson (2010), will go some way towards changing this.

# REFERENCES

Abelson, R. P. (1963). Computer simulation of "hot" cognition. In: S. S. Tompkins & S. Messick (Eds), *Computer Simulation of Personality* (pp. 277–298). New York: Wiley.

Allen, J. (1902). *As a Man Thinketh*. Camarillo, CA: De Vorss [reprinted 1999].

American Psychiatric Association (1994). *Diagnostic and Statistical Manual of Mental Disorders* (4th edn). Washington, DC: American Psychiatric Association.

Anscombe, G. E. M. (1958). Modern moral philosophy. *Philosophy, 33*: 1–19.

Aristotle (1955). *The Ethics of Aristotle*. Harmondsworth: Penguin Books.

Armstrong, D. M. & Malcolm, N. (1984). *Consciousness and Causality*. Oxford: Blackwell.

Arnold, M. B. (1960). *Emotion and Personality*. New York: Columbia University Press.

Ayer, A. J. (1936). *Language, Truth and Logic*. London: Gollancz.

Ayer, A. J. (1968). *The Origins of Pragmatism*. London: Macmillan.

Bakhtin, M. M. (1981). *The Dialogic Imagination: Four Essays*. Austin, TX: University of Texas Press.

Bartley, W. W. (1988). Theories of rationality. In: G. Radnitzky & W. W. Bartley (Eds), *Evolutionary Epistemology, Rationality, and the Sociology of Knowledge* (pp. 205–216). La Salle, IL: Open Court.

Barwise, J. & Perry, J. (1983). *Situations and Attitudes*. Cambridge, MA: MIT Press.

Bate, W. J. (1979). *John Keats*. London: Chatto & Windus.

Baxandall, M. (1985). *Patterns of Intention*. New Haven, CT: Yale University Press.

Beck, A. (1963). Thinking and depression: I. Idiosyncratic content and cognitive distortions. *Archives of General Psychiatry, 9*: 324–333.

Beck, A. T. (1964). Thinking and depression: 2. Theory and therapy. *Archives of General Psychiatry, 10*: 561–571.

Beck, A. T. (1976). *Cognitive Therapy and the Emotional Disorders*. New York: International Universities Press.

Beck, A. T., Freeman, A. & Associates (1990). *Cognitive Therapy of Personality Disorders*. New York: Guilford Press.

Beck, A. T., Rush, A. J., Shaw, B. F. & Emery, G. (1979). *Cognitive Therapy of Depression*. New York: Guilford Press.

Beisser, A. R. (1972). The paradoxical theory of change. In: J. Fagan & I. L. Shepherd (Eds), *Gestalt Therapy Now: Theory, Techniques, Applications* (pp. 88–92). Harmondsworth: Penguin Books.

Berne, E. (1961). *Transactional Analysis in Psychotherapy*. New York: Evergreen.

Berne, E. (1964). *Games People Play*. Harmondsworth: Penguin Books.

Bloor, D. (1976). *Knowledge and Social Imagery*. London: Routledge & Kegan Paul.

Blum, J. M. (1978). *Pseudoscience and Mental Ability: The Origins and Fallacies of the IQ Controversy*. New York: Monthly Review Press.

Boden, M. A. (1977). *Artificial Intelligence and Natural Man*. Brighton: Harvester.

Bond, F. W. & Dryden, W. (1996). Why two, central REBT hypotheses appear untestable. *Journal of Rational-Emotive and Cognitive-Behavior Therapy, 14*: 29–40.

Bond, F. W. & Dryden, W. (2000). How rational beliefs and irrational beliefs affect people's inferences: An experimental investigation. *Behavioural and Cognitive Psychotherapy, 28*: 33–43.

Boring, E. G. (1950). *A History of Experimental Psychology*. New York: Appleton-Century-Croft.

Boring, E. G. (1963). *History, Psychology, and Science*. New York: Wiley.

Brazier, D. (1995). *Zen Therapy*. London: Constable.

Bridgman, P. W. (1927). *The Logic of Modern Physics*. New York: Macmillan.

Brinkmann, S. (2006). Mental life in the space of reasons. *Journal for the Theory of Social Behaviour, 36*: 1–16.

Broadbent, D. E. (1958). *Perception and Communication*. London: Pergamon.

Brock, T. D. (1988). *Robert Koch: A Life in Medicine and Bacteriology*. Madison, WI: Science Tech Publishers.

Brown, G. & Beck, A. T. (1989). The role of imperatives in psychopathology: A reply to Ellis. *Cognitive Therapy and Research, 11*: 121–146.

Brown, P. (1989). *The Body and Society*. London: Faber & Faber.

Bunge, M. (1967). *Scientific Research*. Berlin: Springer-Verlag.

Bunge, M. (1984). What is a pseudoscience? *Skeptical Inquirer, 9*: 36–46.

Bunge, M. (1996). In praise of intolerance to charlatanism in academia. In: P. R. Gross, N. Levitt & M. W. Lewis (Eds), *The Flight from Science and Reason* (pp. 96–115). New York: New York Academy of Sciences.

Burke, T. (1994). *Dewey's New Logic: A Reply to Russell*. Chicago: University of Chicago Press.

Butterfield, R. (2004). Letter. *The Guardian*, 4 March.

Carnegie, D. (1948). *How to Stop Worrying and Start Living*. Bungay: Chaucer Press.

Carroll, B. E. (1997). *Spiritualism in Antebellum America*. Indianapolis, IN: Indiana University Press.

Carroll, J. B. (Ed.) (1956). *Language, Thought, and Reality: Selected Writings of Benjamin Lee Whorf*. Cambridge, MA: Technology Press.

Chomsky, N. (1957). *Syntactic Structures*. The Hague: Mouton.

Chomsky, N. (1959). Review of B. F. Skinner's *Verbal Behavior. Language, 35*: 26–58.

Chomsky, N. (1971). The case against B.F. Skinner. *The New York Review of Books*, pp. 18–24.

Cicero (1991). *On Stoic Good and Evil*. Warminster: Aris & Phillips.

Cioffi, F. (1998). *Freud and the Question of Pseudoscience*. Chicago: Open Court.

Clark, D. M. & Fairburn, C. G. (Eds) (1997). *Science and Practice of Cognitive Behaviour Therapy*. Oxford: Oxford University Press.

Claxton, G. (Ed.) (1986). *Beyond Therapy: The Impact of Eastern Religions on Psychological Theory and Practice*. London: Wisdom Publications.

Cobbett, W. (1823). *Cottage Economy*. London: J.M. Cobbett, Fleet Street.

Collins, S. & Pinch, J. (1993). *The Golem: What Everyone Should Know about Science*. New York: Cambridge University Press.

Cooper, T. D. (2003). *Sin, Pride, and Self-Acceptance*. Downers Grove, IL: InterVarsity Press.

Cooter, R. (1980). Deploying "pseudoscience": then and now. In: M. P. Hanen, M. J. Osler & R. G. Weyant (Eds), *Science, Pseudo-Science and Society* (pp. 237–272). Waterloo, Canada: Wilfred Laurier University Press.

Cottingham, J., Stoothoff, R. & Murdoch, D. (1985). *The Philosophical Writings of Descartes* (Vol. 1). Cambridge: Cambridge University Press.

Crawford, T. & Ellis, A. (1989). A dictionary of rational-emotive feelings and behaviors. *Journal of Rational-Emotive and Cognitive Behavior Therapy, 7*: 3–28.

Creath, R. (1996). The unity of science: Carnap, Neurath, and beyond. In: P. Galison & D. J. Stump (Eds), *The Disunity of Science: Boundaries, Contexts, and Power* (pp. 158–169). Stanford: Stanford University Press.

Crisp, R. & Slote, M. (1997). *Virtue Ethics*. Oxford: Oxford University Press.

Crombie, A. C. (1994). *Styles of Scientific Thinking in the European Tradition* (Vol. 1). London: Duckworth.

Crook, J. & Fontana, D. (Eds) (1990). *Space in Mind: East-West Psychology and Contemporary Buddhism*. Shaftesbury: Element.

Curley, E. M. (1978). *Descartes against the Sceptics*. Oxford: Basil Blackwell.

Danziger, K. (1997). *Naming the Mind*. London: Sage.

Danziger, K. (2008). *Marking the Mind: A History of Memory*. Cambridge: Cambridge University Press.

Darnton, R. (1984). *The Great Cat Massacre and other Episodes in French Cultural History*. Harmondsworth: Penguin Books.

Davidson, D. (1980). *Essays on Actions and Events*. Oxford: Oxford University Press.

Davidson, K. (2002). *Cognitive Therapy for Personality Disorders*. London: Arnold.

Dawkins, R. (1976). *The Selfish Gene*. Oxford: Oxford University Press.

De Grey, A. D. N. J., Gavrilov, L., Olshansky, S. J., Coles, L. S., Cutler, R. G., Fosself, M. & Harman, S. M. (2002). Antiageing technology and pseudoscience. *Science, 296*: 656.

Deatherage, O. G. (1980). Mindfulness meditation as psychotherapy. In: S. Boorstein (Ed.), *Transpersonal Psychology* (pp. 209–240). Palo Alto, CA: Science and Behavior.

DeCarvalho, R. J. (1991). *The Growth Hypothesis in Psychology: Humanistic Psychologies of Abraham Maslow and Carl Rogers*. Lampeter: Edwin Mellen Press.

Dewey, J. (1896). The reflex arc concept in psychology. *Psychological Review, 3*: 357–370.

Dewey, J. (1938). *Logic: The Theory of Inquiry*. New York: Henry Holt.

Dixon, T. (2006). *From Passions to Emotions: The Creation of a Secular Psychological Category*. Cambridge: Cambridge University Press.

Dolby, R. G. A. (1996). *Uncertain Knowledge: An Image of Science for a Changing World*. Cambridge: Cambridge University Press.

Dryden, W. (1984). *Reason and Therapeutic Change*. London: Whurr.

Dryden, W. (1990). *Rational-Emotive Counselling in Action*. London: Sage.

Dryden, W. (1991). *A Dialogue with Albert Ellis: Against Dogma*. Milton Keynes: Open University Press.

Dryden, W. & Still, A. W. (1998). REBT and rationality: philosophical approaches. *Journal of Rational-Emotive & Cognitive-Behavior Therapy, 16*: 77–99.

Dryden, W. & Still, A. W. (1999). When did a psychologist last discuss "chagrin"? America's continuing moral project. *History of the Human Sciences*, 12: 93–110.

Dryden, W. & Still, A. W. (2006). Historical aspects of mindfulness and self-acceptance in psychotherapy. *Journal of Rational-Emotive & Cognitive-Behavior Therapy*, 24: 3–28.

Dryden, W. & Still, A. W. (2007). Rationality and the shoulds. *Journal for the Theory of Social Behaviour*, 37: 1–23.

Dryden, W., Ferguson, J. & Clark, T. (1989). Beliefs and inferences: A test of a rational-emotive hypothesis: 1. Performing in an academic seminar. *Journal of Rational-Emotive & Cognitive-Behavior Therapy*, 7: 119–129.

Duncker, K. (1945). On problem solving. *Psychological Monographs*, 58 (Whole Number 270).

Dupré, J. (1983). The disunity of science. *Mind*, 92: 321–346.

Eddy, D. M. (1982). Probabilistic reasoning in clinical medicine: Problems and opportunities. In: D. Kahneman, P. Slovic & A. Tversky (Eds) *Judgment Under Uncertainty: Heuristic and Biases* (pp. 249–267). New York: Cambridge University Press.

Eliot, T. S. (1951). Shakespeare and the Stoicism of Seneca. In: *Selected Essays* (pp. 126–140). London: Faber & Faber.

Ellenberger, H. F. (1970). *The Discovery of the Unconscious: The History and Evolution of Dynamic Psychiatry*. London: Allen Lane.

Ellis, A. (1946). The validity of personality questionnaires. *Psychological Bulletin*, 43: 385–440.

Ellis, A. (1950). An introduction to the principles of scientific psychoanalysis. *Genetic Psychology Monographs*, 41: 147–212.

Ellis, A. (1955a). New approaches to psychotherapy techniques. *Journal of Clinical Psychology*, 11: 207–260.

Ellis, A. (1955b). Psychotherapy techniques for use with psychotics. *American Journal of Psychotherapy*, 9: 452–476.

Ellis, A. (1956). An operational reformulation of some of the basic principles of psychoanalysis. In: H. Feigl & M. Scriven (Eds), *The Foundations of Science and the Concepts of Psychology and Psychoanalysis* (pp. 131–154). Minneapolis, MN: University of Minnesota Press.

Ellis, A. (1957a). Rational psychotherapy and individual psychology. *Journal of Individual Psychology*, 13: 38–44.

Ellis, A. (1957b). Outcome of employing three techniques of psychotherapy. *Journal of Clinical Psychology*, 13: 344–350.

Ellis, A. (1958). Rational psychotherapy. *The Journal of General Psychology*, 59: 35–49.

Ellis, A. (1960a). There is no place for the concept of sin in psychotherapy. *Journal of Counseling Psychology*, 7: 188–192.

Ellis, A. (1960b). Mowrer on "sin". *American Psychologist, 15*: 713.

Ellis, A. (1962). *Reason and Emotion in Psychotherapy.* Secaucus, NJ: Citadel Press.

Ellis, A. (1974). *Humanistic Psychotherapy: Rational-Emotive Approach.* New York: McGraw-Hill.

Ellis, A. (1976). The biological basis of human irrationality. *Journal of Individual Psychology, 32*: 145–168.

Ellis, A. (1977). The basic clinical theory of rational-emotive therapy. In: A. Ellis & R. Grieger (Eds), *Handbook of Rational-Emotive Therapy* (pp. 3–34). New York: Springer.

Ellis, A. (1984–1985). Yes, how reasonable is rational-emotive therapy? *Review of Existential Psychiatry and Psychology, 19*: 129–134.

Ellis, A. (1987). A sadly neglected cognitive element in depression. *Cognitive Therapy and Research, 11*: 121–146.

Ellis, A. (1991). My life in clinical psychology. In: C. E. Walker (Ed.), *The History of Clinical Psychology in Autobiography* (pp. 1–37). Pacific Grove, CA: Brooks/Cole.

Ellis, A. (1994). *Reason and Emotion in Psychotherapy: A Comprehensive Method of Treating Human Disturbances* (revised edn). New York: Carol Publishing.

Ellis, A. (2006). Rational Emotive Behavior Therapy and the mindfulness based stress reduction training of Jon Kabat-Zinn. *Journal of Rational-Emotive & Cognitive-Behavior Therapy, 24*: 63–78.

Ellis, A. & Bernard, M. (1986). What is rational-emotive therapy (RET)? In: A. Ellis & R. Grieger (Eds), *Handbook of Rational-Emotive Therapy* (Vol. 2) (pp. 1–30). New York: Springer.

Ellis, A. & Harper, R. A. (1961). *A Guide to Rational Living.* Englewood Cliffs, NJ: Prentice Hall.

Emerson, R. W. (1977). Montaigne; or, The Sceptic. In: M. van Doren (Ed.), *The Portable Emerson* (pp. 488–513). Harmondsworth: Penguin Books.

Emerson, R. W. (n.d.). *Essays and Representative Men.* London: Collins.

Endersby, J. (2009). Lumpers and splitters: Darwin, Hooker, and the search for order. *Science, 326*: 1496–1499.

Epictetus (1955). *The Enchiridion.* Indianapolis, IN: Bobbs-Merrill.

Epictetus (1995). *The Discourses of Epictetus* (2nd edn). London: J. M. Dent.

Epstein, M. (1995). *Thoughts without a Thinker.* New York: Basic Books.

Erskine, A. (1990). *The Hellenistic Stoa: Political Thought and Action.* London: Duckworth.

Erwin, E. (1997). *Philosophy and Psychotherapy.* London: Sage.

Evans, C. S. (1984–1985). Albert Ellis' conception of rationality: How reasonable is rational-emotive therapy? *Review of Existential Psychiatry and Psychology, 19*: 129–134.

Farr, R. M. (1983). Wilhelm Wundt (1832–1920) and the origins of psychology as an experimental and social science. *British Journal of Social Psychology, 22*: 289–301.

Feigl, H. & Scriven, M. (Eds) (1956) *The Foundations of Science and the Concepts of Pyschology and Psychoanalysis*. Minneapolis, MN: University of Minnesota Press.

Fields, R. (1992). *How the Swans Came to the Lake* (3rd edn). Boston: Shambala.

Fodor, J. A. & Pylyshyn, Z. (1981). How direct is perception? Some reflections on Gibson's "Ecological approach". *Cognition, 9*: 139–196.

Folsom, C. (1984). Anger, dejection and acedia in the writings of John Cassian. *American Benedictine Review, 22*: 219–248.

Foucault, M. (1965). *Madness and Civilization*. New York: Pantheon.

Foucault, M. (1977). *Discipline and Punish*. Harmondsworth: Penguin Books.

Foucault, M. (1980). Two lectures. In: C. Gordon (Ed.), *Power/Knowledge: Selected Interviews and Other Writings 1972–1977* (pp. 78–108). Brighton: Harvester Press.

Frankl, V. E. (1967). *Psychotherapy and Existentialism: Selected Papers on Logotherapy*. Harmondsworth: Penguin Books.

Freud, S. (1949). *Collected Papers* (Vol. 4). London: Hogarth Press.

Fuller, R. (1986). *Americans and the Unconscious*. London: Oxford University Press.

Galison, P. (1997). *Image and Logic: A Material Culture of Microphysics*. Chicago: University of Chicago Press.

Galison, P. & Stump, D. J. (1996). *The Disunity of Science: Boundaries, Contexts, and Power*. Stanford, CA: Stanford University Press.

Gardner, M. (1952). *In the Name of Science*. New York: G. P. Putnam's Sons.

Gardner, M. (1957). *Facts and Fallacies in the Name of Science*. New York: Dover.

Gardner, M. (2000). *Did Adam and Eve Have Navels? Debunking Pseudoscience*. New York: W.W. Norton.

Garner, W. R., Hake, H. W. & Eriksen, C. W. (1956). Operationism and the concept of perception. *Psychological Review, 63*: 149–159.

Garske, J. P. & Anderson, T. (2003). Toward a science of psychotherapy: Present status and evaluation. In: S. O. Lilienfeld, S. J. Lynn & J. M. Lohr (Eds), *Science and Pseudoscience in Clinical Psychology* (pp. 145–175). New York: Guilford Press.

Gendlin, E. T. (1981). *Focussing*. New York: Bantam Books.

Gendlin, E. T. (1997). *Experience and the Creation of Meaning*. Evanston, IL: Northwestern University Press.

Germer, C. K., Siegel, R. D. & Fulton, P. R. (2005). *Mindfulness and Psychotherapy*. New York: Guilford Press.

Gibson, J. J. (1959). Perception as a function of stimulation. In: S. Koch (Ed.), *Psychology: A Study of a Science* (Vol. 1) (pp. 456–501). New York: McGraw-Hill.

Gibson, J. J. (1979). *The Ecological Approach to Visual Perception*. Boston: Houghton Mifflin.

Giddens, A. (1976). *New Rules of Sociological Method*. New York: Basic Books.

Gieryn, F. (1999). *Cultural Boundaries of Science: Credibility on the Line*. Chicago: University of Chicago Press.

Gigerenzer, G. (2000). *Adaptive Thinking: Rationality in the Real World*. New York: Oxford University Press.

Gigerenzer, G. & Selten, R. (Eds) (2000). *Bounded Rationality: The Adaptive Toolbox*. Cambridge, MA: MIT Press.

Gilbert, P. (Ed.) (2005). *Compassion: Conceptualisations, Research and Use in Psychotherapy*. London: Routledge.

Goddard, D. (1956). *A Buddhist Bible* (2nd edn). London: Harrap.

Goldstein, J. & Kornfield, J. (1987). *Seeking the Path of Wisdom: The Path of Insight Meditation*. Boston: Shambala.

Goleman, D. (1977). *The Varieties of the Meditative Experience*. London: Rider.

Good, J. M. M. (2000). Disciplining social psychology: A case study of boundary relations in the history of the human sciences. *Journal of the History of the Behavioral Sciences, 36*: 383–483.

Gould, S. J. & Lewontin, R. C. (1979). The spandrels of San Marco and the Panglossian paradigm: A critique of the adaptationist programme. *Proceedings of the Royal Society, London, B 205*: 581–598.

Gross, P. R. & Levitt, N. (1994). *Higher Superstition: The Academic Left and its Quarrels with Science*. Baltimore, MD: Johns Hopkins University Press.

Gross, P. R., Levitt, N. & Lewis, M. W. (Eds) (1997). *The Flight from Science and Reason*. New York: New York Academy of Sciences.

Grünbaum, A. (1984). *The Foundations of Psychoanalysis*. Berkeley, CA: University of California Press.

Guignon, C. B. (1993). Authenticity, moral values, and psychotherapy. In: C. B. Guignon (Ed.), *The Cambridge Companion to Heidegger* (pp. 215–239). Cambridge: Cambridge University Press.

Haaga, D. A. F. & Davison, G. C. (1993). An appraisal of rational-emotive therapy. *Journal of Consulting and Clinical Psychology, 61*: 215–220.

Haakonssen, K. (1996). *Natural Law and Moral Philosophy: From Grotius to the Scottish Enlightenment*. Cambridge: Cambridge University Press.

Hacking, I. (1995). *Rewriting the Soul: Multiple Personality and the Sciences of Memory*. Princeton, NJ: Princeton University Press.

Hacking, I. (1996). The disunity of the sciences. In: P. Galison & D. J. Stump (Eds), *The Disunity of Science: Boundaries, Contexts, and Power* (pp. 37–74). Stanford, CA: Stanford University Press.

Hadot, P. (1995). *Philosophy as a Way of Life: Spiritual Exercises from Socrates to Foucault.* New York: Wiley.

Halmos, P. (1965). *The Faith of the Counsellors.* London: Constable.

Hanen, M. P., Osler, M. J. & Weyant, R. G. (Eds) (1980). *Science, Pseudo-Science and Society.* Waterloo, Canada: Wilfred Laurier University Press.

Hare, R. M. (1952). *The Language of Morals.* Oxford: The Clarendon Press.

Hayakawa, S. I. (1941). *Language in Action: A Guide to Accurate Thinking, Reading and Writing.* New York: Harcourt, Brace and Company.

Hayakawa, S. I. (1952). *Language in Thought and Action: How Men use Words and Words use Men.* London: George Allen & Unwin.

Hayes, S. C. (1984). Making sense of spirituality. *Behaviorism, 12*: 99–109.

Hayes, S. C., Strosahl, K. D. & Wilson, K. G. (1999). *Acceptance and Commitment Therapy: An Experiential Approach to Behavior Change.* New York: Guilford Press.

Hefferline, R. F. (1958). The role of proprioception in the control of behavior. *Transactions of the New York Academy of Sciences, 20*: 739–764.

Heider, F. (1958). *The Psychology of Interpersonal Relations.* New York: Wiley.

Helmholtz, H. von (1962). *A Handbook of Physiological Optics* (3 vols). New York: Dover.

Hempel, C. G. (1959). *Aspects of Scientific Explanation and Other Essays in the Philosophy of Science.* New York: The Free Press.

Hempel, C. G. (1965). *Aspects of Scientific Explanation.* New York: Free Press.

Herbert, J. D., Lilienfeld, S. O., Lohr, J. M., Montgomery, R. W., O'Donohue, W. T., Rosen, G. M. & Tolin, D. F. (2000). Science and pseudoscience in the development of eye movement desensitization and reprocessing: Implications for clinical psychology. *Clinical Psychology Review, 20*: 945–971.

Herrigel, E. (1953). *Zen in the Art of Archery.* London: Penguin Books [reprinted: 2004].

Herrigel, G. L. (1958). *Zen in the Art of Flower-Arrangement.* London: Routledge.

Herzog, M. (1995). William James and the development of phenomenological psychology in Europe. *History of the Human Sciences, 8(1)*: 29–46.

Hinde, R. A. (1970). *Animal Behaviour: A Synthesis of Ethology and Comparative Psychology* (2nd edn). New York: McGraw-Hill.

Hinde, R. A. & Stevenson-Hinde, J. (1973). *Constraints on Learning: Limitations and Predispositions.* London: Academic.

Hines, T. (1988). *Pseudoscience and the Paranormal.* Buffalo, NY: Prometheus Books.

Horney, K. (1937). *The Neurotic Personality of Our Time*. London: Kegan Paul.

Horney, K. (1945). *Our Inner Conflicts*. New York: Norton.

Horney, K. (1950). *Neurosis and Human Growth: The Struggle toward Self-Realisation*. New York: Norton [reprinted with a new foreword 1991].

Hull, C. L. (1943). *Principles of Behavior*. New York: Appleton-Century-Crofts.

Humphreys, C. (1951). *Buddhism*. Harmondsworth: Penguin Books.

Husserl, E. (1964). *The Phenomenology of Internal Time-Consciousness*. Bloomington, IN: Indiana University Press.

Husserl, E. (1965). *Phenomenology and the Crisis of Philosophy*. New York: Harper Torchbacks.

Husserl, E. (1970). *The Crisis of European Science and Transcendental Phenomenology*. Evanston, IL: Northwestern University Press.

Inwood, B. (1985). *Ethics and Human Action in Early Stoicism*. Oxford: Clarendon Press.

Inwood, B. (1993). Seneca and psychological dualism. In: J. Brunschwig & M. C. Nussbaum (Eds), *Passions and Perceptions: Studies in Hellenistic Philosophy of Mind* (pp. 150–183). Cambridge: Cambridge University Press.

Jacobson, A. & Berenberg, A. N. (1952). Japanese psychiatry and psychotherapy. *American Journal of Psychiatry*, 109: 321–329.

Jacobson, J. W., Mulick, J. A. & Schwartz, A. A. (1995). A history of facilitated communication: science, pseudoscience, and antiscience. *American Psychologist, 50*: 750–765.

Jacoby, R. (1975). *Social Amnesia: A Critique of Conformist Psychology from Adler to Laing*. Hassocks: Harvester.

James, W. (1890). *The Principles of Psychology* (Vols 1 and 2). New York: Henry Holt.

James, W. (1899). *Talks to Teachers on Psychology*. New York: Henry Holt [reprinted: 1910].

James, W. (1902). *The Varieties of Religious Experience*. London: Longmans, Green.

James, W. (1926). *The Letters of William James* (Vol. 1). London: Longmans.

James, W. (1956). *The Will to Believe*. New York: Dover.

Johnson-Laird, P. N. (1983). *Mental Models*. Cambridge: Cambridge University Press.

Johnson, W. (1939). The treatment of stuttering. *Journal of Speech Disorders*, 4: 170–172.

Johnson, W. (1946). *People in Quandaries: The Semantics of Personal Adjustment*. New York: Harper

Jones, M. L. (2006). *The Good Life in the Scientific Revolution: Descartes, Pascal, Leibniz and the Cultivation of Virtue*. Chicago: Chicago University Press.

Kabat-Zinn, J. (1990). *Full Catastrophe Living: Using the Wisdom of your Body and Mind to Face Stress, Pain, and Illness*. New York: Delacorte.

Kabat-Zinn, J. (1994). *Wherever You Go, There You Are: Mindfulness Meditation in Everyday Life*. New York: Hyperion.

Kabat-Zinn, J. (2005). *Coming to Our Senses: Healing Ourselves and the World through Mindfulness*. New York: Piatkus.

Katz, N. (Ed.) (1983). *Buddhist and Western Psychology*. Boulder, Colorado: Prajna Press.

Katz, N. (2006). *Zen and the Art of Crossword Puzzles*. Cincinnati, OH: Adams media.

Kipling, R. (1977). *Selected Poems*. Harmondsworth: Penguin Books.

Kirsch, I. (2009). *The Emperor's New Drugs: Exploding the Antidepressant Myth*. New York: Basic Books.

Koch, R. (1882). *Essays of Robert Koch*. Westport, Connecticut: Greenwood Press [reprinted: 1987].

Kohlberg, L. (1963). Development of children's orientations toward a moral order. *Vita Humana, 6*: 11–36 [*Human Development*].

Korzybski, A. (1948). *Science and Sanity* (3rd edn). Lakeville, CT: International Non-Aristotelian Publishing.

Krantz, D. L. (1972) Schools and systems: The mutual isolation of operant and non-operant psychology as a case study. *Journal of the History of the Behavioral Sciences, 8*: 86–102.

Kraut, R. (2010). Aristotle's Ethics. In: E. N. Zalta (Ed.), *The Stanford Encyclopedia of Philosophy* (Summer 2010 Edition), http://plato.stanford.edu/archives/sum2010/entries/aristotle-ethics/ [last accessed 23 January 2012].

Krishnamurti, J. (1954). *The First and Last Freedom*. London: Victor Gollancz [reprinted: 1972].

Kuhn, T. S. (1962). *The Structure of Scientific Revolutions*. Chicago: University of Chicago Press.

Laing, R. D. (1965). *The Divided Self*. Harmondsworth: Penguin Books.

Lakatos, I. (1970). Falsification and the methodology of scientific research programmes. In: I. Lakatos & A. Musgrave (Eds), *Criticism and the Growth of Knowledge* (pp. 91–195). Cambridge: Cambridge University Press.

Langer, E. J. (1989). *Mindfulness: Choice and Control in Everyday Life*. London: Harvill [reprinted: 1991].

Latour. B. (1987). *Science in Action*. Milton Keynes: Open University Press.

Laudan, L. (1983). The demise of the demarcation problem. In R. Laudan (Ed.), *The Demarcation between Science and Pseudo-Science* (pp. 7–35). Blacksburg, VA: Virginia Polytechnic Institute and State University, Center for the Study of Science and Society.

Laudan, R. (Ed.) (1983). *The Demarcation between Science and Pseudo-Science*. Blacksburg, VA: Virginia Polytechnic Institute and State University, Center for the Study of Science and Society.

Lave, J. (1988). *Cognition in Practice*. Cambridge: Cambridge University Press.

Leahey, T. H. & Leahey, G. E. (1983). *Psychology's Occult Doubles: Psychology and the Problem of Pseudoscience*. Chicago: Nelson-Hall.

Lenoir, T. (1979). Descartes and the geometrization of thought: The methodological background of Descartes' *Géométrie*. *Historia Mathematica, 6*: 355–379 [*History of Mathematics*].

Lentricchia, F. (1988). *Ariel and the Police*. Madison, WI: University of Wisconsin Press.

Lilienfeld, S. O., Lynn, S. J. & Lohr, J. M. (Eds) (2004). *Science and Pseudoscience in Clinical Psychology*. New York: Guilford Press.

Linehan, M. M. (1993a). *Cognitive-Behavioral Treatment of Borderline Personality Disorder*. New York: Guilford Press.

Linehan, M. M. (1993b). *Skills Training Manual for Treating Borderline Personality Disorder*. New York: Guilford Press.

Long, A. A. (1974). *Hellenistic Philosophy*. London: Duckworth.

Long, A. A. (1986). *Hellenistic Philosophy* (2nd edn). London: Duckworth.

Long, A. A. (2002). *Epictetus: A Stoic and Socratic Guide to Life*. Oxford: Oxford University Press.

Long, A. A. & Sedley, D. N. (1987). *The Hellenistic Philosophers*. Vol. 1. *Translations of the Principle Sources with Philosophical Commentary*. Cambridge: Cambridge University Press.

Luchins, A. S. (1942). Mechanization in problem-solving: The effect of *Einstellung*. *Psychological Monographs, 58 (Whole number 248)*.

MacIntyre, A. (1981). *After Virtue: A Study in Moral Theory*. London: Duckworth.

Mahoney, M. J. (2004). *Cognitive and Constructive Psychotherapies: Theory, Research and Practice*. New York: Springer.

Mahoney, M. J. & Gabriel, T. J. (1987). Psychotherapy and cognitive sciences: An evolving alliance. *Journal of Cognitive Psychotherapy, 1*: 39–59.

Mahoney, M. J., Lyddon, W. F. & Alford, D. J. (1989). An evaluation of rational-emotive theory of psychotherapy. In: M. Bernard & R. DiGiuseppe (Eds), *Inside Rational-Emotive Therapy* (pp. 69–94). San Diego, CA: Academic Press.

Marlatt, G. A. (2002). Buddhist philosophy and the treatment of addictive behavior. *Cognitive and Behavioral Practice, 9*: 44–49.

Martin, L. H., Gutman, H. & Hutton, P. H. (eds) (1988). *Technologies of the Self: A Seminar with Michel Foucault*. London: Routledge.

Maslow, A. H. (1971). *The Farther Reaches of Human Nature*. Harmondsworth: Penguin Books.

May, R. (1958). *Existence: A New Dimension in Psychiatry and Psychology*. New York: Simon and Schuster.

May, R. (1969). *Love and Will*. New York: W.W. Norton.

Mayr, E. (1982). *The Growth of Biological Thought*. Cambridge, MA: Harvard University Press.

McMahon, J. (1996). *The Contribution of Albert Ellis to Cognitive Behavioral Psychotherapy*. PhD thesis, University of Wales.

McNally, R. J. (2003). Pseudoscience resurgent? A reply. *The Scientific Review of Mental Health Practice*, 2: 115–116.

Medawar, P. B. (1969). *The Art of the Soluble*. Harmondsworth: Penguin Books.

Meehl, P. & MacCorquodale, K. (1948). On a distinction between intervening variables and hypothetical constructs. *Psychological Review*, 55: 95–107.

Michael, M. & Still, A. W. (1992). A resource for resistance: Power-knowledge and affordance. *Theory and Society*, 21: 869–888.

Mill, J. S. (1843). *A System of Logic*. London: Longmans, Green [reprinted 1898].

Miller, G. A. (1956). The magical number seven, plus or minus two. *Psychological Review*, 63: 81–97.

Miller, P. & Rose, N. (1994). On therapeutic authority: Psychoanalytical expertise under advanced liberalism. *History of the Human Sciences*, 7(3): 29–64.

Mitchell, T. (1991). *Colonising Egypt*. Berkeley, CA: University of California Press.

Mitchell, T. (2002). *Rule of Experts*. Berkeley, CA: University of California Press.

Montaigne, M. de (1987). *An Apology for Raymond Sebond*. London: Penguin Books.

Montaigne, M. de (1991). *The Complete Essays*. London: Penguin Books.

Moore, W. E. (1970). *The Professions: Roles and Rules*. New York: Russell Sage Foundation.

Morgan, C. L. (1894). *An Introduction to Comparative Psychology*. London: Scott.

Morrison, R. G. (1997). *Nietzsche and Buddhism: A Study in Nihilism and Ironic Affinities*. Oxford: Oxford University Press.

Morvay, Z. (1999). Horney, Zen, and the real self: Theoretical and historical connections. *American Journal of Psychoanalysis*, 59: 25–35.

Mowrer, O. H. (1950). *Learning Theory and Personality Dynamics*. New York: Wiley.

Mowrer, O. H. (1960a). Some constructive features of the concept of sin. *Journal of Counseling Psychology, 7*: 185–188.

Mowrer, O. H. (1960b). "Sin": The lesser of two evils. *American Psychologist, 15*: 301–304.

Murphy, G. & Murphy, L. B. (1968). *Asian Psychology.* New York: Basic Books.

Murray, D. J. (1995). *Gestalt Psychology and the Cognitive Revolution.* Hemel Hempstead: Harvester Wheatsheaf.

Nanavira Thera (1987). *Clearing the Path: Writings of Nanavira Thera (1960–1965).* Colombo, Sri Lanka: Path Press.

Neisser, U. (1967). *Cognitive Psychology.* New York: Appleton-Century-Crofts.

Newton-Smith, W. H. (1981). *The Rationality of Science.* London: Routledge & Kegan Paul.

Nicolson, M. (1991). The social and the cognitive: Resources for the sociology of scientific knowledge. *Studies in the History and Philosophy of Science, 22*: 347–369.

Nietzsche, F. (1889). *Götzen-Dämmerung, oder: Wie man mit dem Hammer philosophert.* Leipzig: C.G. Naumann.

Nietzsche, F. (1968). *Twilight of the Idols and The AntiChrist.* Harmondsworth: Penguin Books.

Nussbaum, M. C. (1994). *The Therapy of Desire: Theory and Practice in Hellenistic Ethics.* Princeton, NJ: Princeton University Press.

Nyanaponika Thera (1962). *The Heart of Buddhist Meditation.* London: Rider.

O'Donohue, W. & Vass, J. S. (1996). What is an irrational belief? Rational-emotive therapy and accounts of rationality. In: W. O'Donohue & R. F. Kitchener (Eds), *The Philosophy of Psychology* (pp. 304–316). London: Sage.

Ong, W. J. (1983). *Ramus, Method and the Decay of Dialogue.* Cambridge, MA.: Harvard University Press.

Onians, C. T. (1959). *Shorter Oxford Dictionary.* Oxford: Clarendon Press.

Padesky, C. A. (2004). *Harnessing Hope and Reducing Relapse: Engaging Clients in CT for Depression.* Cognitive Workshop, London, 12–13 May, 2004.

Panizza, L. A. (1991). Stoic psychotherapy in the middle ages and renaissance. In: M. Osler (Ed.), *Atoms, Pneuma, and Tranquility* (pp. 39–66). Cambridge: Cambridge University Press.

Passmore, J. (1966). *A Hundred Years of Philosophy.* Harmondsworth: Penguin Books.

Peale, N. V. (1996). *The Power of Positive Thinking.* New York: Ballantine Books.

Pembroke, S. G. (1971). Oikeiosis. In: A. A. Long (Ed.), *Problems in Stoicism* (pp. 114–149). London: The Athlone Press.

Perls, F., Hefferline, R. H. & Goodman, P. (1951). *Gestalt Therapy: Excitement and Growth in the Human Personality.* London: Souvenir Press [reprinted 1972].

Perry, R. B. (1948). *The Thought and Character of William James.* Cambridge, MA: Harvard University Press.

Phillips, D. C. (2000). *The Expanded Social Scientist's Bestiary: A Guide to Fabled Threats to, and Defenses of, Naturalistic Social Science.* Lanham, MD: Rowan and Littlefield.

Piaget, J. (1932). *The Moral Judgement of the Child.* London: Kegan Paul.

Piaget, J. (1971). *The Biology of Knowledge.* Edinburgh: Edinburgh University Press.

Pirsig, R. M. (1974). *Zen and the Art of Motorcycle Maintenance.* London: Bodley Head.

Plato (1970). *The Dialogues of Plato* (Vol. 4: The Republic). Trans. Benjamin Jowett. London: Sphere Books.

Poirier, R. (1987). *The Renewal of Literature: Emersonian reflections.* New York: Random House.

Poirier, R. (1992). *Poetry and Pragmatism.* Cambridge, MA: Harvard University Press.

Popper, K. R. (1962). *The Open Society and its Enemies.* Vol. 2. *Hegel & Marx* (4th edn). London: Routledge & Kegan Paul.

Popper, K. R. (1968). *The Logic of Scientific Discovery.* London: Hutchinson.

Popper, K. R. (1972). *Conjectures and Refutations: The Growth of Scientific Knowledge.* London: Routledge & Kegan Paul.

Popper, K. R. (1976). *Unended Quest: An Intellectual Autobiography.* London: Fontana.

Popper, K. R. (1978). *Objective Knowledge: An Evolutionary Approach.* Oxford: Oxford University Press.

Porter, N. (1869). *The Human Intellect.* New York: Charles Scribner.

Potter, J. & Wetherell, M. (1987). *Discourse and Social Psychology.* London: Sage.

Price, A. W. (1994). *Mental Conflict.* London: Routledge.

Quine, W. V. O. (1953). *From a Logical Point of View.* Cambridge, Massachusetts: Harvard University Press.

Quinn, S. (1988). *A Mind of Her Own: The Life of Karen Horney.* New York: Addison-Wesley.

QuotesL.com (n.d.) www.quotesl.com/adlai_stevenson [accessed 21 January 2012].

Reed, E. S. (1982). Darwin's earthworms: A case study in evolutionary psychology. *Behaviorism, 10*: 165–185.

Reed, E. S. (1988). *James J. Gibson and the Psychology of Perception.* New Haven, CT: Yale University Press.

Reed, E. S. (1990). Space perception and the psychologist's fallacy in James's *Principles*. In: M. G. Johnson & T. B. Henley (Eds), *Reflections on the Principles of Psychology: William James after a Century* (pp. 231–247). Hillsdale, NJ: Lawrence Erlbaum.

Reed, E. S. (1997). *From Soul to Mind: The Emergence of Psychology, Erasmus Darwin to William James*. New Haven, CT: Yale University Press.

Reynolds, D. K. (1976). *Morita Psychotherapy*. Berkeley, CA: University of California Press.

Rhys Davids, T. W. (1895–1910). *The Questions of King Milinda* (Vol. 1). London: Curzon [reprinted: 2001].

Richards, B. (1989). *Images of Freud: Cultural Responses to Psychoanalysis*. London: J.M. Dent & Sons.

Richards, G. (1995). "To know our fellow men to do them good": American psychology's enduring moral project. *History of the Human Sciences, 8(3)*: 1–24.

Richards, I. A. (1926). *Science and Poetry*. New York: Haskell House Publishers [reprinted: 1974].

Richardson, R. D. (1995). *Emerson: The Mind on Fire*. Berkeley, CA: University of California Press.

Rieff, P. (1960). *Freud: The Mind of the Moralist*. London: Gollancz.

Robertson, D. (2010). *The Philosophy of Cognitive-Behavioural Therapy (CBT): Stoic Philosophy as Rational and Cognitive Psychotherapy*. London: Karnac.

Robinson, D. M. (1993). *Emerson and the Conduct of Life: Pragmatism and Ethical Purpose in the Later Work*. Cambridge: Cambridge University Press.

Rogers, C. (1974). *On Becoming a Person*. London: Constable.

Rogers, C. (1990). Toward a modern approach to values. In: H. Kirschenbaum & V. L. Henderson (Eds), *The Carl Rogers Reader* (pp. 168–185). London: Constable.

Rorty, R. (1967). *The Linguistic Turn: Recent Essays in Philosophical Method*. Chicago: Chicago University Press.

Rorty, R. (1980). *Philosophy and the Mirror of Nature*. Oxford: Basil Blackwell.

Rorty, R. (1985/1986). Texts and lumps. *New Literary History, 17*: 1–16.

Rosenberg, A. (1994). *Instrumental Biology, or, The Disunity of Science*. Chicago: Chicago University Press.

Rosenberg, H. (1987). *Impasse and Interpretation*. London: Tavistock Publications.

Ross, A. (Ed.) (1996). *Science Wars*. Durham, NC: Duke University Press.

Ross, C. A. & Pam, A. (1995). *Pseudoscience in Biological Psychiatry: Blaming the Body*. New York: Wiley.

Safran, J. D. (Ed.) (2003). *Psychoanalysis and Buddhism: An Unfolding Dialogue*. Somerville, MA: Wisdom Publications.

Sagan, C. (1995). *The Demon-Haunted World: Science as a Candle in the Dark.* New York: Random House.

Samuels, A. (1989). *The Plural Psyche: Personality, Morality and the Father.* London: Routledge.

Schön, D. A. (1983). *The Reflective Practitioner: How Professionals Think in Action.* New York: Basic Books.

Sedlar, J. W. (1982). *India in the Mind of Germany: Schelling, Schopenauer and their Times.* Washington, D.C.: University Press of America.

Segal, Z. V., Williams, J. M. G. & Teasdale, J. D. (2002). *Mindfulness-based Cognitive Therapy for Depression: A New Approach to Preventing Relapse.* New York: Guilford Press.

Segall, S. R. (Ed.) (2003). *Encountering Buddhism: Western Psychology and Buddhist Teachings.* Albany, NY: State University of New York Press.

Self-improvement-ebooks.com   (n.d.).   http://jamesallen.wwwhubs.com [last accessed 17 May 2011].

Seligman, M. E. P. (1995). The effectiveness of psychotherapy: The *Consumer Reports* study. *American Psychologist, 50*: 965–974.

Seligman, M. E. P. (2002). *Authentic Happiness: Using the New Positive Psychology to Realize Your Potential for Lasting Fulfillment.* New York: Free Press.

Seneca (1928). *Moral Essays* (Vol. 1). London: Heinemann.

Seneca (1962). *Ad Lucilium Epistulae Morales.* Cambridge, Massachusetts: Heinemann [*Moral Letters to Lucilius*].

Sharp, D. S. (1914). *Epictetus and the New Testament.* London: Charles H. Kelly.

Sharpe, R. A. & McMahon, J. (1997). Identity and constructivism: Grounding the self in Rational Emotive Behavior Therapy. *Journal of Rational-Emotive & Cognitive-Behavior Therapy, 15*: 31-47.

Shermer, M. (2002). *Why People Believe Weird Things: Pseudoscience, Superstition, and Other Confusions of our Time.* New York: Owl Books.

Shotter, J. (1983). "Duality of structure" and "intentionality" in an ecological psychology. *Journal for the Theory of Social Behaviour, 20*: 19–41.

Simon, H. A. (1956). Rational choice and the structure of environments. *Psychological Review, 63*: 129–138.

Skinner, B. F. (1931). The concept of the reflex in the description of behavior. *Journal of General Psychology, 5*: 427–458.

Skinner, B. F. (1945). The operational analysis of psychological terms. *Psychological Review, 52*: 270–277.

Skinner, B. F. (1950). Are theories of learning necessary? *Psychological Review, 57*: 193–216.

Skinner, B. F. (1953). *Science and Human Behavior.* New York: Free Press.

Skinner, B. F. (1972). *Beyond Freedom and Dignity.* London: Jonathan Cape.

Skinner, B. F. (1977). Why I am not a cognitive psychologist. *Behaviorism, 5*: 1–10.

Snyder, N. J. (2006). "William Whewell". In: Edward N. Zalta (Ed.) *The Standard Encyclopedia of Philosophy*. http://plato.stanford.edu/archives/win2006)/entries/whewell/ [Last accessed 29 January 2012].

Sokal, A. D. & Bricmont, J. (1998). *Intellectual Impostures*. London: Profile Books.

Sorabji, R. (2000). *Emotions and Peace of Mind*. Oxford: Oxford University Press.

Spencer, H. (1860). *First Principles*. London: Williams & Norgate [reprinted: 1904].

Spiegelman, J. M. & Miyuki, M. (1985). *Buddhism and Jungian Psychology*. Phoenix, AZ: Falcon Press.

Stebbing, S. (1944). *Philosophy and the Physicists*. Harmondsworth: Penguin Books.

Stevens, S. S. (1935). The operational basis of psychology. *American Journal of Psychology, 47*: 323–330.

Stevens, S. S. (1939). Psychology and the science of science. *Psychological Bulletin, 36*: 221–263.

Still, A. W. (1986). The biology of science: An essay on the evolution of representational cognitivism. *Journal for the Theory of Social Behaviour, 16*: 251–266.

Still, A. W. (2001). Reflections on Loughborough realism. *History of the Human Sciences, 14(3)*: 108–113.

Still, A. W. (2001). Marginalisation is not unbearable. Is it even undesirable? *Journal of Rational-Emotive & Cognitive-Behavior Therapy, 19*: 55–66.

Still, A. W. & Dryden, W. (1998). The intellectual origins of Rational Psychotherapy. *History of the Human Sciences, 11(3)*: 63–86.

Still, A. W. & Dryden, W. (1999). The place of rationality in Stoicism and REBT. *Journal of Rational-Emotive & Cognitive-Behavior Therapy, 17*: 143– 164.

Still, A. W. & Dryden, W. (2003). Ellis and Epictetus: Dialogue vs. method in psychotherapy. *Journal of Rational-Emotive & Cognitive-Behavior Therapy, 21*: 37–55.

Still, A. W. & Dryden, W. (2004). The social psychology of "pseudoscience": A brief history. *Journal of the Theory of Social Behaviour, 34*: 265–290.

Still, A. W. & Good, J. M. M. (1992). Mutualism in the human sciences: Towards the implementation of a theory. *Journal for the Theory of Social Behaviour, 22*: 105–128.

Still, A. W. & Good, J. M. M. (1998). The ontology of mutualism. *Ecological Psychology, 10*: 39–63.

Stockdale, J. B. (1995). Testing Epictetus's doctrines in a laboratory of human behaviour. *Bulletin of the Institute of Classical Studies, 40*: 1–13.

Suppes, P. (1978). The plurality of science. In: P. D. Asquith & I. Hacking (Eds), *PSA 1978* (Vol. 2) (pp. 3–16). East Lansing, MI: Philosophy of Science Association.

Suzuki, S. (1970). *Zen Mind, Beginner's Mind*. New York: Weatherhill.

Suzuki, D. T., Fromm, E. & Martino, R. (1963). *Zen Buddhism and Psychoanalysis*. New York: Grove Press.

Tart, C. T. (Ed.) (1969). *Altered States of Consciousness*. New York: Wiley.

Tart, C. T. (Ed.) (1975). *Transpersonal Psychologies*. London: Routledge & Kegan Paul.

Taylor, E. (1996). *William James on Consciousness beyond the Margin*. Princeton, NJ: Princeton University Press.

Teasdale, J. D. (1976). The loneliness of the long-distance runner. In: H. J. Eysenck (Ed.), *Case Studies in Behaviour Therapy* (pp. 77–95). London: Routledge & Kegan Paul.

Teasdale, J. D., Segal, Z. V. & Williams, J. M. G. (1995). How does cognitive therapy prevent relapse and why should attentional control (mindfulness) training help? *Behaviour Research and Therapy*, 33: 225–239.

Thich Nhat Hanh (1976). *The Miracle of Mindfulness*. Boston: Beacon.

Tiles, M. (1984). *Bachelard: Science and Objectivity*. Cambridge: Cambridge University Press.

Tilly, C. (2006). *Why? What Happens When People Give Reasons … And Why*. Princeton, NJ: Princeton University Press.

Tolman, E. C. (1932). *Purposive Behavior in Animals and Men*. New York: Century.

Tolstoy, L. (1983[1869]). *War and Peace*. Oxford: Oxford University Press.

Trilling, L. (1942). The progressive psyche. *Nation*, 12: 215–217.

Trumble, W. R. & Stevenson, A. (Eds) (2003). *Shorter Oxford Dictionary* (5th edn). Oxford: Oxford University Press.

Turkle, S. (1979). *Psychoanalytic Politics: Jacques Lacan and Freud's French Revolution*. London: Burnett Books.

Van Rillaer, J. (1991). Strategies of dissimulation in the pseudosciences. *New Ideas in Psychology*, 9: 235–244.

Varela, F. J., Thompson, E. & Rosch, E. (1993). *The Embodied Mind: Cognitive Science and Human Experience*. Cambridge, MA: MIT Press.

Veyne, P. (2010). *When our World became Christian*. Cambridge: Polity Press.

Vygotsky, L. (1962). *Thought and Language*. Cambridge, MA: MIT Press.

Walach, H. & Kirsch, I. (2004). Herbal treatments and anti-depressant medication: similar data, divergent conclusions. In: S. O. Lilienfeld, S. J. Lynn & J. M. Lohr (Eds), *Science and Pseudoscience in Clinical Psychology* (pp. 306–330). New York: Guilford Press.

Wallace, R. K. (1970). *The Physiological Effects of Transcendental Meditation*. Los Angeles, CA: Students' International Meditation Society.

Wallis, R. (Ed.) (1979). *On the Margins of Science*. Keele: University of Keele (Sociological Review Monographs).

Wallis, R. (1985). Science and pseudo-science. *Social Science Information*, 24: 585–601.

Warder, A. K. (1974). *Introduction to Pali* (2nd edn). London: Pali Text Society.

Watson, J. B. (1913). Psychology as the behaviorist sees it. *Psychological Review, 20*: 158–177.

Watts, A. (1951). *The Wisdom of Insecurity: A Message for an Age of Anxiety.* London: Rider [reprinted: 1979].

Watts, A. (1961). *Psychotherapy East and West.* New York: Pantheon Books.

Weber, M. (1946). *From Max Weber: Essays in Sociology.* New York: Oxford University Press.

Wells, A. (1997). *Cognitive Therapy of Anxiety Disorders.* New York: Wiley.

Wertheimer, M. (1961). *Productive Thinking.* London: Tavistock Publications.

Wessler, R. L. (1992). Constructivism and rational-emotive therapy: A critique. *Psychotherapy, 29*: 620–625.

Wessler, R. L. (1996). Idiosyncratic definitions and unsupported hypotheses: Rational Emotive Behavior Therapy as pseudoscience. *Journal of Rational-Emotive and Cognitive-Behavior Therapy, 14*: 41–61.

West, M. A. (1979). Meditation: A review. *British Journal of Psychiatry, 135*: 457–467

Whewell, W. (1840). *The Philosophy of the Inductive Sciences: Founded Upon Their History.* London: J.W. Parker.

Whitehead, A. N. (1933). *Adventures of Ideas.* Harmondsworth: Penguin Books.

Whitehead, A. N. (1978). *Process and Reality.* New York: Free Press.

Wiley, T. (2002). *Original Sin: Origins, Developments, Contemporary Meanings.* New York: Pauline.

Williams, R. (1976). *Keywords: A Vocabulary of Culture and Society.* London: Fontana.

Winch, P. (1958). *The Idea of a Social Science and its Relation to Philosophy.* London: Routledge & Kegan Paul.

Wittgenstein, L. (1922). *Tractatus Logico-Philosophicus.* London: Routledge & Kegan Paul.

Wittgenstein, L. (1953). *Philosophical Investigations.* Oxford: Blackwell.

Wolpert, L. (1992). *The Unnatural Nature of Science.* London: Faber and Faber.

Xenakis, J. (1969). *Epictetus: Philosopher-Therapist.* The Hague: Martinus Nijhof.

Yalom, I. D. (1980). *Existential Psychotherapy.* New York: Basic Books.

Yeoman, L. A. (1991). *Heart-work: Emotion, Empowment and Authority in Covenanting Times.* PhD Thesis, University of St Andrews.

Young, T. (1961). *The Toadstool Millionaires.* Princeton, NJ: Princeton University Press.

Yurchak, A. (2006). *Everything Was Forever, Until It Was Too Late: The Last Soviet Generation.* Princeton, NJ: Princeton University Press.

# INDEX